THE MAGIC OF CONCEPTS

THE MAGIC OF CONCEPTS

History and the Economic in Twentieth-Century China

REBECCA E. KARL

DUKE UNIVERSITY PRESS

Durham and London

2017

© 2017 Duke University Press
All rights reserved
Printed in the United States of America
on acid-free paper ∞
Typeset in Minion Pro and Gill Sans
by Westchester Book Group

Library of Congress Cataloging-in-Publication Data
Names: Karl, Rebecca E., author.
Title: The magic of concepts : history and the economic in
    twentieth-century China / Rebecca E. Karl.
Description: Durham : Duke University Press, 2017. |
    Includes bibliographical references and index.
Identifiers: LCCN 2016035966 (print) |
    LCCN 2016037766 (ebook)
ISBN 9780822363101 (hardcover : alk. paper)
ISBN 9780822363217 (pbk. : alk. paper)
ISBN 9780822373322 (e-book)
Subjects: LCSH: China—Economic policy—1912–1949. |
    China—Economic policy—1976–2000. |
    China—History—20th century—Historiography. |
    China—Politics and government—History—20th century.
Classification: LCC HC427 .K27 2017 (print) |
LCC HC427 (ebook) | DDC 330.0951/0904—dc23
LC record available at https://lccn.loc.gov/2016035966

Cover photo: Motion blur in the Shanghai Sightseeing
Tunnel. Sean Pavone / Alamy Stock Photo.

FOR DAVID.

WITH LOVE AND IN MEMORY.

YOU WILL ALWAYS BE MY PERSONAL CONCEPT OF MAGIC.

CONTENTS

In the past decade, for reasons of temperament and circumstance, I have immersed myself in university activism. Among others, I have supported graduate student unionization, opposed the offshored branding of education and the casualization of labor regimes at New York University (NYU), worked to shine a light on the horrific labor abuses tolerated by NYU in its construction of a campus in Abu Dhabi, organized against NYU's physical expansion in and destruction of its New York City neighborhood in Greenwich Village, helped lead the movement of no confidence against NYU's erstwhile president John Sexton, and worked for many years in the Faculty Senate against the overwhelming trend toward the dilution of faculty governance in academic affairs and the hypostasized growth and gross empowerment of administrative managerialism at the NYU–New York campus and in NYU's global imperium. I also have spent the past decade writing and then trying to figure out how to turn these critical essays into the academically—demanded and—validated monograph: such is the grip of convention, even for someone such as myself, who otherwise has flouted a good number of its dictates. Finally, I decided to ignore the convention: these are and really should be linked essays. They are thematically linked by a long-standing intellectual-historical project and *problematique*; and they are linked by my sense of a necessary critical politics that is at once scholarly and born of my life as a professor of Chinese history and activist at NYU at this particular historical juncture.

The essays were written in the shadow of the historical transformations in China and the institutional transformations shaping my everyday life at NYU, transformations that feature the centrality of both China and NYU to what I deem to be noxious neoliberal trends of and in the world today. I have written widely for an internal NYU audience on my sense of those transformations and their trampling of academic integrity, faculty autonomy, and intellectual life. The topics covered in this book can be considered my sense of transformations in China. The essays cannot help but reflect the fact that the institution for which I work is run according to many antidemocratic, retrograde culturalist, politically oppressive, and unjust economic principles, whose 1930s and 1980s/1990s Chinese intellectual instantiations I examine and critique here. In these days of generalized market-centrism, ahistorical globalism, antilabor consumerism, and purportedly apolitically "correct" culturalism, this book of critical reflection presents itself as a history of the present; that is, it is emphatically in and of its global and local place and its time, although alas it can only ever be quite imperfectly so.

More happily, these essays also are the product of many years of interaction with and learning from a number of people in my life, many of whom have defied conventions in one way or the next. I am pleased to acknowledge them here. Harry Harootunian has long been as steadfast and challenging an interlocutor as he has been a generous friend and mentor; Lin Chun continually has inspired me with her personal integrity, intellectual honesty, and political acumen; Dai Jinhua has been a constant source of friendship and grounded feminist critique of the inequalities and injustices of Chinese and global society and culture; and Angela Zito's deeply ethical, thought-provoking, and humorous approach to life and the academy have been a steady cause of stimulation and enjoyment. I am fortunate to know and to have worked with each of them. I also want to salute here my comrades at NYU(-NY): our struggles must continue, in solidarity and in hope!

Many marvelous graduate students, now in the professoriate or other careers, have been central to the conceptualization and writing of different parts of this book over the years it has taken to produce it. I want to acknowledge in particular Nakano Osamu, Chen Wei-chih, Maggie Clinton, Zhu Qian, Max Ward, Lorraine Chi-Man Wong, Jane Hayward, and Andy Liu. In classes and beyond, they accompanied me on a program of theoretical and empirical reading, while intellectually challenging me at every step. My NYU life would be much impoverished were it not for the seriousness and serendipity of these students and of their worthy successors.

Over the years these essays have taken shape, I have received funding and assistance from various places for other projects. Those projects were not completed, as it was these studies that continually grabbed and held my attention. So, I owe very belated thanks to the ACLS/NEH Area Studies Fellowship, the once intellectually vibrant NYU International Center for

Advanced Studies (now defunct), the Modern History Institute at the Academia Sinica in Taiwan, and the Department of History at Tsinghua University in Beijing. At some point, each gave me money and/or time and/or space to work, think, and engage in dialogue. In Taipei, Peter Zarrow, Yu Chien-ming, Shen Sung-ch'iao, Julia Strauss, and P'an Kuang-che helped make my stay productive and enjoyable. At Tsinghua, Wang Hui, Ge Fei, and Qi Xiaohong were particularly helpful. In addition, I have been invited to many places to present parts of most of these works. Henrietta Harrison invited me to Harvard's Fairbank Center; T. J. Hinrichs had me to Cornell; Andre Schmid and Ken Kawashima arranged for two visits at the University of Toronto; Bryna Goodman organized a talk at the University of Oregon. Bruce Cumings invited me to the University of Chicago; Eugenia Lean hosted me at the Columbia Modern China Seminar; Jane Hayward invited me to Oxford; Viren Murthy asked me to present at a joint University of Chicago/People's University conference in Beijing and subsequently, along with Louise Young, invited me to the University of Wisconsin–Madison. Dai Jinhua had me to the Beijing University Department of Chinese; Wang Hui arranged for me to teach some of this material at Tsinghua; Lin Chun invited me to the London School of Economics; Michael Dutton and Sanjay Seth had me at Goldsmiths; and the amazing Harriet Evans coaxed me to present at the University of Westminster. Finally, Tina Chen lured me (in winter no less!) to Winnipeg. Discussions with varied audiences assisted me in clarifying the arguments and pushed me to be more intellectually ambitious. Naturally, those named and those not are absolved of any responsibility for what I made of their contributions, comments, critiques, and skepticisms.

Parts of this book have been published elsewhere. Portions of the first essay were published in *The Material of World History*, edited by Tina Mai Chen and David Churchill (2015); a very preliminary version of the second essay was published in *Historien: A Review of the Past* (Greece 2005); and another version has been published in Chinese in an anthology edited by Lydia Liu, titled, in English, *World Order and Civilizational Stages: New Theories and Scholarship* (2016). Parts of the fourth essay were published in Chinese in *Marxism and Reality* (Beijing 2013) and other parts in *boundary 2* (2005); a portion of essay five was published as part of the aforementioned *boundary 2* article. This previously published material has been thoroughly reworked.

I thank my editor at Duke University Press, Ken Wissoker, for his solid support for me and my work. I am particularly grateful to the readers for the press who challenged, encouraged, and assisted me in innumerable ways. The copyeditor, Sheila McMahon, was heroic in her efforts. Finally, I am obliged to my student Xu MengRan, who helped me prepare the manuscript for final submission and to Zhu Qian for the index. As I have now come to expect, the production team at Duke was spectacular.

As always, my family has supported me in big and small ways. At an early moment in writing, my mother, Dolores Karl, generously lent me her house on Long Island to use as a retreat; she kept siblings, kids, and dogs at bay for the requested period of time. While I was there, Charlie and Lee ensured I had good food and companions at least once a week. Miranda Massie provided an early sounding board for some of the work as it was being thought. The Bell/Calhoune/St. Vil/Ennis/Massie families—adults and kids—have kept me laughing, company, and tethered to life as it is lived in real time. And through everything, F. David Bell was a challenging and marvelous best friend and partner: for his consistent ability—despite all—to find levity in our lives, I dedicate this book to him. I am deeply grieved that he did not live to see this book published. He was and will continue to be my personal spark, my very own concept of magic.

Introduction

Repetition and Magic

Just when they seem engaged in revolutionizing themselves and things, in creating
something that has never yet existed, . . . they anxiously conjure up the spirits of
the past to their service and borrow from them names, battle cries and costumes in
order to present the new scene of world history in this time-honored disguise and
this borrowed language.

—KARL MARX, *Eighteenth Brumaire*

In the late 1930s and early 1940s, Wang Yanan, an economic philosopher
and prominent cotranslator (with Guo Dali) into Chinese of David Ricardo,
Adam Smith, and Karl Marx's three-volume *Das Kapital*, among others,
published a series of critiques of contemporary political economic theory
in various social scientific journals in China of his day.[1] With topics ranging over aspects of "the economic" as science and social practice, as philosophy and concept, nine of the essays were reprinted as a book in 1942.[2] The
anthology's lead piece, "On Economics," announces Wang's basic position:
"Economics is a science of practice [*shijian de kexue*]; it is a science that
forms itself in the course of practice; and it is only in its significance and
utility in practice that it can be correctly and efficaciously researched and
understood."[3] Rejecting economics as either pure theory or pure empiricism,
Wang was adamant that "the economic" was a philosophy of human behavior and thus, as an academic disciplinary practice, should retain and be
based in a dynamic relation to everyday materiality. The economic as
a social phenomenon had to be derived from and return to historicized
practice as a matter of and in the very conceptualization of social life at any
given moment in time. For Wang, attempts to grasp economic concepts
ahistorically—through the externalization of concepts that detaches them

from the social realities and the historicity of their own emergence—were no more than manifestations of metaphysical or idealist ideology. By the same token, he maintained that the opposite of metaphysical idealism, that is, positivistic empiricism, was also untenable as it represented an evasion of universal economic laws established in and by capitalism as a global process. While metaphysical idealism was too removed from everyday life and social practice in its insistence on ahistorical categorical absolutes, positivism served to bypass the unevenly structured materiality of global social practice through an overemphasis on specificity and a rejection of structural analysis.[4]

On Wang's account, in the 1930s and 1940s, the two malevolent trends of idealism/metaphysics and positivistic empiricism were exemplified in China and globally by two flourishing contemporary schools of economics: the Austrian School (metaphysical) and the (German) New Historicists (positivistic empiricism). Wang reserved his most scathing critique for the Austrian School, which, he believed, had thoroughly infiltrated global mainstream and jejune Chinese economics circles with simplistic theories. For Wang, the Austrian School was the more dangerous because it appeared the most commonsensical.[5] Yet the positivist-empiricist trend as exemplified in the German New Historicists was also troubling to Wang, as many economists of the time (in China as elsewhere) seemed content to delve into endless empiricist detail, thus forsaking attention to theoretical systematicity, historicized social practice, and conceptual rigor. In Wang's estimation, the endless pileup of empirical detail merely led to a historical analytical impasse of repetitive difference, particularly, as was usually the case, when such empiricism was unaccompanied by historically cogent and materially specific conceptualization.

In accordance with his jaundiced view of the major global trends, Wang's assessment of social scientific inquiry, including economics, in the China of his day was also withering. His general observation on this issue pointed to what he deemed the worst of all worlds in China's research practices since the late nineteenth century. These practices entailed the necessary wholesale importation into China of political economy as a discipline and science due to imperialist capitalism and its attendant cultural-intellectual impositions; the subsequent ill-fitting application of this imported discipline and science to Chinese reality; and, finally, the arrival by Chinese scholars at what appeared to be an altogether logical choice of conclusions: either the theories were faulty and one did not need them because Chinese reality exceeded or lagged behind the theorization, or the theories were fine and Chinese reality was somehow at fault for their ill fit. These two conclusions, Wang noted, corresponded almost exactly to empiricist exceptionalism (a wing of the positivist camp) and metaphysical universalism. One particular target of Wang's critique in the 1930s for his simultaneous propensity toward empiricist exceptionalism *and* metaphysical universalism—as well as for what Marx might have called his conjury of the past to minimize the newness of the present—was the economist and later (in)famous demographer Ma Yinchu.[6] In the late 1930s, Wang castigated Ma for his willful distortion of Adam Smith's liberalism and his neglect of the historical conditions through and in reaction to which Smith produced his late eighteenth-century study, *Wealth of Nations* (which had been fully translated by Wang and Guo Dali in the late 1920s).[7] According to Wang, Ma's distortion of Smith and neglect of China's specific history had become the premise of his famous book, *Transformation of the Chinese Economy* [*Zhongguo Jingji Gaizao*].[8] Of particular concern to Wang was Ma's cavalier attitude toward concepts along with the way Ma based his argument about the reform of the Chinese economy upon a condemnation of the Chinese people for being a "loose plate of sand" (*yipan sansha*), referring to their lack of political organization.[9] According to Wang, this "looseness" seemed to demonstrate for Ma a Chinese hyperindividualism, proving that "the Chinese people do not need liberalism" of either the political or the economic variety.[10]

In his equating of the particularity of China's sociopolitical structure to the concept of liberalism and his consequent distortion of the historicity of China and of the concept of liberalism, Wang accused Ma, among other things, of "playing" (*wannong*) with concepts, here specifically by reducing liberalism to a purported individualism that equated in China to a lack of political organization. This conceptual "playing" allowed Ma (and others, such as close associate and Fudan University economist Li Quanshi) to acknowledge a given concept as the basis for a given theory (thus, to recognize its supposed universalism), reduce the theory/concept to a commonsensical or vulgar core (thus to turn the theory into an ahistorical metaphysics), proclaim the reduced core irrelevant for China because China's reality did not fit its (now distorted) content (hence to exceptionalize China), and thence to proceed to analyze China's situation as if it were divorced from theory, as if concepts floated free of and could be abstracted from the materiality of their relevance, *and* as if China's reality were entirely outside the realm of common theorization and historical materiality. In Wang's analysis, Ma's simultaneous discarded universalism and derived exceptionalism was no mere methodological choice. Rather, it became and was intended to be a truth-claim about Chinese exceptionalism that could only ever be intensely ideological.[11] That is, rather than exploring categorical abstractions in their concrete historical content and manifestations, Ma appeared to be appealing to a category-free content that seemed to transcend history altogether.[12] Wang encapsulated this type of conceptual conjuring and ideological ahistorical claim to truth under the rubric of the "magic of concepts" (*gainian de moshu*).[13]

The "magic of concepts" is a felicitously suggestive formulation. Taking a cue from Wang Yanan's phrase in relation to the problem of history as repetition and conjury named in Marx's *Eighteenth Brumaire*, the current book explores some of the normative conceits—concepts—that have come to inform the study of modern Chinese history, not only in the United States but in China and more generally.[14] By the same token, the following essays are sometimes not so much about China *as such* as they are about conceits—concepts—of history, philosophy, and culture as thought through China in the 1930s and 1990s. Let me explain: The normative conceits of social scientific inquiry taken up in the following essays were systematically established in the 1930s in China (although most had piecemeal origins from an earlier period) through a number of contestations and debates enmeshed in ongoing global and Chinese discussions over the nature of conceptualization in the context of a global crisis in political-economic approaches to history more generally. The essays in this book reflect on and document some of the contours of those contestations and debates, many of which revolve around the content and scope of what constitutes "the economic" in concept and social life. In the wake of the demise of Maoist socialism and global revolution in the 1980s and 1990s, many of the formerly most contested of these conceits were rediscovered or redeployed to become *the* central pillars of social scientific and humanities inquiry for a new age of global Chinese studies, in China as elsewhere. While some find in this redeployment evidence for a rupture in or a continuity of Chinese historical inquiry within a strict national historicist periodization (ruptural because the supposed linearity of "modern Chinese history" was severed by the so-called aberration of socialism; continuous because China's 1930s modernization can be sutured to the 1990s pursuit of capitalist modernization as if socialism meant nothing), the following essays reject such a national historicist method or premise. Instead, I suggest that a more productive way to think of these redeployments is in the terms of repetition offered by Marx in the *Eighteenth Brumaire*. My point is emphatically *not* to erase the socialist moment but rather to track how it has become eminently erasable through the resumption of normative (capitalist) social scientific conceptualization in the 1990s. The monologic dialogues I am setting up, therefore, primarily are between the 1930s and the 1980s and 1990s; in this sense, I am not aiming (and failing) at tracking the furious political battles of the 1980s over the prospects for socialism in China. That latter very important task is being undertaken by others and elsewhere.[15]

To my end, the essays in this book track loosely or rigorously the multi-faceted discussions in China and globally in the 1920s–1940s (glossed as "the 1930s") as well as in the 1980s–1990s on "the economic" and its conceptual links to social practice and social life more generally. I pay more attention in both eras to the academic rather than the Party or political side of these debates. The attempt is to understand how certain central concepts emerged—through an alchemy of common sense, debate, scientific truth-claim, and global scholarly consensus—as settled concepts of historical inquiry, which then become repeated in different eras, as if de facto and yet de novo. This is the problem named by repetition in Marx's sense. That is, repetition is a form of temporalization, an understanding of history as hereditary through a performative enactment of a spectral return, ghosts often "resuscitated in mythical form" in the service of a reactionary politics.[16] Repetition then is a problem of the dead haunting the living—what Marx called the vampiric—that produces a sense of ostensible continuity, or yet again, of never-ending circling. Marx evokes the vampire figure to name a political economy of the dead: a world soaked in blood and hauntings. I argue that the vampiric nature of the political economy of the modern world can be demonstrated in a historiography of magical concepts in social scientific inquiry. To illustrate this, each essay moves between the 1930s and the 1990s, where the move-between is intended not to erase the existence of the middle—that is, the often-disappeared socialist moment—but rather to illustrate how the very occlusion and disappearing of the socialist moment help produce the historiographically repetitive magic of concepts that, in the practice of social scientific inquiry, erases challenges to its own normative assumptions through its smooth renarration of history in "objective" terms. That is, crudely, socialism is treated as unobjective and thus ideological, while capitalist social science is considered normative and hence objective; this allows for the challenge that was socialism to be dismissed without serious analysis. Thus if in the 1930s the conceptual landscape was open to debate and question—where concepts were acknowledged to carry ideological weight—after the beginning of the 1980s and certainly by the 1990s, the landscape came to be foreclosed by the repudiation of critique and the rewriting of histories in globally accepted "objective" scholarly terminology, where ideologies are hidden in capitalist (social scientific) normativity. In this sense, then, the relation of the vantages between and within each essay is at once conceptual and material, where each takes on both a self-contained and a connected set of issues. The internal and external relations within and among them are products of actual material linkages; but more explicitly in this book, they are presented as products of the conceptual conflations created by and through particular social scientific premises of comparison and equivalence. They are, in other words, connected through ghostly conjury, repetition, magic.

Rather than take China's 1930s as continuous with (or ruptural from) the 1980s–1990s under the rubric of a supposedly singular national-cultural subject of history called "China"—a China that seemingly went off the (capitalist) tracks in the 1950s–1970s, only to rejoin those (capitalist) tracks in the 1980s onward—I seek to trouble the stable subject of a singular national history or conceptual community, not by deconstructing the state's narrative nor by denying the deep historicity of China as a sometimes-unified polity or loose and dispersed historical unity in heterogeneity, but by taking different eras within the supposed national time-space and the similar conceptual languages within the supposed wholeness of "Chinese academic language" as problems in comparison and of critical repetition. As Marx evokes in the *Eighteenth Brumaire*, conceptual conjury is often mobilized to envelope history in a "magic cap,"[17] to produce history as a problem of continuity, to dress up dissimilar but seemingly repetitive events in disguise and re-present them as new. In this sense, my intranational comparative strategy intends to bypass ongoing and by now (in my opinion) altogether dead-end debates in the China field about continuity and rupture in China's modern history while at the same time reconfiguring how we might speak of this history as both Chinese and global. In view of the fact that debates on the economic are not unique to China even though they occurred in China in unique ways, the relationality and comparability critically exposed and historically elaborated in the essays in this book focus on how "the economic" came to be detached from a historical philosophy of everyday life and practice in the 1930s and some of the ways this detachment came to be critically apprehended. This detachment helped render economic categories transhistorical, which in turn helped yield a flat terrain of history usually glossed as national space or transnational region, national history, world history, or some other spatialized and naturally temporalized category of an untroubled chronological variety. This flatness was taken up anew in the 1980s and 1990s in the name of professional and objective inquiry after the supposed more ideologically charged socialist period. The book's essays thus individually and collectively also address philosophical problems of comparability/equivalence and historical conceptualization, as well as historical problems of the relationship between concept and practice. In this reading, the magic of concepts, as the name of the problem of uncritical historical repetition and truth-conjury, is a crucial trope for and entry into my discussions and elaborations.

Of Magic and Concepts

A long anthropological tradition takes magic as a ritualized key to everyday practice in precapitalist ("primitive") societies. A more recent revision of that tradition has critiqued the opposition between magic and rationality, primitivity and modernity by demonstrating that the operations and the productions of magic in and by societies are thoroughly enmeshed in modern processes. Of course Marx long ago asserted and demonstrated, through his analysis of the commodity fetish, the essentially enchanted nature of the modern world. Three major historical approaches to magic have evolved and been developed from the anthropological/sociological literature: a Weberian approach to the role of charisma in leadership regimes, or charisma as the magic of the leader; a Foucauldian/Heideggerian approach to representation in relation to "the real" where the two are, to one degree or the next, set in opposition to one another; and a Marxist/Benjaminian approach to commodity fetishism as an ideological and social form of reification.[18] Each of these illustrates a certain aspect of the relationship of magic to modernity, where magic operates not as the primitive remnant or occulted exotic but rather as a crucial aspect of the very modern global processes of state formation, language-reality mediations, social formation, and capitalist political economic procedures. Each paradigm suggests, in addition, a relationship of magic and conjury to modern temporality and social conceptualization. Indeed, as Jean Baudrillard noted some time ago in addressing the problem of the "magical thinking of ideology": "Ideology can no longer be understood as an infra-superstructural relation between a material production . . . and a production of signs. . . . Ideology is thus properly situated on neither side of this split. Rather, it is the one and only form that traverses all the fields of social production. Ideology seizes all production, material or symbolic, in the same process of abstraction, reduction, general equivalence and exploitation."[19]

My interest does not reside in adjudicating among the various approaches. Rather, I suggest how we might cast the problem of magic into a historical frame: when and how did magical thinking—here specifically in the realm of the economic—become possible and relevant in China? When and how did the economic become ideology, if we understand ideology in Baudrillardian terms as a process of "abstraction, reduction, general equivalence and exploitation" tied not only to a local social formation but a global set of contingencies and structures figured in the (inevitable) noncorrespondence between concept and material history? Is "magic" a process only of negative conjury, of fetishization and repetitive performativity, or can magic point to something more socially generative and critical?

Working backward from the questions raised above, philosophically we can say that magic evokes certain lived dimensions of temporal disjuncture forced by the modern generalization of abstraction and the condition of historical displacement. As the sociologist Henri Lefebvre noted in this regard, magic evokes a past that has disappeared or is absent; as part of social life, it resurrects the dead or the absent by achieving a "repetition or the renewal of the past." In this sense, magic "can challenge what has been accomplished and act as though what is is not."[20] For Lefebvre, this imagined renewal and repetition of the past represents a form of everyday life that does not allow for an accumulation of time in the manner understood by historians or social scientists as chronological linearity or national continuities. Rather, the centrality of magic to the ostensibly seamless establishment of a relationship between past and present precisely signals a form of nonaccumulation. That is, magic can signal productively the reorganization of time around a series of moments that may recall, but cannot be said to be continuous with, one another. This form of temporality is what critic Daniel Bensaïd has called "punctuated anachrony,"[21] a syncopated quality that can help explain why everyday life—as moment and routine, as repetition and renewal—forms the crux of Lefebvre's philosophical and historical investigations into modernity. As *creative* mediator, magic is crucial to the necessary ambiguity of modern everyday life: it is part of the quotidian suturing of incommensurate temporalities and thus participates in the disjunctive rituals that comprise the everyday. At the same time and often more persuasively or in more saturated fashion, in practical social life, magic is crucial as ideological illusion.[22]

In this dual but often contradictory sense—as necessary suture and as illusion—magic suggests a lived form of reciprocal historicity mediated by disjuncture rather than continuity.[23] It thus can indicate how modern temporality can be understood and articulated as objectified experience, even as it is constructed out of severe historical displacement.[24] Ritual and magic hence are part and parcel of conventionalization, by helping render the modern experience of sociotemporal displacement into an objectified quotidian.[25] Yet, as anthropologist Marilyn Ivy has cogently put it, it is the conventionality of ritual and magic that compels belief: "Only the force of society can insure that the conventional is believable."[26] To the extent, then, that social-scientific languages and concepts create conventionality both in academic inquiry and as a general common sense—thus, to the extent that these concepts mediate between past and present in a seemingly seamless "objective" fashion, abolishing temporality even as they appeal to continuous chronology—they fall squarely within the realm of conceptual (as opposed to lived) magic as here understood.

The problem of magic also suggests epistemological issues in the practice of conceptual history. As historical philosopher Reinhart Koselleck has noted with regard to conceptual histories: "Investigating concepts and their linguistic history is as much a part of the minimal condition for recognizing history as is the definition of history as having to do with human society.... Any translation [of concepts] into one's own present implies a conceptual history.... Obviously, the reciprocal interlacing of social and conceptual history was systematically explored only in the 1930s."[27] Indeed, as a historical datum, a concern with concepts as abstractions—their linguistic and historical specifications as well as their realms of reference—was shared by many scholars and activists in China, as elsewhere, in the 1930s and beyond. Thus, while numerous debates in China at the time—including the social history debate and the agrarian economy debate, among others—were about the urgency of contemporary revolutionary politics, as historian Arif Dirlik has argued,[28] yet they were also and importantly about specifying the scope of concepts that could mediate different yet common realities of and in the 1930s world.[29] Here, Koselleck's periodizing—originally derived from German scholarly practice but readily recognizable as transcending that particular historical case—is indicative of the global capitalist 1930s experience of general dislocatedness and crisis, the increasing domination of abstraction over life in general, and the corresponding desire to fix understanding of that generalized condition into universal "objective" conceptualization.

By the same token, Koselleck's caution that concepts have a linguistic history is at the same time obvious and endlessly complex as a historical problem; yet it is just part of the larger issue raised by conceptual history. For, although we can certainly register the historical specificity of the 1930s as an extended moment during which the historicity of concepts and their linguistic definitions/equivalences were confronted quite directly in China as globally, our concern cannot stop at the idealist level of conceptual history as a linguistic, translational, disciplinary, or even functional history of concepts. That is, rather than be limited by what, in current academic parlance, goes by the methodological label of the translatability of, or establishment of, equivalence between concepts—whether from foreign to native soil or from past to present/present to past[30]—we need to be attentive to the historical conditions of necessity for the incorporation of concepts, not only as textual affect but as material effect into specific historical situations. In this sense, while many recent theorists have taken up the question of translation as the crux of the philosophical problem of sociohistorical forms of mediation, they often do not specify that this form of mediation is particular to the historical conditions of modernity. In other words, they do not recognize adequately, as part of their interpretive practice or premise, that the re-enchantment of the world in and through the dominance of the commodity form raises the problem of "translatability" as a historical/philosophical problem of a particular form of mediation specific to an era of social abstraction where "equivalence" can only be given in the abstract. Without this specificity, the historical problematic of translatability cannot exist philosophically as a historicized problem of abstraction pertaining to a particular extended historical moment. Rather, it can only exist as a mechanical problem of language equivalence. Here, then, for translation as a method to have historical analytical purchase beyond a mechanical or technical applicability, it must be seen as a particular historicized form of mediation, as part of the complex problem of modern historical abstraction.[31]

In this regard, we should recognize, as anthropologist James Clifford writes, that "all broadly meaningful concepts . . . are translations, built from imperfect equivalences."[32] By the same token, as I just argued, a focus on translatability as (the search for) equivalence is insufficient to historical explanation and problematization. Instead, what is needed is attention to what historical anthropologist John Kraniauskas analyzes as the contested and violent material process rendering translation historically necessary to produce and reproduce the global uneven processes of historical materialization characteristic of modernity.[33] This is what Brazilian literary critic Roberto Schwarz calls, in an ironic or even sardonic gesture, "misplaced ideas."[34] This process of "misplacement" (so close to, but so far from, displacement!) is rooted in modern imperialist-colonialist encounters: those encounters that produced global unevenness as a necessary premise of all social relations, meanwhile producing abstraction as a necessary mode of social reproduction. In other words, these are not matters merely of discursive appropriation, of genealogies of particular words (vocabulary or language change) or representational practices in disciplinary regimes or techniques. Rather, these are issues embedded within and produced through the broad historical conditions informing and forcing appropriative activity, as a matter of language and power, to be sure, but, more materially, as a matter of and in the production of the everyday and its conceptualization as an uneven yet simultaneous form of modern global social life within the abstracting processes of capitalist expansion and reproduction in different local parts of the globe simultaneously.

Thus, unlike Koselleck or Clifford, whose formulations of the problem of equivalence ultimately are irresolvable (there can never be perfect linguistic, historical, or social equivalence),[35] the "magic of concepts" or magical concepts, in Wang Yanan's sense as well as in the sense evoked in the essays in this book, does not register only a linguistic, self-reflexive, or method-ological impasse. For, all of those merely lead to a historical-conceptual dead end or increasingly circular or involuted modes of analysis that ultimately lead to claims of cultural or historical exceptionalism. Rather, the "magic of concepts" is at one and the same time a condemnation of a lack of historical-conceptual reflexivity as well as a potentially generative call for an engagement with the conceptual complexity of history as lived global and local experience and social practice. It is from the specificity of those processes of production and reproduction of the social experience of every-day life that the significance and utility of various concepts for analysis of social life are derived. It is also from that experience that these con-cepts gain the ability to indicate the contours of a possible futurity that is *of the world* rather than exceptionally apart from the world as either a utopian nowhere or an idealized recovery of some distant (nonexistent) past. What the magic of concepts indicates is that to ignore the dialectic between concepts, history, and the present/future is to deny the relational temporal dimensions of the historicity of concepts. And, to do that is to engage in sleights of hand, methodologically and, more importantly, ideo-logically. Indeed, denying such a dialectic upholds a pursuit of normative conventionalization and thence of a politically and socially truncated ver-sion of extant common sense, in which futurity—and with it, politics—can be erased as utopian and thus unthinkable.

China Studies, Concepts, Translations

While the relationship of concept to history has arisen insistently in China studies—most recently, since the 1980s onset of the rethinking of the role of Marxism/Maoism in Chinese history—discussions of and proposed reso-lutions to the concept/history problem often continue to be stuck in a cycle of nativist/foreign (Chinese/Western) claims. In the most general of terms, recently what we can call China-centered scholars (those who take the contestation of Eurocentrism in history as a key target of critique so as to recenter Chineseness) as well as "national essence" (*guocui*) scholars (those who take the discovery of the revival and/or survival of native traditions as a key goal of writing history and understanding the past) insist that foreign ("Western") concepts can only ever collide with Chinese reality, that such concepts can never be adequate to China's reality. This nativist or neonativist tendency (whether invoked by Chinese or non-Chinese scholars, by national essence or anti-Eurocentric scholars) recapitulates a frequent refrain in area studies more generally. That is, the area (whichever one) is so historically different and unique as to be sui generis, culturally so different as to be describable only in its own conceptual terms. Yet problems raised by the adequacy of concepts to history cannot be construed so narrowly as a problem of the operationalization of native method, as a genealogy of native concepts, or as the establishment of pure equivalence in application between a unique culture and a set of concepts derived from a geographical or temporal elsewhere.[36] For, it is the specific conditions through and in which concept and history are mediated—the structured historical conditions demanding mediation—that must form the core of concern among those analyzing disjunct histories (whether the disjunctures are spatial or temporal or, more likely, both), if reifications of imputed native authenticity or of some external conceptual unity are not to be elevated and valorized. This problem is discussed variously in the first and fourth essays in this book in a relatively concerted fashion. For example, as discussed in the fourth essay, so far as Wang Yanan is concerned, China's conditions were shaped by what he called its "hypocolonized" (*cizhimindi*) situation in the global 1930s.[37] Putting aside for the moment the contestedness of the term *hypocolonization* and its relation to semicolonization (problems that are particular to a form of Chinese historiography), we can recognize this condition (whatever it might describe or name) as one of forced mediation. In such a condition of historically forced mediation, as Roberto Schwarz points out, "anyone who uses the words 'external influence' is thinking . . . of the cultural alienation that goes with economic and political subordination."[38] Since the process of subordination—or of historico-cultural alienation—is raised by the problem of concept-history mediation in the era of imperialism as a violently enforced necessity, asserting an authentic native reality in the form of a primordially existing social excess outside conceptualization and historical materialization can only appear as evasion, ideology, or, in short, magic. What appears—or what some analysts wish to preserve—as a social space of untouched authenticity can only be the mystified or reified domination of concepts over life.

It is precisely from the premise of global capitalist unevenness that Wang Yanan refused the idea that there is a primordial Chinese social reality outside conceptualization and historical materialization. For him, the geographical problem of "Eurocentrism" was the historical problem of capitalism. As he recognized, there is a historically specific experience to which the importation of concepts corresponds. In addressing this issue in the 1930s, Wang Yanan wrote witheringly of those who mobilized a China-centered, self-referential conceptual universe to grasp their current situation: "If they want to understand things this way as a mode of 'self-fulfillment,' of course they are free to do so; but they actually are advocating for it: using conclusions that bear no relation to reality in order to suit the demands of reality."[39] For Wang, this so-called nativist-based methodology only managed to evade substantive engagement with China's contemporary (nonreducible) problems. Not only did it work to inscribe an enduring China as a mythical real standing outside the historicity of imperialist-capitalist imposition, but it also inscribed a counterpart "West" that was also outside history. It failed, then, to grapple with the actuality of abstracted social relations as a fact of the modern capitalist world. With his deep suspicions about Chinese exceptionalism as well as a culturally reduced "West," and his simultaneous cautions about proper thinking about political economic theoretical concepts, Wang's concern about imported concepts rarely revolved around their applicability to China or their "sinification," as it were. For such concerns he had only contempt. Instead, his concern was with the coerced ways in which conceptual imports arrived (through capitalist imperialism and invasion, thus as commodities in a fully fetishized and ideological sense) and the consequently mechanical or slavish ways in which many in China either "applied" them or rejected them out of hand. Indeed, Wang's emphasis on the dialectic between practice and concept points to the inevitable mediated nature of conceptualization in an era of forced interaction (the inevitably mediated nature of the temporal present of global capitalism).

In Wang's understanding, the importation into China of political economic theory was irrevocably marked by the continuously violent and ongoing historicity of incorporation, and the concrete materiality of the transculturation and enforced modes of mediation as actually lived social processes. The question posed for Wang hence was not whether imported theory and concepts fit Chinese reality or Chinese reality fit imported theory and concepts: this mode of posing the question was a red herring as well as an alibi for lazy thinking. In Wang's view, the tendential global reach of capitalism through its violent expansion over the world already had imposed upon all countries and societies a partially universal character in the form of a shared set of economic, social, political, and cultural problematics. These shared problematics were the inevitable condition produced by and resulting from the historical formation of capitalism as a global systemic structure and the increasing abstractions in and of life. To the extent that post–Opium War China (1840s and beyond) had become firmly embedded in the global capitalist system—a fact that, for Wang, was not in doubt—classical or postclassical political economy, which derived from and arose to explore and explain capitalism, were eminently relevant to China's contemporary reality. And yet for Wang the generalization of capitalism and of the economic theory tied to it clearly did not erase the historical specificity of China's current situation. To the contrary, it rendered that temporal specificity—or contemporaneity—historically concrete, globally synchronous, and legible. In other words, China's specificity could be seen only in relation to the generality rendering it visible. In this sense, capitalism and China could not be treated as external to one another; they had to be seen and researched as mutually constitutive of, albeit obviously not reducible to, each other.

Here, the fact of a universalizing capitalism was not the problematic aspect of the use of political economic theory in China, as universalizing capitalism had forced China into political economy's theoretical and material ambit. Global capitalism could not be understood without China; China could not be understood without global capitalism. What most troubled Wang was the magic wielded by his fellow economists and social scientists (Chinese and foreign), who erased the global generality of the current situation, so as to protect a purportedly enduring and untouched Chinese reality—a genuine and unsullied native sphere—outside it. This magic already had become a method and an ideology; it had become a widespread and seductive process of conjury premised upon retrospectively constructed false temporal (national) continuities as well as conceptual conflations and reductions. Its primary content was the instantiation of an ahistorical culturalist essence attached to a would-be nation-state, serving not to connect China to its history and past but rather to sever China from historicity in general and from the contemporary moment in particular. Yet, by the same token, Wang was also quite certain that those who denied China's specificity in order to apply some set of theories from "advanced" countries and philosophies in mechanical and unmediated fashion were also at great fault. Indeed, his lifelong project was to think through and elucidate how Chinese reality and global universal capitalist socioeconomic theory could be united analytically, historically, and for the specification of a global present and a national future, whose futurity could not be foretold.

In Wang's view, it was necessary to turn attention to the concretization of the philosophy of political economy in China as a specific practice linked to its global systemic nature. It was, hence, futile to concentrate on the foreign origins of the concepts. A critique of Eurocentrism—its posited unitary historical teleology, and its linguistic-discursive impositions—was necessary but not adequate. In this sense, Wang's endeavor, at its most abstract, can be seen as answering Henri Lefebvre's demand that modern philosophy be recalled to its original vocation by "bringing it back into the sphere of real life and the everyday without allowing it to disappear within it."[40] The essays in this book are intended as a modest contribution to that project as against the detachment of philosophy and the economic from everyday life as adequate to sociohistorical inquiry.

The Essays

Each of the essays that compose this book was written for a specific occasion or in answer to a specific historical question raised in the China field or in academic practice generally. They were written over a period of a decade and intended, originally, to be crafted into a monograph. I instead have decided to just leave them as intellectually connected essays. Each essay, therefore, is a self-contained argument while also receiving amplification and elaboration in relation to the other essays. The topics represent some of the things I have been thinking and teaching about for the past decade. They also can be considered as a first approach to Wang Yanan and his circle of thought. A monograph that takes up Wang more centrally is in progress; I hope there to elaborate more clearly on some of the emergent themes here, and to take up interlocutory aspects of Wang's thought that are inadequately developed in the present volume.[41]

The first essay, "The Economic, China, World History: A Critique of Pure Ideology," explores the recent debates about the nature of the eighteenth- and twentieth-century Chinese economy. The essay examines the instantiation of an ideology of "the economic" as a form of implicit or explicit comparison that sutures past to present in magical fashion. Fundamentally antihistorical, "the economic" is an empiricist conceptual methodology that now dominates—as it did in the 1930s, albeit differently—much inquiry into modern Chinese history. The essay discusses how "the economic" became a dominant mode of writing world history: critically in the 1930s and normatively in the 1990s.

"The Economic and the State: The Asiatic Mode of Production" moves to a discussion of the centrality of the untheorized central state in Chinese history. By exploring the significances of the Asiatic mode of production as a form of statist culturalism—in the 1930s and, in a very different register with utterly different resonance, in the post-Mao period—this essay brings to visibility the magic of the ahistorical state as a default narrator or narrative center of national and imperial thinking.

"The Economic as Transhistory: Temporality, the Market, and the Austrian School" and "The Economic as Lived Experience: Semicolonialism and China" both centrally take up Wang Yanan and his critique of liberalism and incipient neoliberalism (the Austrian School) from a non-Communist Marxist perspective. Wang's critique of the Austrian School of economics, as discussed in the third essay, along with his elaboration of "semicolonialism" as the lived experience of imperialist capitalism in China's 1920s–1930s, as discussed in the fourth essay, were intended to bring economics back to its roots in everyday life. The reappearance in the 1990s of the doctrines of neoliberalism (in Hayekian form) and issues of semicolonialism (in cultural postcolonial form) are taken up in counterpoint.

The final essay, "The Economic as Culture and the Culture of the Economic: Filming Shanghai," compares two films about Shanghai—one from the end of the 1940s and one from the 1990s—and about economy, culture, and China's imagined historical trajectory. The comparative discussion illumines how the economic becomes thoroughly culturalized by the 1990s. A brief afterword concludes the volume.

CHAPTER I

The Economic, China, World History

A Critique of Pure Ideology

Do not build on the good old days, but on the bad new days.
—BERTOLT BRECHT, "Conversations with Brecht"

One of the more enduring academic legacies of the Cold War has been the continuing domination of historical problem consciousness by a focus on the economic as history. Now no longer necessarily pertaining to or drawing upon an old-style Eurocentric (or American/Japanese style) modernization theory, nevertheless, "successful" modern history continues to be understood as the rationalization of state and society in the efficient development of productive resources and labor power, coupled with economic openness to the outside world abetted by an already existing, recently revived, or newly cultivated cultural disposition toward industriousness and personal enrichment, all of which feeds national wealth, power, and capital accumulation on a global scale. Named "capitalist" or not, these concerns with economic success have been folded into the congeries of empirical studies that have animated recent inquiry into China in its current conjoining to the booming field of what is called *world history*. In this combination, modernization cannot be treated merely as a discursive problem, nor as a metaphysical symptom of the dominance of Hegelian teleological history in national narrative.[1] Rather, it must be seen as the material instantiation of a system of ideological power relations privileging a supposedly normative set of socioeconomic, political, and cultural practices as the center of contemporary *and* historical interpretation and desire. The conceptual institutionalization of these relations is what I call a pure ideology.

The recent manifestation and ascendance academically of this pure ideology has come in the form of world history as an economic history

story, a form that aggressively revises parts of the previous Cold War variety of world history that narrated the cultural history of the singular genetic rise of "the West" and the economic realization of its imaginary, particularly its cultural and intellectual prowess. This Cold War narrative is now often (and correctly) dismissed as pure Eurocentrism (where "the West" is historically European and then, since the 1950s, American and Japanese). Previously excluded from such a narrative because of what was understood to be its cultural and political unfitness, China and the *longue durée* of Chinese history have now been adduced quite profitably to the new world history as an economic story. In this metamorphosed new-style world history, China has not so much converged with the West as become the latent phoenix rising from the ashes of past glory and temporary abjection to new-style commanding heights.

This essay critically focuses on this new sinocentric world history, as it is narrated through the modality of economic normativity as universal history. I argue that the academic institutional premise for the internationalization, transnationalization, or globalization of histories in a universal economic form serves ideologically as a tactic for smuggling a certain type of normative expectation back into the center of the global narrative. I am concerned in particular with how these normative economic expectations dominate inquiry into as well as determine the very ideology of world history as an object of knowledge. I build my argument from the perspective of Chinese historiographical concerns with the economic at two particular junctures: the 1930s and the 1990s—loosely periodized; each is an axial moment for the rewriting and rethinking of Chinese history in its relation to world history. While in the 1930s, the concepts used to write and think these histories were still contested, by the 1990s, the social scientificity of economic inquiry had been settled. By contrasting the critical 1930s to the normative 1990s, I wish to suggest that the current supposedly depoliticized social scientificity achieves a seamless joining of China to the new world historical paradigm by establishing that cultures can be diverse (and this is where contemporary world history departs most radically from the culturally exclusive Eurocentric modernization theory of the Cold War period), even while economic pursuits (if not their forms) are said to be normatively similar (as evidenced in the quantitative flattening of differences). It is thus the economic—as quantitative social scientific method—that becomes the pure ideology of China and/in world history, and it is the current thorough multiculturalization—in the guise of multiplicity of forms—of this normativity that authorizes and legitimates such purity.

The purpose of my exploration and critique is twofold. I wish to examine the ideological foundations in current scholarship of the recentering of China in world history as a supposedly postideological endeavor. When Eurocentricism is taken to be the content of hitherto-existing ideology, and normative economics is taken to be the anti-ideological anti-Eurocentric orthodoxy, then the opening of the purview of world history to non-Europe can claim not only legitimacy but some success. As Eurocentricism is the commonsensical target of almost all scholarship on China these days, all one needs to prove one's anti-Eurocentric bona fides often enough is to eschew certain terminologies and analytics (such as "capitalism," which is supposedly so thoroughly "Western" or "European" as to be unsayable in relation to non-Euro-American societies!). Yet this most narrow view of ideology merely turns a historical economic-political problem (capitalism and its global expansion) into an ahistorical cultural one (Eurocentrism); by gesturing to banish the cultural bias, such studies assume that the economic-political and historical ones melt away as well. Yet the quantitatively measured normativity of economics is anything but postideological or postcultural, as it is premised upon the affirmation of what counts as the economic as a social scientific fact. Since social scientific modes of inquiry are born of the transformations of European and American societies into capitalist ones, what counts as relevant activity and practice is limited. Whether economics is defined in Marxist (capitalist) or Smithian (market-driven) terms—to name one recent (spurious) distinction that has captured a certain academic imagination[2]—is of little consequence on this meta-ideological scene, since that particular dispute over the "name of history" is merely another way to solidify a national continuity ("Chinese history") as an object of cognition while deflecting all inquiry into the centrality of "the economic" to the quantitatively measurable standard of a priori practices.[3]

Second, in exploring the pure ideology of the economic, I wish to highlight the importance of discussions of the economic in the 1930s and 1990s, where the echoes and yet vast differences between these two decades allow me to investigate how China and/in the world is shot through with the historically specific character of the era informing the emergence of the problem. That is, with the increasing reifications of the global (the world) itself—where "the world" can only mean the mainstream world of limitless capital accumulation—the very historicity of the problem of China and/in the world floats free in time and space. The process of reification, I would argue, is rendered particularly visible in its social-academic establishment in the 1930s and 1990s, when the problem of world history and the problem of Chinese history were both in great contention. As a consequence of my focus on the reification of the world as the global accumulation of capital, in the following critique I purposely skip China's socialist period (the 1950s–1980s), precisely because socialism did in fact, albeit quite unsuccessfully, pose a challenge to the reifications of "the world" as the capitalist teleology of all histories.[4] Indeed, the vengeful acceptance and ideological instantiation of "the world" in its 1990s reified form of neoliberal (market) capitalist norms can be indexed to the serial repudiations globally of socialism's erstwhile systemic challenge.

The Economic Trinity

In my usage, pure ideology refers, on the one hand, to a form of Gramscian hegemony: a social common sense secured through a class process whose historical tracks are concealed.[5] As Antonio Gramsci notes in this regard: "Every time the question of language surfaces . . . it means that a series of other problems are coming to the fore: the formation and enlargement of the governing class, the need to establish more intimate and secure relationships between the governing groups and the national-popular mass, in other words, to recognize the cultural hegemony."[6] The establishment of a supposedly postpolitical economic history along with its dispassionate scientific language wielded by a technocratic/scholarly class of experts is one of the more recent global hegemonic projects; its cultural reach and appeal are certainly not confined to China studies, of course, but that is the arena of particular interest here. That interest in part can be said to reside in the fact that the incorporation of China into the pure ideology of the postpolitical global economic history project has yielded an entirely new cottage industry in the "reorienting" of world history around a Chinese center. In the idiom of Gramscian hegemony, one could say that the pure ideology of contemporary China studies, ostensibly freed from overt coercion by the U.S. state or Eurocentric academic conventions as well as from Maoist socialist straitjackets, has passed into the Žižekian sublime. It acts as pure form rather than necessary content; it is both the most commonsensical and the most unattainable object of desire and thus must be continually striven for as if "it" exists.[7]

On the other hand, in a Kantian sense, pure ideology refers to a structure of thinking where knowledge is premised on subjectivist experience. The subjectivization of the *historical real* points to a process of self-validating legitimation through a naturalization of the relation among experience, subjectivity, and truth.[8] The contemporary dominance of the economic as history, particularly as such an approach is adduced to humanistic, culturally essentialist, and identitarian arguments based upon the antihistorical foundationalism of perdurable culture and impermanent experience, draws upon this Kantian structure.[9] It affirms that human behavior and experience of the world is always-already economic, in the classical political-economistic sense. With the ostensible universalization of developmentalist dreams— the so-called China dream included—in a neoliberal ideological form, the tendential refashioning of social scientific inquiry into a handmaiden of a corporatized and militarized functionality of knowledge and value is all but complete.[10] In its critical and complicit analytics, the pure ideology of the economic is an epistemological, historiographical, and historical problem: it is a problem of our present.

When one looks at recent trends in China studies, particularly in their relation to recent trends in world history, the high-profile, ongoing reevaluation of China's pre-nineteenth-century economy looms as exemplary of this type of pure ideology. The economic-history-as-world-history trend has nicely dovetailed with the latest disciplinary call for internationalizing histories (as if nineteenth-century China weren't already international by virtue of having been assaulted by imperialist-capitalist aggressions!) even as histories are also enjoined to be more micro, local, and experiential. Beyond the internationalizing imperative—so-called China-centered histories—the new turn has academic roots in and substantively contributes to the rush toward global or world history, now written in an economically universal while benignly culturally diverse idiom. (The universality of the economic is animated and facilitated by the celebration of postpolitical cultural diversity.) In this version, the practice of world history informs a general turn away from studies of historical imperialism, colonialism, and violent aggression in favor of inclusionary narratives derived from a multipolar model of civilizational cultures and particularisms. At the same time as the China-and/in-the-world trend has become central to and by the postcolonial unmasking of Eurocentrism, it also has become important in the attempts to rescue China for (a unique) or from (a Eurocentric) modernity. The types of universalisms, then, are different between then and now: where previously universalism pointed to convergence with Europe (and America or Japan), now universalism points to culturally particular developmentalism and growth as pure ideological desire for success and state-national power. In such a guise, this trend presents itself as something new.

And in some ways it *is* new. Forsaking the older scholarly conventions of a stagnant China vegetating in the teeth of time as compared to a dynamically progressive Europe; forsaking, as well, the dreaded "Western impact" theory of Chinese history, which held that China needed to be shocked into movement by the superiority of the West, these new histories do, of course, debunk a whole pre- and postwar sinological tradition about China's supposed historical and contemporary unfitness for modernization. (Clearly, the fact that contemporary China is growing wildly helps break down these older prejudices as well.) Yet, rather than mark out genuinely novel theoretical perspectives, the ostensible break from cultural Eurocentrism through the embedding of the Chinese economy into an a priori global (capitalist or market-driven) frame of teleological developmentalism actually entrenches these studies ever more deeply in an economistic paradigm of history, now updated for the anti-Eurocentric and culturally pluralist market-centered neoliberal present. That is, when the trajectory of the pre-nineteenth-century Chinese economy is articulated as a challenge to Eurocentrism as a historiographical cultural problem (e.g., Kenneth Pomeranz's *The Great Divergence*, on which, more below), it immediately can be and is harnessed to buttress arguments for China's alternative or even unique path to modernization or development (e.g., Chinese economist Yao Yang's work on this topic, which represents in many ways the trend toward turning China's "unique path to modernization" into a model of extractable global lessons for the rest of the developing world—the so-called China model of growth). This adaptive adoption is facilitated by the perspective offered in these new works that accept economic growth—whether termed "market" or capitalist or otherwise—as the teleological goal of all history; that accept developmentalism as the one and only viable goal of all historical societies and all viable states and cultures. By pluralizing its cultural forms and historical modes, such scholarship merely relocates the geographical center and chronological scope of the global economy to include China. Indeed, the relocation of the global economy's center to include Ming and Qing China (fifteenth to nineteenth centuries) has turned almost instantaneously into a defense of "development with Chinese characteristics" (a political-cultural claim), which, in turn, represents the ghostly return of one repressed object of modernizationist historical and historiographical desire: the need for a strong central state capable of disciplining and rationalizing society for economic takeoff while building from and reinforcing economistic cultural norms in popular attitudes. While an older modernization paradigm used to be reserved for "the West," the contemporary rise of China opens the world to a new inclusionary impulse promising a more superficially culturally diverse, albeit economically monotone, global space.

With these broad developments in historiographical and historical norms, the current ideological upshot of the trend to affirm China's centrality to world history *avant la lèttre*, as it were, is to legitimate the historical teleology of developmentalist globalization and of China's fitness to be included in "it." This not only endows China with an essentialist genetic historical presence that appears to have primed it for (belated or delayed) historical success, but, more perniciously, it endows the global with intrinsic, inevitable, and ahistorical characteristics, spatialities, and temporalities that predate any historical materialization of the logic of globality itself. It is here where what could be called modernizationism's trinity—the state-cultural complex, economic development, and a priori global connectivity—becomes the pure ideology of China studies at the same time as it becomes the pure ideology of a brave new world. The admixture presents a depressingly complicit pure ideology of China in/and the world.

The Global and China

R. Bin Wong's and Kenneth Pomeranz's separate but related works on the eighteenth-century Chinese economy and state have been crucial in recentering China and China's economy in the new world history. The general impact and academic influence of their work were assisted by the splash made by Andre Gunder-Frank's *Re-Orient*, which provided a *longue durée* economic historical narrative recentering the entirety of the pre-nineteenth-century world upon the "orient," China in particular.[11] In part because Pomeranz and Wong deal explicitly with European comparison—Pomeranz from an economic historical and Wong from an explicit Weberian state-building perspective—a special forum published in the April 2002 issue of *American Historical Review* (*AHR*) featured them alongside several scholars of the early modern European economy in a reconsideration of approaches to world history. In the words of the forum's introducer, Patrick Manning, not only do Pomeranz and Wong "prove the existence of a global economy" in the eighteenth century but, more important, they also place China firmly in one of the centers of this economy—at one of its two "poles"—rather than on the periphery or semiperiphery of Europe, where it had resided in an earlier Wallersteinian world systems schema.[12] Manning goes on to note that the paradigm shift signaled by this new perspective, as buttressed by Gunder-Frank's chronological-geographical extensions of it to the dawn of historical time, partakes of the larger tendency in the academic discipline and pedagogy of economic history to expand "the scale and interactive detail of interpretation."[13]

Despite this lauded expansion, at the end of his introduction Manning almost predictably is reduced to lamenting the continued exclusion of Africa from this brave new world of global history and economic interactivity. It is clear from his introduction, although Manning does not put it this way, that what counts normatively as the global and its attendant economy is *reinforced* by China's inclusion rather than *rethought*. That is, while China's inclusion certainly enhances detail and shifts angles, nevertheless, as currently mobilized, the premise of the old world history model of aggregated fragments remains unchanged: the global sits there waiting for areas to demonstrate their worthiness for inclusion by virtue of their previous or contemporary enthusiasm and aptitude for "development." As a corollary, it is that aggregated enthusiasm and aptitude that proves the global exists. Here, the *AHR* forum overcomes Eurocentrism only through the simplest reliance upon the entirely inadequate principle of national-geographical inclusion.[14] There is no attempt to confront basic conceptual, theoretical, philosophical, or historical problems posed by world history, as the category of the world or the global is posited a priori as an inert space that can be said and proven empirically to exist by being filled in through the aggregation of its ostensible preexisting fragments from a priori preexisting national premises.

By contrast, if taken seriously, the new details and insights might force historians not merely to include China and shift a historical center to that area (and it isn't really "China" we are speaking of, but the Yangzi Delta region) but rather perhaps to explore how the world that came into being by the late eighteenth century, through the expansion now not merely of contingently organized "markets" but of necessary commodity production—actively *underdeveloped* China by incorporating aspects of its productive capacities and formations into an emergent global capitalist system. In other words, if taken seriously, a global view of the eighteenth and nineteenth centuries would put "China" *and* capitalism—the only known global form of *necessary* economic interaction—into a dynamic relation with one another, producing each other rather than merely in inert juxtaposition or comparison to one another. This dialectical view could establish as a central proposition that China and "the world"—that is, the world being made through and by capitalist expansion into China (among other places, of course)—came into being together, as necessarily relationally linked; it would turn China into a constitutive analytic for "the (modern capitalist) world" rather than merely treating China as one more geographical space to be included in a ready-made purview of "the world." This type of materialist global relationality might help spur new kinds of inquiries into the nineteenth century, an extended pivotal moment for China, its fragments, and for the world as well. In these new dialectically related histories, China's supposed decline and the rise of capitalism could be seen to be co-relational and internal to one another, rather than in relations of externality.

In this connection, then, I suggest that a more historically creative and theoretically generative way to think of the global/the world has to begin from the premise that the significance of the world/the global is not transhistorical and that it does not signify in the same way over time. The eighteenth-century world and the nineteenth-century world are two different, if obviously connected, forms of "worlding"; China and/in the world then must be treated as a historically specific topos. In this idiom, the global/the world cannot be said to preexist its constitution *as a logic*, a systemic necessity. That is, the global/the world only can be understood as a historical or critical category of analysis—rather than as a reified spatiality or "thing" waiting to be realized—when it refers to the establishment of a *necessary* and not merely accidental systemic logic of socioeconomic and cultural-political interdependence on a world scale that aspires to draw all, usually violently, into a coerced universal history dominated and tendentially unified by, albeit of course not reducible to, that logic. Comparison between two already constituted (and incommensurable) entities—"The West" and "China"—cannot achieve that critical analytic function. Synchronic historical narrative accomplished through the logic of inclusion also cannot achieve a world history that produces anything other than a reified object of cognition.

Why modern capitalism? As Marx long ago understood and critically exposed, the only historical force of *necessary* (not accidental or epiphenomenal dyadic) global socioeconomic relational interdependence—an interdependence that creates first the possibility of and then the requirement for a universalizing world history—is animated by the logic of global capital accumulation.[15] Unlike previous systems of interaction, the very logic of capitalism as a systemic is always-already global. However, it is global in intensely local ways that need to be treated as inimical to the historical elaboration of cookie-cutter teleologies of internalist development and spontaneous genetic modernization. Thus, on the one hand, for example, no matter how much parity there might be between China and Britain in abstracted economic measurements of calories and other ostensibly stable factors in the eighteenth century (as Pomeranz argues), how these factors signify in a larger historical sense—or what their logic might be—is crucial to our evaluation of what calories mean, even as the late eighteenth-century and early nineteenth-century encounter of Britain and China through an emerging interdependent logic of an expanding global market (in commodities, including in labor-as-commodity) necessarily alters both, while coming to define capitalism itself. On the other hand, then, a critique of Eurocentrism as the cultural conceit of some preexistent category of Europe's/the West's unique genius (necessary as such a critique might be) does little to assist in elaborating or understanding this global logic in its historical becoming or its local iterations. In these senses, the AHR forum's logic of inclusion merely reaffirms a putatively known inert world space realizing itself in geographical fullness, rather than lead to a rethinking of the historical logic of the world as it materially and relationally emerged into being in the eighteenth and nineteenth centuries. It turns out that including China so as to confirm the world as we think we know it is an analytical and conceptual dead end.

Chinese Economic History

Because of its emphasis on broad inclusiveness, where "China" is treated as a known singularity, the 2002 AHR forum did not indicate the then-brewing dispute between Philip Huang and Kenneth Pomeranz over the nature of the eighteenth-century Chinese economy. This dispute appeared in the May 2002 issue of *Journal of Asian Studies* (*JAS*), which was given over to Huang and Pomeranz to air their differences. Each was permitted a set of "seconds," who verified in accompanying articles the authenticity, transparency, equivalence, and working order of the evidence used in the debate (like any dueling pair). With rhetorics sometimes verging on personal attack, each of the articles was nevertheless framed in impeccably "objective" social scientific terms.[16] The controversy includes a large variety of issues, including empirical accuracy and technical points. I am not concerned with those. Rather, below I take up a few major conceptual—or ideological—issues.[17]

The disagreement centers in part on how to evaluate China's (or some geographical fraction thereof, made to stand in for the whole) pre-nineteenth-century economy in the explicit or implicit comparative perspective of a European (or Manchester-British, really) trajectory defined by the development of capitalist social productive relations and state form. In Huang's terms and in implicit comparison, China's economy is characterized by involution, yielding a peculiar, unique, and insurmountable structural impasse preventing it from developing capitalism (the expected norm). For Huang, involution represents change without development, yielding a particular and unique economic form.[18] In Pomeranz's terms and in explicit comparison, China's eighteenth-century economy grew in ways comparable to the British precapitalist economy, yielding equivalent growth through the eighteenth century that, because of ecological constraints, came to lag behind just as Britain found an "escape" in coal-fueled technologies, New World resources, and favorable global conjunctures.[19] For Pomeranz, China demonstrates development, albeit without (European-style or capitalist) growth and modernization.

These positions exhibit real differences in identifying mechanisms of historical change and in social scientific methodology: Huang relies upon an Alexander Chayanov–derived focus on peasant family farming conjoined to a Robert Brenner–derived understanding of socioeconomic change as determined substantively through the internal generation and mutation (or nonmutation) of economic formations. By contrast, Pomeranz relies upon an elaborated Weber-derived comparative focus enhanced by a demographic model postulating the centrality to economic phenomena of the relationship between land, consumption, and population growth. Despite these differences—which, to be sure, lead to almost incompatible quantitative and evaluative conclusions—what the two scholars share is the premise of aptitudes for modernization and developmentalist norma-tivity, whether framed as China's difference from or equivalence to what led to capitalist modernization in England/Europe. By reinforcing the teleological and normalized historicism of industrial modernization as the only form of historically possible or relevant *internal* social development— that is, with development framed within the unidirectionality of history as a nationally bounded internalist proposition—Huang's and Pomeranz's shared premise keeps the authors quite firmly in the very Eurocentric para-digm supposedly being overcome (irrespective of the empirical veracity of either argument). That is, if Euro-American-Japanese-style development remains the norm and the teleological goal, all other trajectories need to be explained in its shadow. Thus, if Europe develops capitalism and China does not, China can only ever fail to be Europe; Eurocentricism remains untouched so long as the emergence of capitalism is assumed to be the *genet-ically* internal privilege of European social transformation, rather than the historically produced outcome of dialectical relationality.

In this iterative paradigm, Eurocentrism/anti-Eurocentrism has become an important way to understand China as *exterior* to capitalism's rise, in Europe or globally. Yet such a perspective has never been adequate to the historical problem of global capitalism—which is a problem of the globally violent nineteenth and twentieth centuries—and thus should be discarded. In its stead, the past and present relationality of China to an emergent and ever-newly-elaborated global and local systemic of capitalist productive relations—understood not merely as an aggregate of fragments but as the violent establishment of a necessary global interdependence—should be a large part of the agenda of world history. Sadly, many China historians and most self-described world historians misrecognize their task as one of including more and more parts of the globe into a normative geographical framework of "the world," an acritical normative positivism that serves no purpose other than to reconfirm "our" world as we think we know it.

The Global as the Grounds of Comparison

To clarify this point as a problem of what I have called pure ideology, I want to bring in a comparison not between China and Europe but between the Huang/Pomeranz economic debate and the agrarian economic debates carried out by Chinese scholars in the mid-1930s. The 1930s present the first extended moment during which China was historiographically embedded in a modern global economic explanatory paradigm, not merely as a discourse (discursive embedding had occurred in the late nineteenth century) but as a way to explain Chinese history itself. One major articulation of this explanatory came through the Debate on the Nature of Agrarian China (*Zhongguo nongcun xingzhi lunzhan*), which took place from 1934 to 1937 in the pages of two major journals, *Agrarian China* (*Zhongguo nongcun*) and *Chinese Economy* (*Zhongguo jingji*). On the surface, and in immediately ideological terms, this debate pitted proponents of the semifeudal designation for China's rural economy, represented by the Agrarian China Society led by Chen Hansheng, against the proponents of the capitalist designation for China's rural economy, represented by Trotskyites, and in a different idiom, by some liberal participants. The agrarian debate proceeded in the shadow of earlier Soviet/European/Japanese Marxist controversies over the Asiatic mode of production (AMP), which had attempted to delineate and argue about the possible parameters of a global history of the local present. (See the next essay in this book.) By the early 1930s, that particular branch of the debate had been (temporarily) muzzled by Stalinist fiat and theoretical dead ends. However, the agrarian debate also proceeded directly on the heels of its more famous kin, the social history debate (*shehui xingzhi lunzhan*), which, as Arif Dirlik long ago demonstrated, attempted to periodize China's historical social formations in universal Marxist and semi-Marxist terms, as a way to understand the country's revolutionary present.[20]

Among many important aspects of these various debates, what is noteworthy for my purposes here is that the agrarian economic debate in 1930s China—as the previous AMP and social history debates—was unabashedly about the ideology and thus the epistemology of economics as disciplinary practice and mode of knowledge production. It was about how to conceptualize the local (rural, national) and global economies in one analytical frame as a historical proposition of the present (and thus of the past). In other words, "the global" was not an a priori reification and neither was "China." More precisely, the agrarian debate was about how to conceptualize the local agrarian problem—particularly the agricultural crisis of the late 1920s and 1930s—in its confrontation with complexly evolving processes connected to the emerging depression-era global economy and the recentering of historical process on the urban, where the global and the city became historically specific yet interlinked sites of modernity, modernization, and catastrophe.[21] In this sense, the global, the urban, and the agrarian were understood historically and dialectically in a dynamic interaction, rather than positivistically as always-already constituted spaces of quantitative factuality; they were understood relationally and materialistically, rather than in an a priori fashion.

Indeed, throughout the agrarian debates, there was little pretense about the objectivity of positivistic empiricism as being adequate to the discipline of economics or to the interpretation of domestic and global social formations. Likewise, there was no lack of recognition that the global was a historically specific, constantly mutating, tendential unity requiring not inclusionism but an explication of its logic at various conjunctural points in history at various levels simultaneously. No doubt, the relative lack of empirical data at that time informed the ways in which various ideological/ epistemological positions often were made to serve specific political parties and factional policies. Thus, what is crucial here is not nostalgia for that particular mode of functional argumentation but rather recognition that operative today is also a form of functionalism, albeit not merely a local, political functionalism (although the recentering of China serves the Chinese PRC state quite beautifully) but also a universal, ideological functionalism that underpins the naturalization of profit and accumulation as the definition of history itself. That is, in the 1930s, the global as a form of materialist conceptualization alongside the practice of economics was still new enough for Chinese thinkers and intellectual practitioners that its conceptual conceits were recognized to be ideological constructs serving ideological goals. This was true in much research the world over, in part due to the global financial panic, which brought the global and the local economic to new levels of crisis and new forms of visibility and questionability.

Rather than reifying the space of the global and the discipline of economics to demonstrate each empirically, the participants in the 1930s economic debates showed great awareness of the importance of ideological-conceptual clarity in the thinking of economic history and particularly in the thinking of Chinese economic history as part of something called world history.[22] The relationships had to be thought and conceptualized at the same time as they were specified, preventing a form of inevitability that, by contrast, characterizes today's work. While today, there is plenty of empirical piling—all that detail Manning lauded in 2002—there is correspondingly little substantive reflection on conceptual issues, particularly surrounding the problem of world history, other than in the sterile terms of inclusionism.[23] The appeal, then, to ideology-free empiricism in the current debate—in English- or Chinese-language scholarship[24]—through its reaffirmation of empiricist positivism as adequate conceptualization and method (no matter how contested the data might be) is symptomatic of the pure ideology of the global and of universal economics as the expected history of the world.[25] This unquestioned affirmation of empiricist objectivism does not only reinforce empiricism as a commonsensical arbiter of a supposedly value-free foundationalism, but this common sense, it transpires, is none other than the teleology that used to be named modernization, but that is now named (negatively) involution (sociocultural failure to modernize: Huang) or development (albeit without modernization: Pomeranz).

The instantiation of the common sense of the empirical appears to lead to an implicit or explicit claim that it suffices to invoke the global (and its ostensible obverse, the local or the national) to banish any intimation of allegiance to the now despised Eurocentrism. This produces, like the more straightforward Eurocentrism albeit in a different register, a universe of naturalized historicism that roams over the expanse of the globe producing comparability, even when the very basis of that comparison—the global—does not yet exist. In short, this type of comparability names the global an ahistorical unity and neutral, inert space, open to all to beg for inclusion in "it" on ostensibly equivalent (if not equal) terms. And it leaves the explanatory and critical vantage of global capitalism—tainted by association with Europe/Eurocentricism—untouched.

The Specter of Japan

At the same time as this supposedly value-free empiricist common sense is hammered home in AHR or JAS, among other places (including in the vibrant debates online on the question), the current reevaluation of the

Chinese economy does not name that which spectrally hovers over the framework like a ghost: not Europe but pre- and postwar Japan's successful modernization. Even more spectrally, there hovers the debate that consumed the Japan studies field in the 1970s about whether the economic successes of the Meiji (1868–1912) and the postwar (1945–1980s) periods were a fundamental rupture with or continuation of the Tokugawa and/or fascist-era economies.[26] I thus take a brief detour through the 1970s Japan debate, as I contend that the current debate on the Chinese economy ideologically and epistemologically recapitulates the earlier Japanese version.

The 1970s Japanese economic debate was academically situated at the intersection of the rise of "people's history" in the social historical field, the coming to fruition of demographic methodologies, and the impasse reached by a certain type of doctrinaire Marxist scholarship, along with the waning of Marxism in Japanese historiography in its increasing convergence with anti-Marxist American historiographical trends. It was also situated at the conclusion of the Brenner–Hill debates in the field of European economic history, fought over the problem of endogenous or exogenous sources of transformation in the transition to capitalism in Europe.[27] Historically, it was situated at the moment of the consolidation of the postwar Japanese economy and at the cusp of what turned out to be the bubble economy. At these multiple intersections, the debate on Tokugawa/Meiji economic history focused on the problem of development or stagnation in Japan's premodern (pre-Meiji) economy. Reduced to their basic ideological contents, the questions were: Did Meiji economic successes (post-1868) occur primarily due to a continuation from the developing late-Tokugawa economy that saw rising living standards, rational demographic behavior, rising differentiation in the agrarian economy, and more widely spread distribution of economic surpluses? Or, conversely, was it stagnation and a deepening crisis in the late-Tokugawa economy that led to peasant immiseration, from which the Meiji-era economy made a dramatic break in order to fashion modern (capitalistic) development? In a break from the then-dominant Marxian historiography, where attention was squarely on agrarian relations of production as a major focus of economic history, the focus in the 1970s and 1980s turned to patterns of circulation, consumption, and demographic behavior.

Prior to the 1970s, it was generally accepted that the Tokugawa economy was at best stagnant and at worst declining. Yet, by the mid-1970s, Sydney

Crawcour was able to succinctly state the new orthodoxy: "Japan's economic modernization followed directly from the internal dynamics of the pre-Restoration economy and . . . the impact of the West was significant in influencing the form that economic development would take rather than in determining whether it would take place or not."[28] Demographers Susan Hanley and Kozo Yamamura echoed: "The stereotype of the breakdown of the feudal economic order has given way to a picture of dynamism, of pervasive changes occurring even in the most remote rural areas. The current theme is growth and development, rather than stagnation and eventual demise."[29] Integral to this new consensus is that growth means "higher living standards." In this view, among other claims, the endemic peasant uprisings of the Bakumatsu (end of the Tokugawa period) were now understood not as rebellions of immiseration and worsening agrarian relations but as rebellions of frustrated rising expectations. Underpinning these assessments, and contrary to past assumptions of decreasing population, the Tokugawa population is said to have grown at a slow but constant rate. Thomas Smith already had noted the anomaly of growing commercialization, better living standards, and slow population growth, since such a pattern diverged so completely from the European experience of high population growth in the late mercantile period. His answer to the paradox was to point to the high incidence of infanticide in Japan, which, he claimed, was practiced "less as a part of a struggle for survival" and more "as a way of planning the sex composition, sex sequence, spacing, and ultimate number of children among peasant families."[30] The claim of rational family planning through equal-opportunity infanticide hardened into the facticity of the late-Tokugawa era experiencing rising standards of living and improved conditions, which the Meiji developed into a fully capitalist economy.

From this very brief review, it seems clear how apparently value-free empiricism turned effortlessly into economic normativity and thence into the pure ideology of modernization. The now near-universally accepted developmentalist view of the late-Tokugawa economy pushes Japan's modernizationist takeoff back to the Tokugawa period from its former location in either the Meiji/Taisho period or in the postwar period. This periodizing helps undercut and erase previous emphases on worsening relations of production in the Tokugawa, thus to mitigate old Western-impact emphases on the cataclysmic rupture of the arrival of the West (so-named, although really it was capitalism that arrived, not "the West"). Meanwhile, the emphasis on the essential continuity of Japanese development and the Japanese nation reaching back at least to the eighteenth century facilitates a comparative interpretation that brings Japan closer to the European model (rendering Japan more European than most of Europe, in fact). Here, then, even while Japan cannot be claimed for inclusion in the global economy prior to the mid-nineteenth century, the purported continuity of internal development makes Japan a unique exception to the rule of nineteenth-century non-European abjection. The pure ideology of modernization and of Japanese exceptionalism is thus spun from ostensibly value-free pure empiricism.

China Reconsidered

Naturally, one major difference between the China and Japan economic debates of the 1970s/today is what they were/are designed to explain. For Japan scholars, the question was to explain the success of Japan in the century of China's humiliation (1840s–1940s), while for China scholars the question always has referred back to the problem of nineteenth-century failure. In this light, returning to the China debates: for Huang, the determinant for China's involution (thus failure) is the transhistorical family unit, where land/labor ratios within the family are determinative in economic-cultural ways of an involutionary socioeconomic cultural structure in the eighteenth through the twentieth centuries. This echoes a certain version of the 1970s Japan debate, even while Huang's version can be seen also in contrast to the 1930s Chinese debates, where the foundations of the Chinese economy were understood as structurally residing in the relations of production—in part family-based, to be sure, but with the family unit embedded as part of a more general social formation based in a spatial-temporal totality that took seriously the ongoing and dynamic production of unevenness regionally and globally. In the 1930s, consensus soon congealed around the determination that these relations had been arrested in place in the nineteenth century in the guise of a semifeudalism produced and reproduced by imperialist capitalism. In this semifeudal form, the obstacle to economic transformation did not reside for many 1930s theorists in an internal structural-cultural family-based ontology (involution) but rather in complex global historical social formations to which imperialist capitalism was key. While the semifeudal argument soon was turned to a different purpose than originally proposed, what the term originally highlighted was the specific historical modes of the materialization of economic practice in China's violent nineteenth-century encounter with capitalism, rather than the arrested cultural-economic ontology proposed by involution. (See the fourth essay in this volume for more on this question.)

Pomeranz, for his part, is more focused on the explicitly comparative aspects of China's pre-nineteenth-century economy while also being more interested in finding similarity and equivalence between China and England. Using a Weberian comparative method, Pomeranz identifies factors that retrospectively seem to explain Britain's success—coal, New World resources, global "accidents"—and finds that they do not exist in China. From this accidental (or, what he sometimes calls contingent) historicity, Pomeranz moves to teleological retrospection and tautologically finds these factors as determinative of Britain's rise and China's decline in the late eighteenth century.[31] But, for example, Pomeranz can only fix on the determining role of coal for Britain by holding the problem of spatial division and integration in an essentially unchanging historical condition. That is, the production of unevenness locally and globally is not integral to his problem consciousness, and thus the units of analysis—the national, the local, or, more insidiously, the global—seem to preexist their constitution and remain in steady relation and mutual significance to one another over time. This, too, echoes a certain version of the Japan debates.

By contrast, in the 1930s debates, the global was seen as a newly emergent, historically specific logic and violently produced (uneven) unity. The analytical challenge—not met then, or now—was to devise ways to think the global immanently at the same time as thinking the local immanently. Pomeranz's attempt to think the local mobilizes the global merely to return us to an unnamed (and, in fact, partially disavowed) Eurocentric conceit of the world revealed in some predetermined image, rather than messily realized in history. Meanwhile, China is treated as an inert space (where the Yangzi Delta stands in for the national unit). Bypassing the conceptual/theoretical problem of what the global might be or might become through the eighteenth-century interactions, Pomeranz merely invokes it so as to banish some obvious epistemological premises that underpin certain assumptions about what a global economy is.[32] In this way, he critiques Eurocentrism but smuggles it in through the back door.

Indeed, a focus on the historical production of uneven spatial division and/or integration within evolving contingent logics and then necessary productive logics would render the global a system of uneven and unstable interdependent relations, rather than an arbitrary and inert aggregate of fragments. This critical approach would present a fundamental challenge to, rather than an endorsement of, world history as normative economic developmentalism. And it would be a challenge to the normativity defined by Europe (or, really Britain) that could constitute a real challenge to historical practice more generally. No mere addition of a new fragment that reconfirms an already constituted whole, China's particular history in relation to capitalism could thus help to reopen certain closed debates about the economic as universal history and the global as that which produces and instantiates a contemporary normativity whose pure ideological sway seems undiminished despite all the nominal challenges launched against it.

Conclusion

Finally, then, I will reiterate that the entirely necessary historiographical and cultural-ideological struggle against Eurocentrism cannot be waged sinocentrically or Japanocentrically, or "centrically" at all. As we have seen, the Japanocentric bid for inclusion in a universalist teleology of fitness for capitalism merely reinforces Eurocentric historicism of the old world historical variety: Europe had a special genius; Japan somehow also had it. Meanwhile, the appeal to Chinese exceptionalism (Huang) leaves the paradigm untouched and merely reinforces Chinese culturalism, even as the appeal for China's superior inclusion in the global (Pomeranz) also does nothing to alter the paradigm of an extant world revealed. The inclusionary impulse merely adds a worthy member—now China—into the mix while facilitating the nationalist Chinese conviction that the world did indeed once upon a time and could/will once more center on China. By the same token, in these mutations we can see how the significance of the global has been altered: from a temporally marked teleological stagist universalism, it has become an inert space sitting out there waiting to be realized. Neither version is satisfactory, as both recapitulate major pillars of Eurocentricism and revolve around the inadequate piling on of ever-newer sets of empirical work harnessed to already prepared models of explanation. They depend in other words on the economic as a magical concept that spirits away before it all conceptual historicities in order to arrive at historical truths.

Given this, in my view, new departures in world history need to be engaged as a theoretical-conceptual overhauling of historical assumptions and historical questions. One point would be to call for clarity: not for purportedly ideology-free (pure empirical) scholarship but rather for scholarship that recognizes its own premises and historical conditions of possibility. Without such clarity, the neoliberal culturalist mode will always provide a comfortable refuge for magical thinking. This clarity is not best accomplished by holding the global outside history as a Hegelian transcendent *Geist* or spatial spirit waiting to be realized; nor is it best achieved in Weberian fashion by making all things that happen in the world comparably equivalent and commensurate in an empiricist fullness but historical void. Otherwise the abstraction of violence inherently produced by capitalism and rationality will be reproduced as the violence of abstraction that speaks more to current hegemonic desires than to historically specifiable modalities. And that hegemony merely returns us to prior magical conceptual conceits rather than forcing us to rethink China, the world, and how they became integrally related to one another through global capitalism in new generative, irreducible, and productive fashions.

CHAPTER 2

The Economic and the State

The Asiatic Mode of Production

If we examine this fact of transition more closely . . . we must here banish from our minds the prejudice in favor of duration, as if it had any advantage as compared with transience: the imperishable mountains are not superior to the quickly dismantled rose exhaling its life in fragrance.

—G. W. F. HEGEL, *The Philosophy of History*

[The state's] route is terror, its method, ideology.

—REINHART KOSELLECK, *Critique and Crisis*

In a 1937 commentary on the study of Chinese economic history, the translator, social scientist, and economic philosopher Wang Yanan wrote of the mistaken views of the Asiatic mode of production (AMP) hitherto offered by Soviet, Hungarian, Japanese, and Chinese scholars. Reflecting on the recently concluded multinational Marxist debates on social history, revolutionary strategy, and global history, in which the AMP had been one among many issues in contention, Wang condemned the characteristic AMP claim to historical exceptionalism. This claim—upheld equally, albeit differently, by Georgi Plekhanov, Joel Kotkin, and L. I. Madyar (all 1930s critics or proponents of AMP) and by their various followers, including Karl Wittfogel and a host of Chinese and Japanese social scientists and historians—was wrong, Wang wrote, because "China's socioeconomic development never escaped from the common categories of human world history; rather it belongs, along with other non-Chinese Asian societies, to these categories. In this sense, the 'Asiatic mode of production' which has been seen as exceptional, simply does not exist [as such]."[1] In Wang's view, the problem to be solved by socioeconomic historical analysis in the 1930s was *not* to explain China's supposed exceptional deviation from some "normal" (European) path; nor was it to explain China's supposed historical stagnation or longevity as a matter of either cultural shame or pride. The point also was not to pose a false "alternative" historical path purportedly offered by an "Asian" difference from Europe. Rather, for Wang, the point was to start from the current situation in 1930s and 1940s China and the world, so as to specify China's contemporary socioeconomic characteristics in order to figure out a way forward. This was to be done by understanding the historical modes of social relations, reproduction, and expanded reproduction that had shaped the particular contours of China's social formation and that, when confronted with capitalism in the nineteenth century, helped determine the form of social, economic, and political transformation into the current moment (the 1930s and 1940s).

Wang's concern with China's social formation is situated at a moment during which there was an urgently perceived necessity among Chinese social commentators to integrate a Chinese national history with world history, or world economic history. While explorations into and translations (from the Japanese, primarily) of "universal" (*tongshi*) histories had been ongoing since at least the end of the Qing dynasty (1870s onward), it was only in the 1930s that Wang and others began to analyze the underlying theoretical and thus historical premises of world historical categories of inquiry. Important in these debates often were considerations about the status of China in a civilizational discourse of social stages, which defined social formations in national spatial terms and in linear chronological time. That is, in line with Enlightenment-informed, colonially reinforced histories of the so-called proper division and process of history (derived from idealized versions of "Western" history underpinned by an abstracted Hegelian-Weberian specification of the prerequisites for and conditions of modern sociopolitical and economic life), China's supposed continuous national history was thought to need to conform to the already universalized categories provided by mainstream classical political economy and Marxist theory. The primary effort among social scientists and historians in the 1930s, therefore, emphatically was not to mark China's difference from these supposed universal stages; rather, the effort was to find concepts adequate to China's specific history in the context of the demanded civilizational universalisms mapped elsewhere. While this effort yielded—as it had earlier in France, Scotland, and England—some of the first materialist histories of Chinese political and social life, nevertheless the necessity to shoehorn a newly developed Chinese *national* history into predetermined *universal* stages also produced problems that could neither be properly explained nor properly addressed in the given terms. These efforts, however inadequate to the task as given, emerged not only from a domestic revolutionary necessity but from a newly current and newly important requirement to write China-the-nation in and into the idiom of world history.

In this essay, I recall how the AMP as theory as well as the writing or narrating of China's history were intimately entangled throughout the twentieth century in the writing of world or global history.[2] I build upon the general ideological contours of world or global history as written in the 1930s and revived in the 1990s already sketched in the first essay in this book. Yet, before I move into my consideration of the AMP, I should note explicitly: I have no intention of arguing that AMP can or should be rescued. While certain postcolonial theorists have attempted to resurrect the AMP as an enabling principle of global difference (e.g., Gayatri Spivak), and certain Chinese theorists have attempted to resurrect it in the name of an elemental Chinese difference (e.g., most recently, Tu Chenglin),[3] in my opinion, the AMP died an appropriate death in the 1930s and should remain dead. However, as with magical concepts more generally and the nature of modern repetition, despite its repeated burials, the AMP seems to rise, zombie-like, from its undead grave at various intervals, as if it can explain *this time* something it never could explain last time. Indeed, in the 1980s, the AMP staged a minor comeback in Chinese historical analysis after almost half a century in eclipse, an undead revival that was intimately tied to the reevaluations of the Mao era and thus to the reassertions of (capitalist-inspired) linear modernization theory and, after an interval, of alternative (nativist) modernity. The waning of revolutionary ruptural historical paradigms and the rise of more continuous nationalistic and capitalist-modernizationist ones in the wake of Mao Zedong's death, along with the reorientation of China's socioeconomics away from socialism toward capitalist-style development, facilitated and almost ideologically demanded this return.

This demand, as it were, arises from the history of the AMP debates. For, ever since the late-1920s/early-1930s debates in China, the Soviet Union, and Japan (among other places) over the AMP, the stigmatized multilinearity of global history inherent in the AMP as a non-European social formation or mode of production had been rejected for a linear historical dogmatism following the historicist path indicated by vulgar Marxist and later vulgar modernizationist convergence theory. (These theories of convergence held that all histories would eventually converge on one point: in vulgar Marxism, that would be Communism through the historicist five-stage theory of historical unfolding and revolutionary materialist dialectics; in modernizationist theory, the convergence point would be American-style capitalism through industrialization, procedural democracy, and rationalization of bureaucracy, individualist citizenry, and profit-driven production.) In the demand to conform, the multilinearity presented by the AMP became a liability both for the unitary nature of the proposed Marxist historicist trajectory of all histories ending with Communism as well as for the modernizationist theory of American hegemony converging on two-party democracy and capitalism. Yet, by the 1980s and 1990s, both the Marxist and the modernizationist versions of the world had been dealt fatal setbacks; in this global context, the AMP was revived first to critique the Maoist state and then in short order to explain China's difference from and yet fitness for contemporary life lived globally.

Second, from the 1930s vantage of China's revolutionary urgency, the AMP's basic coordinates did not answer the needs of the revolutionary present. That is, with the revolutionary ascendance of theories of class struggle—the state as a class-based and class-contained institution, society as a battlefield of class antagonisms, extraction and surplus value as a matter of capitalist *mystification* and savage exploitation, and so on—the nondifferentiated social nature of the AMP appeared anachronistic and distinctly unrevolutionary and undialectical. By the mid-1930s, the AMP was deemed to be an antirevolutionary obstacle to an analysis of China's demanded revolutionary transformation: it did not answer the needs of the revolutionary present or future. It was given a summary burial. The burial at this time was demanded not only by Stalinist orthodoxy—the AMP having been tarred with the Trotskyist brush after 1931 and thus proclaimed dead by fiat[4]— but also by the ideological and practical correlation between the AMP and imperialism, and specifically for China, Japanese imperialism. Indeed, one theoretical prop of Japanese fascist-imperialism, as argued by Japanese Marxist oriental studies scholar Akizawa Shuji, among many others, had been that China's AMP-induced stagnation—its historical failure to develop progressively since the Song dynasty, it was said—was sufficient historical reason for the Japanese invasion of China and the imposition of a Japanese-centered modernizing mission on its society and economy. The

AMP's theoretical and historical emphasis on socioeconomic stagnation hence was generally seen by Chinese analysts in the 1930s as an apologetic for imperialism, not only in relation to China with respect to the Japanese but in relation to India, Ceylon, and Egypt with respect to the British. Other forms of historical inquiry in the 1930s conceptualization of the modern tasks of Chinese national history came to the fore.[5] While the AMP resurfaced from time to time in Chinese discourse (e.g., in the 1950s), as it did periodically in Euro-American-Japanese Cold War discourse, nevertheless, in serious social analyses, the AMP was all but abandoned.

The post-Mao rise of new contemporary social and political tasks and demands led to the exhumation and reexploration of old historical and historiographical issues, many of which—like the AMP—had been long suppressed or bent to other purpose. Freed from the straitjacket of revolutionary necessity and Maoist historical dogmatism, some Chinese historians rediscovered in the AMP not only a *national* but a *comparative imperial* historical paradigm that could explain China's supposedly "distorted" premodern and modern historical trajectory. Here, "distortion" was understood variously to encompass the failure of China to develop capitalism out of a commercialized past (the repeatedly unsprouted sprouts of capitalism, as it were[6]) and also the supposed historical wrong turn of the Communist revolution and the Maoist state itself.[7] At the same time, this rediscovery led historians to reopen the question of China's historical social formation in comparison to other imperial formations considered to have faced similar historical conditions from the premise of analogous foundations— primarily Moghul India and the Ottoman Empire. A flurry of comparative "oriental" or "Eastern" or "Asian" (*dongfang*) histories emerged in the 1980s and 1990s in Chinese scholarship—and soon thereafter, in Euro-American scholarship—along with renewed interest in empire studies (as opposed to studies of imperialism); these were accompanied in the later 1990s by a rejuvenated interest in Asianism and/or pan-Asianism in general.[8] By the later 1990s, the AMP was transformed from a critique of the Maoist state and from an indicator of negative (peasant) backwardness into a positive theory of national historical-cultural difference and a comparative theory of alternative imperial formations; this new inflection of the AMP seemed to answer the needs of the 1990s Chinese present precisely *because* of its multilinearity, even as the old version of AMP stagnation—negatively valuated from the 1920s onward, in Chinese and non-Chinese studies of China—was turned to positive account through the claim to "five thousand years" of Chinese historical state continuity and cultural patrimony. This later position came to resemble a synthesis of Hegelian, Weberian, and Wittfogelian analytics, albeit now with a positive valuation rather than a negative one (longevity as cultural and state endurance and robustness rather than as stagnant nonchange and stubborn cultural ignorance). By the same token, the continuity of the state—a "despotic" *Chinese* state that supposedly has endured from the Qin-Han through the Communist Party state, with Mao Zedong as "last emperor" (although recently, the current Chinese leader Xi Jinping has emerged as yet another emperor in disguise[9])—became a favored post-1980s American and anti-Communist political science mode of analyzing the degree of political progress (or stasis) charted by China's opening and reform period. This American Cold War political science version is so expected, it requires little analysis. I abandon it to its pure ideological irrelevance for serious analysis.

Below, I seek to understand not only the Chinese recuperation of AMP in the 1990s as a satisfying post- and indeed antirevolutionary nationalist or comparative imperial paradigm but also the symptomatic rise of the AMP as an explanatory schema in Euro-America at just the moment—from the 1960s onward—when capitalism fell into one of its deepest crises and then seemed to pull itself out of that crisis to become the foundation of our contemporary globalized neoliberal moment. Even while specific references to the AMP have by now mostly fallen away (although never completely; the ghost continues to haunt from time to time!), many of its analytical pillars— most particularly, the so-called despotic state—remain only lightly disguised and thus intact. Yet it is also not surprising that the return today of what can be called transhistorical theories of empire—either in a comparativist or in a global continuist mode—under the guise of critical or celebratory "globalization" theory, or under the guise of a critique of the nation-state, tend to rely upon the categories embedded within the AMP for explanatory power.[10] This trend is visible in China studies, most notably in the equating of the Qing with the nineteenth-century British Empire, or the expansionist practices of the Manchus with British and other colonialisms under the rubric of "new Qing history."[11] It is also visible in the popularity of ethnicity and race studies for the Qing, many of which make little effort to differentiate historical moments and instead discursively conflate them with contemporary conceptual understandings.[12] That is, the trend in "empire studies" is visible in the appeal to categories of analysis that are dehistoricized and thus flattened so as to be made commensurable to some predefined and currently trendy object of study. Whatever the other motivations and contexts for these dehistoricized conflationary operations, in this essay, I set them alongside the multifaceted and quite contradictory recuperation of AMP categories in a theoretical-historical frame offered by a consideration of the 1930s/1990s temporalization and retemporalization—that is, repetition—produced by magical concepts.

World Historical Stages and the Basic Coordinates of AMP

It is useful to recall the basic coordinates of the AMP, as they were articulated and congealed over the years into a (contested but relatively stable) systemic designation. I should note that I am entirely uninterested in entering into the almost century-long debates over whether any of this is reflective/descriptive of some historical reality or whether China does or does not conform to the dictates of the AMP. While in the early 1980s revivals of AMP critique in China, the veracity of the match between description and history was rehashed and historians such as Ke Changji and Zhao Lisheng, among others, took up the issue in this empirical vein,[13] it seems far more productive to take the AMP as a symptom of something else. For my part, I take the AMP as a form of world history born of the global capitalist era and not as a descriptor of real-existing societies or geographies. It is an ideology of and in capitalism. In this sense, to my mind, the AMP arose as a historical explanation not for precapitalist formations that exhibit, as Marx wrote long ago, "the unity of [the] individual with the conditions of reproduction" but rather for capitalism, where all unity had been sundered and where "separation [is] posited in wage labor and capital."[14] In other words, the direct relation in precapitalist formations "of the individual to the objective conditions of labor" is not the historical oddity; this direct relation was for the largest part of human history the historical norm everywhere. It is, rather, "the complete emptying out," the "universal objectification as total alienation" where the human "end-in-itself" is subordinated to "an entirely external end"—as in capitalism—that is so odd and indeed irrational that it needs explanation.[15] It is the rational mask of such irrationality against which the question of the AMP (or any so-called precapitalist formation) is posed; thus, the AMP is proposed from the position of a capitalist ideology already on its way toward becoming globally hegemonic, whether through force and violence or via more subtle coercion (the commodity form). In China's 1980s, the AMP was re-posed most clearly and immediately as a form of critique of the Maoist state, but also, in face of the crisis in socialist economics, as a way of reopening the question of the supposed missed transition between precapitalism and socialism in China's modern history, or that question that had been foreclosed by the compressed rush toward communization from the late 1950s onward. The AMP in the 1980s was thus about statism but also about proper stagist social transitions: that is, at the level of political discussion, the question was whether capitalism was inevitable given the problems in socialism, or whether a different answer was possible.[16] The brief open-endedness of this political question soon enough was foreclosed by the willed inevitability of a state-dominated capitalist-type solution.

Yet the problem of stagism was at issue even long before Marx. Indeed, what had made the AMP as a distinct social formation thinkable—or any theory of precapitalist formations, for that matter—is the emergence in the eighteenth century of a stages-theory of social-historical progress. That is, the AMP was thinkable by Marx's time in the mid-nineteenth century because of the prior "discovery" of what historian Ronald Meek has called the "four-stage" theory of societies. Meek traces the stages of society theory back to the French Physiocrats—for whom it was a three-stage model— and the Scottish Enlightenment, where a fourth stage was added. He credits Adam Smith for having first articulated this theory most completely.[17] The innovation of the stages theory of society is that it posited for the first time in historical analysis a theory of social progress that is tied to modes of subsistence, which in turn give rise to appropriate political forms. It is thus the first "materialist" version of history as well as the first potential world-historical narrative of history. This four-stage theory is not only based upon an account of history that focuses on human labor and human intervention into the material world as central to human progress; this theory was said to be operative across the world, in any society and any culture. That is, it was conceptually abstract enough to lay a claim to universalism.

In eighteenth-century France, this theory found its first tentative articulations among the French Physiocrats (Count of Mirabeau and François Quesnay, primarily), who proposed a theory of value that argued for the centrality of agriculture to social production, not as against capitalism (which had yet to develop) but as against mercantilism (the prevailing system, then being destabilized), and thus against the growth in trade and commerce in what they called "ornamentation." For the Physiocrats, commerce not only could not produce value, but it helped empower through consumption and accumulation the "sterile class," who were essentially parasitic on society through their hoarding rather than investing of wealth. What the Physiocrats wished to theorize and concretize was the problem of where value comes from: production or consumption or circulation. They resolved this question by affirming that value emerges from production, although only from agricultural production. Thus, for the Physiocrats, there are three stages of society—hunting, pasturage, agriculture—and they are successive to each other, even though they overlap globally. That is, different societies coexisted in the same global time at different stages of social development, where agriculture represented the acme of human social endeavor. Here, then, we can see that the Physiocrats pioneered the conceptual abstractions of political economy in a context of the imminent disappearance of the primacy of agriculture and the hegemony of mercantilism in France.

Responding to the Scottish situation several decades later, Adam Smith theorized an emergent rather than a disappearing mode of production. Smith's question is exactly the same as was the Physiocrats': how and where is value created? Smith starts from a very different place, as he seems to have realized that the extent of the social division of labor under conditions then coming into being in England and Scotland necessarily implied that the market was taking over a number of socioeconomic functions previously undertaken by other institutions. This leads Smith to add a fourth stage to the three already mentioned: commerce for him is the culmination of human society in this now four-stage theory. As we know, Marx follows from this, posing the same question—how and where is value created?—whereupon he discovered the labor theory of value for capitalism. We need not go into that here. What we need to recall for our context is that precapitalism—including the AMP—becomes thinkable only from within a historicist theory of stages, even if it turns out that the AMP itself cannot really be a stage leading anywhere at all.

The component parts of AMP as a precapitalist formation, as Marx delineated them (and as he reworked parts of these formulations from Baron de Montesquieu, Hegel, Lewis H. Morgan, and others), comprise the primacy of the agrarian community; a state presiding over a "unity" or "totality";

the indistinguishability between tax and rent; the uncertain relationship of wealth to the dissolution or the resistance to the dissolution of landed property and hence, the nondissolution status of commercial/merchant's capital as well as of usurer's capital; and finally, the problem of spatio-temporality in circulation/production, or, what he came to call the dialectic of the social surplus product, which is a dialectic of "necessary time" and "surplus labor." Each of these components at one time or another was of theoretical and historical significance. In the 1920s and 1930s, in Soviet Russia and China (as well as other places), all of these were at issue in the debates over the existence or nonexistence of something that could properly be called the "Asiatic mode of production," as an actually existing stage of and in history.[18] In briefly explicating these component parts, we can get a sense of the contours of the theoretical/historical problematic, as it was repeatedly posed in and for China.

The most significant issue in Marx's version of the AMP—observations on which are scattered over several of Marx's works written at various points in his career—and its major difference from capitalist social relations and forms is that the agrarian community's aim in social productive activity is not the *creation of value* but rather the sustenance of an individual proprietor along with his family and community. The productive community, hence, is the "presupposition," *not* the result, of communal appropriation and utilization of land, and thus the clan system is the premise of the community, not its outcome. Because value is not its aim or its mode, this self-perpetuating system endures not because of ideological/cultural stagnancy, as Weber has it in his *Religions of China* (and many subsequent theorists claimed), but rather, as Marx put it, because of the specific historical form that economic relations take in the AMP and their successful resistance to dissolution (G, 471–72).

According to Marx, the AMP is characterized by the combined manufacture and agricultural product within the village community, membership in which is premised upon belonging to the clan/community in which one has subjective/objective existence (G, 492); the self-sustaining nature of village economy, which "contains all the conditions of reproduction and surplus production within itself" (G, 473); and the fact that the individual never enters into a relationship of freedom toward property (G, 494). In this formation, there is a direct relationship of the individual to the natural conditions of labor—that is, to land—not as private owner but as possessor of his own means of production. The surplus product thus appears as real appropriation through labor (*C*, 3:927). The premise of the community is that property is only communal and thus the individual is not distinct from the community, which yields the nondistinction between the individual subject and the collective subject. And because the direct producer is the possessor of his means of production, exploitation—or real appropriation of surplus product—appears to be a function not of *possession* by members of the exploiting class but rather of *extra-economic compulsion* (*C*, 3:926), or of relations of production that are noneconomic (i.e., political/ideological: corvée labor, etc.).[19] The upshot of this social formation is that the individual "never becomes a proprietor but only a possessor; he is at bottom himself the property, the slave of him in whom the unity of the commune exists [i.e., the despot]" (*G*, 493). This is what Marx called "general slavery" (*G*, 495).

We could note here how Hegel's idealist notion of "general equality before the emperor"—in his *Philosophy of History*—that renders all equally enslaved gets turned by Marx into a materialist argument founded upon relation to land and property, appropriation, and labor. And yet Marx agrees with Hegel on the problem of subjectification. For Hegel, historical process is a question of coming to self-consciousness—the spirit manifesting itself in this self-consciousness; for Marx, self-consciousness can only become a problem historically when labor has been alienated, or objectified. For one set of cultural reasons, self-consciousness is not a possibility contemplated by Hegel for oriental societies; and for another set of materialist reasons, it is not a possibility for Marx in AMP, because there is no objectification/subjectification dialectic: there is but subjectification.

It becomes clear here that one part of the explanation for the historical duration of AMP societies is that they endure longest because the individual does not become independent vis-à-vis the commune. There is a self-sustaining circle of production due to the unity of agriculture and manufacture, and the "indifferent unity of town and country" (*G*, 474). Because there is no contradiction inherent in the social formation or the mode of production and extraction, AMP societies reproduce themselves endlessly. (One can see how this set of ideological coordinates, originally intended to condemn Asiatic societies as stagnant, has now been all but embraced by contemporary China's phony Marxist state in its pursuit of "harmony" in a culturalist-statist vein.[20])

The second component of the AMP is the state. The commune does not exist as a political body (*G*, 483). In this sense, Marx identifies the state as the "comprehensive unity standing above the little communities," which "appears as higher proprietor or as sole proprietor with real communities only as hereditary possessors" (*G*, 472). Unity, thus, is "realized in the form of the despot," where surplus product—including surplus labor—belongs to this higher unity. He goes on to note that "the communal conditions of real appropriation through labor, *aqueducts*, very important among the Asiatic peoples; means of communication, etc., then appear as the work of higher unity—of the despotic regimes hovering over the little communes" (*G*, 474). (In the 1920s and 1930s, the debating point here became: if all states are the product of class relations, what is the class basis of the AMP state? And, what would be the status of irrigation: does it produce the despot or is it the consequence of the despot?[21] More infamously, by the 1940s and 1950s Cold War, anti-Communist former Marxists such as Karl Wittfogel began to reduce the AMP to an oriental despotic state essence, reduced to its irrigation functions.) In Marx, the state confronts individuals directly as simultaneously landowner and sovereign: "Here the state is the supreme landlord . . . there is no private landed property, though there is both private and communal possession" (*C*, 3:427). Therefore, the state extracts the surplus product through compulsion and "compulsion makes the possibility [of extraction] a reality" (*C*, 3:928). The oriental despotic state-form, having been passed down from Montesquieu as a cultural attribute, is here articulated by Marx as the unity that extracts via compulsion the communal surplus produced in labor. (By the time of Weber, the oriental state was developed as a cultural-rational bureaucratic form.) It is thus simultaneously a political, economic, cultural, and social element, with no hierarchy of instances to separate these functions from one another. It is an undifferentiated totality. Yet, more important even, the state and its relations to society are entirely transparent: there is no economic mystification (however much religion or superstition there may have been in lived life). The transparency of the relations stands in absolute difference to the magic, vampiric, enchanted fetishization of social relations under capitalism.

Third, the state enacts this simultaneous performance of landlord and sovereign through rent and its indistinguishability from tax. The rent/tax distinction arises only within capitalism for Marx, because in precapitalist formations there has not been a separation between land and labor, and thus land does not appear as anything other than a natural material of production. In precapitalist conditions such as the AMP (among other such formations), rent is the mode of exploitation of the direct laborer by landlord and sovereign (the state), and it corresponds as a mode of appropriation to the function of surplus-value in the capitalist mode of production. In precapitalist societies rent is not based upon surplus-value since there is no such thing as a separation of the laborer from his/her means of production; rather, rent is premised upon the political/ideological subordination of the direct producers to the state (nonproducers). Essentially a payment for the right of use of the land, rent is extracted extra-economically, through political compulsion (thus transparently). The tax/rent coincidence posited by Marx—no matter its specific form—is the cornerstone of his differentiation between precapitalism and capitalism *as historical formations of valorization and appropriation of surplus.*

Finally, there is the status of commercial, merchant, and usurer's capital in precapitalist formations. Marx is clear that usurer's capital cannot of its own accord dissolve or maintain social formations, even though it can be a powerful assistant in both. As he notes: "Where the means of production are fragmented, usury centralizes monetary wealth. It does not change the mode of production, but clings to it like a parasite and impoverishes it. It . . . forces reproduction to proceed under ever more pitiable conditions" (*C*, 3:731). The real problem comes with commercial and merchant's capital, and the key passage here reads:

> Trade always has, to a greater or lesser degree, a solvent [dissolving] effect on the pre-existing organizations of production, which in all their various forms are principally oriented to use-value. But how far it leads to the dissolution of the old mode of production depends first and foremost on the solidity and inner articulation of this mode of production itself. And what comes out of this process of dissolution, i.e. what new mode of production arises in place of the old, does not depend on trade, but rather on the character of the old mode of production itself. (*C*, 3:449)

In Marx, it is clear that commerce/trade is a dynamic factor in any society, and yet it cannot dictate *the form or direction* of any social transition: for example, in antiquity commerce/trade yields slavery, where in the modern world it yields capitalism. Moreover, other than when it serves industry— as in capitalism—commerce is basically parasitic. What remains ambiguous, and as Arif Dirlik long ago noted in his discussion of this passage with regard to the Chinese social history debates of the 1930s, is what specific factors dictate the succeeding mode of production and how much dissolution is enough dissolution before a new mode comes into being. Why and how does commerce/trade extend beyond small regions so as to become an integral element in the transition from feudal to capitalist society (as with the sixteenth and seventeenth centuries in Europe)? In short, is commerce/trade a cause or a result of transformation? And if a result, then something external rather than internal to the social formation in question is responsible for transformation.[22] These questions, in various forms, beset the 1920s and 1930s discussions and have been raised over and again in all subsequent discussions of Chinese economics and history (among others). They are part and parcel of a stage-theory of history that relies upon a notion of "transition" between chronologically linked phases expected of all societies/peoples/nations.

In sum, the component parts of AMP—the unity of the agrarian community; the state and its mode of expropriation (rent); along with usury, merchant/trade capital as parasitic and/or dynamic albeit not determinative—were fully debated in their contested individual historical existences and in their purported systematicity in 1930s China (as in Japan and Soviet Russia). And yet, in Marxist and other stagist theories of state and political economy, the AMP can never be anything more than a residual category—not capitalist, not feudal, and apparently leading nowhere without external impetus. In this sense, with Hegel, Marx, Weber, and into the 1930s and beyond, the stagist perspective was not Physiocratic—about rescuing agriculture from immanent disappearance and reconcretizing value in rural production; rather, stagism came to be about global and universal vantages on the tendential totalizing of abstract capitalist social relations. In colonial perspectives, the AMP and other precapitalist formations functioned as theories of living social forms that needed to be transformed into useful arenas of colonial-capitalist extraction and primitive accumulation. In the view of critical political economists from China (and elsewhere) in the 1930s, the question was how to reconceptualize these extant living forms as forms in and through which (semi)colonized people lived their everyday lives and through which they lived encounters with global capital.

From my proposed vantage, then, the significance of the 1930s Chinese debates lies in how they explicitly sought to link narratives of an emergent

"Chinese" history with an emergent "world" history in the idiom of a contested normalization of capitalism and supposed universal global stages. As we have seen in the first chapter in this book and will see below, these debates reemerged in the 1980s and 1990s, first as a way of rearticulating Chinese Communist Party (CCP) policy away from Maoist statism and soon as a way of reorienting contemporary Chinese history away from revolution and toward the (normative capitalist) world; by the mid-1990s, the signification came to revolve around ways of retaining within China's new class-stratified and commodified social formation some cultural "Chinese characteristics" as a matter of social ideology and CCP state hegemony. In this latter "culturalist" idiom, the historiographical, philosophical, and ideological problem of national-cultural endurance (now substituting for revolutionary rupture) also reemerged as a major motif of history-writing and thinking. This problem was intertwined with the question of historical "transition": what was China's post-Mao transition transitioning toward and how? By the mid-1990s, this previously tensely fraught political question was all but foreclosed not only by political fiat but socioeconomically as well: the transition was a state-mandated ongoing affair that could provide ideological cover for all manner of inequities and injustices; it was named "socialism with Chinese characteristics"—or a so-called primary stage of socialism—which seemed to indicate CCP sociopolitical supremacy and wild capital accumulation on and in a global scale.

The AMP, Transitioning, and the Rebirth of Culture

The philosophical-historical problem of transition is often a key component to social interpretive strategy. Philosophically, the vexed problem of transition is necessarily linked, dialectically or linearly, to the problem of universal historical temporalization. As Hegel well understood, this was not "merely" a problem of how to read the past narratively as a continuous part of the present; rather, and more importantly, it was a problem tied to a critique of the present. Indeed, while Hegel in the "Oriental World" section of his *Philosophy of History* seems to validate transience over duration—we can recall his insistence that the "eternal standstill" of the Orient was its fatal flaw—nevertheless, his general insistence on a methodologically necessary historical totalization complicates this picture. As philosopher Peter Osborne has pointed out, Hegelian totalization displaces the meaning of temporality to the other,[23] shifting the burden of continuous time to the Orient while preserving transient or transitional time for the Western/ German world. To the extent, then, that "continuity" and "transition" have subsequently become popular concepts and ideologies of historical analysis, they have become so by being transformed into what Hegel called "bad infinities": that is, they have expanded to unmanageable levels of abstraction or contracted to microlevels of specificity by representing ostensibly depoliticized truth-claims on historical and present reality.

An old answer to the ostensible conundrum presented by transition and continuity in Chinese history was to deny that there was a conundrum at all. Historical questions were posed so as to preclude contradiction: China's long-lived imperial political, economic, and cultural formations were seen as enduringly stable as well as impervious to a transition to the modern. All apparent change, no matter of what magnitude, could be construed to be enduringly, reproductively, and repetitively Chinese. This, after all, is the central message of Weber's 1920s study, *Religion of China*, where China's bureaucracy can never be transformed into the modernized and industrialized bureaucratic state required of modern societies, and, differently, in Hegel's vision, where perdurable historicity—transience, transition, progress—was simply not within the purview of the Chinese empire's durational expanse. The AMP is a (quasi-Marxist) conceptualization of this durational expanse as a social formation.

The global realignments of the 1990s, the fall of Communism in the Soviet Union and Eastern Europe, as well as the post-1989 Chinese national pursuit of development, wealth, and power at any social cost have led to a resurgence of what might be called "transitionology" in contemporary Chinese (and Russian) socioeconomic and political commentary. Clearly, this problem was never totally absent from Euro-American scholarship, as the concepts of "convergence," "belatedness," or "takeoff" central to modernization theory might remind us. However, the problem has been reborn theoretically in a different register: as a debate over the problem of the multilinearity of historical paths or, more recently, in the language of postcolonialism, of "alternative modernities." In this perspective, many of the older controversies—for example, the AMP—have come back to the center of intellectual, policy, and historiographical contention precisely because they reflect and respond to, while simultaneously articulating, the problematics of global capitalism.

In this light, the AMP can be seen as a magic concept, a ghost haunting the historiographical field. For, while the old stagnation theory of Chinese history as endurably unchanging has been thoroughly and appropriately rejected, solutions to the question of China's imperial longevity (as conflated with a continuous national narrative) have been found in many different types of formulations. For the economy, "involutionary change," or "change without development," or the oscillating ascendance of two primary modes of production with no one mode dominant have been proffered as competing explanatory paradigms for endurance with change.[24] For the apparent persistence of certain social formations from the Song through the late Qing dynasty, "resilience"[25] has gained favor; and, for metacultural continuity, a congenial reformulation of the stagnant "Confucian civilization" thesis into a theory of dynamic Confucian culturalism, "alternative modernity," Smithian, or entrepreneurial, and so on are now offered as cutting-edge cultural studies approaches to China's enduring historical heritage and contemporary global ascendance. What is distinctive about these recent attempts at exploring the old problem of continuity and transition from new angles and evidence is their renewed reliance upon concepts of "culture," where, often, the apparent endurance of cultural-social formations is now evaluated positively as a glue for, rather than negatively as an obstacle to, economic development. It is for this reason that "culture" looms large in my analysis: I contend that "culture" in its broadest senses has been substituted for sociopolitics and political economy in much contemporary analysis.

At one level of analytical rigor, it can be said that all of these formulations grapple with genuine issues; that is, the issues are genuine in the sense of being seen today as problems requiring historical explication. Yet, by the same token, such problems can only be seen as genuine if they are transformed into historical problematics, understood in the sense of the Lukácsian ideological real: that is, as a historically necessary reification that corresponds to and articulates a particular historical moment. On this view, the ideologically real is a category of modern social life internal to the constitution of that social life and it cannot be seen as a function of an extrinsic imposition.[26] Consequently, one can view the Hegelian philosophical problematic of transience/duration or transition/continuity as well as the importance accorded to "culture" in Hegel and at present as significant or internal to the China field today.[27] However, rather than represent timeless and enduring problems of Chinese history (as Weber and Hegel both presented it and as many in China studies today continue to present), transience/duration is a fundamental *political* problem of modern and contemporary social life and thought. Its arrival in China as a mode of inquiry can be dated to the 1920s and 1930s, and its renewed currency in China studies today must be viewed in that light. That is, rather than a transhistorical problem, transience and duration are problems in and of history. This is quite evident in the resurgence staged by the AMP in 1980s and 1990s Chinese historical analysis after more than a half century in eclipse (there was a 1950s recapitulation of the debates, but that was shut down with the Great Leap Forward).

As noted above, in the early 1980s, the AMP arrived in part as a way to readjudicate the relationship between global categories of historical analysis and China's specificity. In the wake of the translation (in 1980) of Umberto Melotti's 1977 book on the Third World—written with the backdrop of the global theories of "underdevelopment" very much in view[28]—and in the context of the death of Mao Zedong and the unknowability of the immediate future in and for China, the early resurgence of AMP theory can be seen at least in part as a weapon in the furious political struggle waged over the suitability of capitalism for and in China of the 1980s. In this context, the AMP was history, but more important, it was an anticapitalist politics. The AMP as inquiry and analysis did not emerge as part of a general rethinking of the stagism of Marxist modes of production—this rethinking has never really happened in China, as Marxism as a serious mode of thought has gone into a historical nosedive and transition theory has become naturalized. Rather, the AMP emerged as part of and has remained a reinterpretation of *Chinese* history and a reorientation of *Chinese* historiography in the post-Mao period. That is, rather than present itself as an engagement with universal historical categories as a matter of rethinking certain premises of world history, the resurgence of the AMP was tied to China's national socioeconomic and political form. While in the 1980s, China's future path lay in the balance and debates over the AMP were part of what might have tipped the intellectual balance toward noncapitalist solutions to socialism's crises, by the 1990s, the resurgence points to the contemporary global process of what Timothy Bewes calls the "ideological corrosion of the possibility of anything other than what exists."[29] An investigation into this latter process of reification in its articulation to the AMP concerns me next.

Good-Bye to Revolution: AMP, Modernization, and Capitalist Convergence

In the late 1920s/early 1930s debates over the AMP in the Soviet Union and China, among other locations, the stigmatized multilinearity inherent in this theory of divergent historical paths had been rejected in favor of a unilinear historicist dogma.[30] The rejection of multilinearity was as tied to vulgar Marxist stagist historicism (a stagism no longer historically progressive, as it had been with the Physiocrats, but rather historiographically confining) as it was tied to capitalist modernization. Both versions of historical analysis posited a theory of historical convergence rather than continued divergence. In the 1980s revival of the AMP, multilinearity was used initially to argue for the pursuit of a noncapitalist path to modernization in face of the collapse of Maoism. However, soon enough, multilinearity as a cultural proposition became quite attractive, not only in China but in Euro-American postcolonial theory as well as among economic historians of China in the United States intent on countering Eurocentric biases (see the first essay in this volume). With a new appreciation for "difference," one aspect of the AMP's stigmatism—its difference from supposed Eurocentric normality—is overcome.

In a different vein, in the 1930s, the AMP's basic coordinates did not answer the needs of the past as it appeared in China's revolutionary present. The AMP yielded only circular stagnation, not revolutionary contradictions and ruptures. Now, all over the world and quite clearly in China, the present is decidedly post- or even antirevolutionary, as domestic stability (in Xi Jinping's Chinese parlance, "harmony") has become the positive watchword for all proponents of foreign investment, economic growth, and sociopolitical development. In much scholarship, the investigation of social conflict in the guise of class analysis and struggle has become anathema; conflict has become understandable only if detached from the production of class difference, and reattached to the status aspirations of rising social constituencies. The AMP's posited classlessness and its insistence on sociocultural political unity have metamorphosed into today's ideal harmonious society of unified national sentiment under a powerful state.

Finally, skepticism about and rejection of the AMP in the 1920s and 1930s was informed by the observed correlation between AMP theory and the practice of imperialism, both as a chronological coincident (the theory rose just as modern imperialism waxed strong) and as an apologetics for invasion and socially transformative colonization.[31] Today, however, now that economistic development is all the rage parading under the guise of globalization as a universal positive good, imperialism, however deplored politically and culturally in China and elsewhere, is often favorably associated with examples of successful postwar economic progress: in East Asia, particularly with the progress shown by the ex-Japanese colonies, Taiwan and South Korea, and more recently exemplified by the advocacy of the advantages of colonization as witnessed in Nobel laureate Liu Xiaobo's theories of China's backwardness.[32] The waning of revolutionary historical paradigms, the rise of more nationalistic albeit global culturalist-developmentalist ones in the 1990s, and the reorientation of Chinese socioeconomics in the 1980s toward growth and the accumulation of national wealth at any cost curiously facilitated the return of the AMP to historiographical attention and plausibility. Good-bye to revolution, indeed!

What connects the chronological transitionism to the spatiality in which it is said to work itself out? It is in the sense of the ideological real—reification—as a particular form of historicity that the "missing link" as a fundamental historical and ideological gap—or, to give it a philosophical name, aporia—as it relates to the AMP becomes interesting. The "missing link" could refer in a very specific sense to the theory, initially popularized in 1931 by the Soviet economic theorist Mikhail Godes, that Marx, in his inclusion of the AMP in the sequence of universal historical stages in the preface to *A Contribution to the Critique of Political Economy* (1859), was merely providing, in the absence of adequate research, a "missing link" to the development of private property in precapitalist societies.[33] Godes's "missing link" theory further held that, once empirical research had demonstrated the invalidity of the AMP (by the 1870s), Marx, but mostly Friedrich Engels, abandoned the category. This postulation led Godes to conclude that the AMP was not legitimate as a fully mature Marxist historical category. The issue went no further at that time, as the late 1920s/early 1930s debates surrounding the AMP, of which Godes's theory was a major part, soon led to its elimination from the Stalinist codification of the five-stage theory of universal historical progression and a consequent insistence on the unilinearity of all histories.[34]

Not being under the same strictures as Godes and his unfortunate comrades in Stalinist Russia, we can note that, in a more general sense, the "missing link" concept articulates an unstated but implicit centrality of an a priori temporally conceived spatial boundedness, most easily captured in the ideology of the nation-state, an entity *extrinsically* and ahistorically linked to a preexisting global universal time-space (whether of competing nation-states, in the classical theories of international relations; or of capital, in Marxian and non-Marxian theories of development; or, yet again, of Weberian modernization and Hegelian *Geist* as embodied in state forms). In this explicit and yet implicit reliance upon the nation-state as the necessary category for global historical inclusion, there resides the peculiarly and particularly unmarked and yet crucial missed historiographical linking of "modes of production" to nation-time (diachronic chronology) and nation-spaces (geographic unity) by the 1920's. As Anne M. Bailey and Josep R. Llobera wrote some years ago, "The 'nationalization' of revolution [with 1917] had its parallel in the 'nationalization' of evolution, whereby the history of nations was interpreted as a succession of modes of production. . . . The merging of world history and national histories as a sequence of universal stages is perhaps partly a product of the nationalization of revolution."[35] This merging was foreshadowed by the Physiocrats and the four-stage theory of society—which, however, had yet to be linked decisively to a nation-state formation.

It is within the realm of this merging that the contemporary appeal of multilinearity appears as a reified metahistorical truism and compensatory gesture (the missing link) in our era of global capital. As with the missing link between evolutionary modes of production and the nation-state for a previous theorization of Marxist revolutions, the resurgence of the AMP in relation to China's contemporary modernization and renationalization of history is thus perhaps less anachronistic than we might first think. That is, the renationalization of history in China through a culturalist reappropriation of continuity and persistence after the global revolutionary moment— in which the revolution was national, to be sure, but also, and importantly, part of a transnational socialist moment that (unsuccessfully) attempted to demystify and dislodge capitalism at a global level[36]—is less difficult to apprehend. It is in this sense that we can see the symptomatic rise of the AMP as an internalizing explanatory schema of China and the world, where "China" and "the world" are held as externalities rather than internal to one another. The problem of externality, then, poses the problem of convergence (or even transcendence).

For years now, the postwar modernizationist conceit of global "convergence" has not only been disproved in practice, but it appeared to have been discarded as theory. We can recall, briefly, the core claim of that conceit from the 1950s through the 1970s: stated in its strongest terms, modernization theory posited that the convergence of the undeveloped and developed nations was both desirable and possible through the correct deployment of national and bilateral economic, cultural, and social development policy. One primary arena through which such convergence was to be accomplished was in the realm of "values" or in what Max Weber and many after him strove to understand as the substructure (or superstructure, if one is a vulgar Marxist) that provided societies with whatever coherence they possessed or professed to possess. While numerous prescriptions for achieving such convergence were proffered, the manifest failures of the practices of modernization and the full-scale assault on the premises of the theory beginning in the 1970s seemed to render the issue obsolete. Yet "convergence" has been reborn, in altered form, as "globalization theory." This latter position posits the fulfillment of a decentered global empire composed of autonomous states in a regime of convergent commerce and free trade, into which all are coerced or, more importantly, formally subsumed.[37] As Justin Rosenberg has pointed out, in the process of positing such claims, globalization theorists have renaturalized precisely those fetishized categories that previous theorists—Marx and Weber, primarily— had worked to problematize: primary among them, "values" (Weber) and "value" (Marx) as dehistoricized cultural and economic categories of analysis.[38] (As we will see in the fifth essay, reborn "values" can also come under the rubric of "mentalité.")

Even as modernizationist "convergence" theory was being subjected to assault by skeptics and critics, the path to its rebirth as globalization theory was augured from the left in the early 1970s in the guise of critique. This articulation emerged out of the debacles of 1960s French and Italian radicalism, as well as from the challenges that decolonization and the failures of modernization in much of the world posed to Marxist theory and practice. Succinctly articulated by Jacques Camatte, a French Marxist, in his 1973 essay "Against Domestication," this ostensibly critical theory posited that capitalism was now converging with its essential self.[39] Unlike some Marxian theories of the time, such as Latin American dependency theory, which emphasized the underdevelopment and consequent local and global unevennesses reproduced by the capitalist world system, theories of the self-convergence of capital—of real subsumption, in short, where "values" and "value" seem to be conflated—while laying bare the false capitalist claims of benefit to all, nevertheless began to take capitalism's own self-definition and self-representation as their premise.

The self-convergence of capitalism was understood as a geographically and temporally homogenizing mode: rather than being historicist—that is, diachronic or historically stagist—it was globally synchronic. This formulation of temporal-spatial convergence links this type of critique to some versions of contemporary "empire" and "globalization" theory, a link revealed in a telling passage of Camatte's essay, where he defines this 1970s moment as the moment of capitalism's convergence with the AMP. He notes that in Marx's theory of the AMP, revolts in the system effectively regenerated it, spawning the constant imperial reconsolidation that accounts for the AMP's durability and imperviousness to transition. In the light of nontransition as a viable historical mode of systemic reproduction, he notes that what was being witnessed in the 1970s was the convergence between the AMP, where classes could never become autonomous but rather were constantly reinscribed into the imperial order, and the capitalist mode of production (CMP), where classes were being absorbed, thus yielding the regeneration of capitalism and *its* imperviousness to transition.[40] In a later essay (1976), Camatte further specified that the convergence of which he wrote was between the despotism of CMP's bourgeois democracy and that of the AMP's generalized slavery.[41]

In part an attempt to explain the resilience of capitalism through what had looked like its death throes in the 1960s and 1970s, Camatte's explanation of a convergence between the AMP and the CMP can be said to operate within what Georg Simmel called, following Hegel, an *eternal present*. That is, it operates as a symptom of a particular historical situation understood to be a defining moment of the historical itself, much in the way that Lukács explained Hegel's concept of *Geist* in the 1930s. According to Lukács, *Geist* was Hegel's attempt to resolve an impossible historical contradiction in the twin contexts of the failure of the Napoleonic revolution and of what to Hegel appeared as the end of revolutionary history.[42] As both historical symptom and what Lutz Neithammer calls *posthistoire* prescription,[43] Hegel's account of the cumulative perennial traces of time as congealed in an eternal present (Simmel's phrase) allowed him to construct a totalizing history of an unfolding and a return, thus joining in identity philosophical immanentism and temporality as history, even while displacing time unto the other. As Hegel summarized in his *Philosophy of History*, "While we are thus concerned exclusively with the Idea of Spirit, and in the History of the World regard everything as only its manifestation, we have, in traversing the past . . . only to do with what is *present*; . . . Spirit is immortal; with it there is no past, no future, but an essential *now*."[44] It could be said this articulation is echoed, much more crudely, in what Slavoj Žižek called George W. Bush's doctrine: "paranoiac logic of total control over some *future* threat" in which "the loop between the present and the future is closed.[45] Given that current American neoconservatism is linked, philosophically, to a Francis Fukuyama–type of posthistoire, itself a version of right-Hegelianism, this linkage is not arbitrarily invoked.

In this light, we can note that, since the 1970s, there has been an increase in theories—from the left and the right—that configure the older conceit of convergence into an *eternal present* of capital, now renamed either "globalization" or empire (here, Hardt and Negri's *Empire* can be seen as paradigmatic).[46] And, similar to modernization theory, albeit in a different political register, these theories of an *eternal present* of capital/empire present themselves as an opening to politics—in Hardt and Negri's terms, a politics of the "multitude"; in Hegelian or Weberian terms, a politics of a class-specific civil society. Yet, as Camatte reminds us with his postulated AMP/CMP convergence, these are really a politics of systemic regeneration. For, as Peter Osborne has pointed out with regard to Hegelian temporality, "the constitutive role of the past in the speculative predetermination of the future . . . might be seen as part of a politics of the present; at another level, it crowds out politics . . . by prematurely imposing the perspective of a future which absolutizes existing relations to the past."[47] I suggest that it is precisely in this absolutizing gesture that Camatte's theory of capitalist convergence into general slavery can be linked to Hardt and Negri's *Empire*, whose core content is composed of the concept of a global imperial formation, real capitalist subsumption, and absorption of classes into an undifferentiated multitude. As I will explain below, it is also precisely in such a mode that the AMP can be joined to national modernization programs under cultural-statist auspices, as happened in China in the 1990s.

First, however, this conjoining can perhaps most easily be seen in Gilles Deleuze and Félix Guattari's articulation of the theory of contemporary capitalism as a regime of real subsumption. In the middle of their *Anti-Oedipus*, Deleuze and Guattari have a subchapter titled "The Barbarian Despotic Machine." It begins:

> The founding of the despotic machine or the barbarian socius can be summarized in the following way: a new alliance and direct filiation. The despot challenges the lateral alliances and the extended filiations of the old community. He imposes a new alliance system and places himself in direct filiation with the deity: the people must follow. . . . The despot is the paranoiac: there is no longer any reason to forego such a statement . . . provided one sees in paranoia a type of investment of a social formation.[48]

Later in the section, Deleuze and Guattari clarify that their conceptualization of this "despotic machine" derives from Marx's brief comments in the *Grundrisse* on the AMP. As they put it: "It remains to be said that, in order to understand the barbarian formation, it is necessary to relate it not to other formations in competition with it temporally and spiritually, . . . but to the savage primitive formation that it supplants by imposing its own rule of law, but that continues to haunt it. It is exactly in this way that Marx defines Asiatic production."[49] In this haunting and haunted formation, the state appears "as the cause of the collective conditions of appropriation," where the socius "has ceased to be the earth" and "becomes the body of the despot," a body identified as the "megamachine" of the state, or that "body without organs" that fully encodes all residents, precisely *not* territorially but through deterritorialization: that is, through a common subjection to an imperial inscription rather than only through filiation to community and soil.[50] Taking a cue from what Marx calls the real subsumption of labor under capital, which ostensibly follows upon the formal subsumption that marks capital's early period, Deleuze and Guattari posit the AMP as the universalized real subjection of "residents" to the state as despot. This real subsumption as absolute subjection is then linked to their current (1970s/1980s) moment of deterritorialized capitalism by transposing the historical tension between formal and real subsumption—that is, their historically coextensive relationship that produces global unevenness—into the despotically subjected imperial global formation of the present. In short, then, for Deleuze and Guattari, the reduction of the sources of sociopolitical power to the body of the despot—as in classical AMP theory—and the real subsump-tion/subjection of "residents" into the universalized machine/regime yields a convergence of state and capital in a deterritorializing move toward des-potism/general slavery.

Clearly, Deleuze and Guattari, along with Hardt and Negri, and Ca-matte, among others, intend their theories of global capital as critiques rather than as celebrations; they are also intended as a way to theorize new forms of subjectivity and new forms of resistance to what they designate an all-encompassing system. Yet, helpful as this theorization might be for an analysis of the production of subjectivities under capitalism as a total social form, as Jason Read has argued, such a theorization nevertheless cannot account for the historical unevennesses produced in and by capitalism as a global formation.[51] Indeed, such theorization erases the historicity of the coextensive relationship between formal and real subsumption that forms the core of the historical movement of capital and its distinctive uneven social formations globally.

Taking up the latter problem—the production of unevenness—concurrently with the emergence of these versions of AMP/CMP conver-gence, other 1960s and 1970s theories posited the AMP not as a theory of convergent *identity* at the level of global despotism/empire of capital but rather as a theory of colonial difference and historical unevenness. Point-ing equally to the failures of modernization in theory and practice, while reintroducing specific historicities into the problem of global analysis, from the 1960s onward, and particularly with Africanist anthropologists in France (such as Claude Meillasoux and, differently, Samir Amin[52]), these quasi-recuperations of AMP, or of interest in pre- or noncapitalist modes of production more generally, led to an exploration of the historical relation-ship of expansive capitalism to local dependence on the domestic commu-nity for the supply of labor-power. That is, AMP and investigations into pre- or noncapitalist societies inspired theorizations not of empire/despotism/real subsumption but of historical imperialism, with particular focus on formal subsumption and community-family relations as restructured sites for the reproduction of labor-power for capitalist empires. These theories at one and the same time rearticulated AMP as a synchronic social forma-tion within imperialist capitalism—as a coextensive relationship—while also distancing themselves from classical anthropology's reliance upon kinship theory as forms of social (or tribal) cohesion. Most important for my purposes here is how these anthropological revivals differ from the versions just mentioned: that is, they differ in their understanding of local social relations as basic structuring elements through which capitalism simultaneously is constituted as a lived everyday experience of the historical while becoming globalized as abstract historicity. Thus, rather than posit a universalized common mode of subjection or real subsumption in some global despotic "body without organs" in an *eternal present* of capital (or of pre- or noncapitalist kinship community), these theories enter the problematic through the intimate historical investigation of the reproduction of labor-power and primitive accumulation through which capitalism and the world market constituted themselves and each other as locally lived and global experiences and simultaneously. (For more on this, see essay 4 in this volume.)

The AMP and China

Finally we arrive back at China, which presents us with a version of AMP recuperation that is premised upon neither *identity* nor *colonial difference* but rather upon *national (cultural) difference*. This version, rather than collapsing historical imperialisms into abstracted "empire," instead collapses "empire" into nation by naturalizing it. In 1980s China, initially, the AMP came to be seen by some commentators as a way of rescuing China from Maoist revolutionary statism and an attendant historicist unilinearity that posited capitalism as the only plausible post-Mao path forward. It was, hence, a scholarly argument in support of a particular political project in the post-Mao period. And yet the AMP had other inflections at the very same time, which came to signify more enduringly, as it turns out.

In the post-Mao rise of new social and political tasks and demands, old historical and historiographical issues, many long suppressed by a dogmatized Maoism and by incantatory cliché, were exhumed. In this process, by the late 1980s Chinese historians rediscovered in the AMP a *national* and thus a *comparative imperial* historical paradigm that could explain China's "distorted" premodern and modern historical trajectory (where distortion is understood as the failure of China to develop capitalism out of a commercialized past, as well as the modern historical "wrong turn" or aberration of socialism itself). Conceiving China in *extrinsic* relation to the modern world—that is, as an a priori and ahistorical unity—was a comparative impulse engaged initially through the retrospective optic of comparing the economic and global fate of nations (India, Turkey) that emerged in the twentieth century from modern imperialism. More recently, in both China and the United States, the comparative focus has been transformed by converting these national units into the incommensurable units of the historical empires from which they ostensibly emerged, thus yielding a deracinated perspective on comparative empires.[53] In this way, by the late 1980s, the AMP came to be incipiently articulated as both a nationalized theory of historical difference and a comparative theory of (always-already nationally constituted) imperial formations.

It is in this dual form that AMP seemed to answer the needs of the modernizing Chinese present, as the old AMP stagnation stigma was turned by the 1990s to positive account through the statist-culturalist claim to "five thousand years" of Chinese historical continuity. Operating as a marker of a posited Chinese national-culture *difference* as *posthistoire* modernization prescription at the end of revolutionary history, *and* as a comparative imperial perspective aimed to substantiate ostensibly commensurate historical trajectories globally, these recuperations by and large recast AMP in terms of a national historically continuous dialectic between the so-called Asiatic state and the rural order, a dialectic in which China was still deeply enmeshed. Thus, alongside the political reanimations of the AMP out of a leftist desire to forestall capitalist transition, there emerged a historicist and conservative impulse.

The first of the major recuperative essays on this topic emanated from a reading of the aforementioned Melotti's *Marx and the Third World*. The author, political economist Wu Dakun, agreed with Melotti that the technological stimulation of *productive forces* was the only key to and relevant measure of development (as against Mao's emphasis on transforming the relations of production) and that Soviet bureaucratism (named "semi-Asiatic") and historically continuous Chinese statism (full-fledged "Asiatic") were to blame for stifling these productive forces.[54] Wu Dakun's basic redefinition of AMP emphasized, in a version of Karl Wittfogel's long-despised caricature, the oriental despotic nature of bureaucratism particular to China, the transformation of which would lead to the long-suppressed flourishing of rural production and the reorientation of the primordial dialectic onto a new path.

Not surprisingly, this rendition of Marxism as a theory of technologized modernization was soon to find its echo (conjuncturally, not causally) in official policy, with the 1987 unveiling of the theory of the "primary stage of socialism." This latter theory basically holds that Maoist overemphasis on transforming relations of production (that is, class struggle) was premature and had to be discarded for the prior task of the building of productive forces (that is, capitalist-style modernization). One key component to the early practice of this "primary stage" of socialism called for the retreat of the state from agricultural production, which temporarily boosted productivity and rural income in the early 1980s. As numerous Chinese intellectuals have pointed out, however, these gains were temporary—lasting at most until 1986–87, when pressures for urban reforms vitiated the rural gains.[55] In ideological terms, then, the choice was made in the early Deng era to "catch up" with "the West"—that is, capitalist countries—at the absolute expense of a socialist agenda, thus recuperating in explicit form the modernizationist trope of the time lag and reproducing the displacement of temporality so effectively suggested by Hegel and internalized as comparative method by Weber.

In a different vein, historian Ke Changji proclaimed in the early 1980s that Maoist-inspired communes in fact represented the resurrection of primitive AMP communal society, long deemed to have hampered agrarian productivity and hindered the primitive accumulation of capital and thus the transition of China from a precapitalist to a capitalist order. In a definitive departure from Marxism, Ke identified "Asiatic" as an enduring rather than historically transcended economic category of rural communal production held in place through the "general slavery" imposed by the despotic state. As such, for Ke, the disbanding of communes and the retreat of the Asiatic state—here, the Communist state—from the rural order were required for the transformation of China's enduring Asiatic precapitalist communal society (that is, Chinese socialist society) into a modernized (capitalist) one.[56]

Curiously, however, the stagnation in the gains obtained by ostensibly unblocking the AMP/socialist state's dialectic of state/agricultural production led by the late 1980s not to a critique of capitalism and capitalist techniques but to a further exploration and refinement of the theoretical purview of the AMP. Indeed, in this moment of the AMP's resurrection, as these and many similar essays indicate, those most critical of Maoism in the early 1980s were initially most forceful in arguing for the revival of the AMP as a legitimate but negative category of historical and contemporary analysis. Whatever the political motivations involved, their collapsing of Chinese history into an *eternal standstill* of Asiatic statism—now linked to Maoist CCP policy—through the AMP became an anti-Maoist and, more important, an antisocialist proscription and prescription simultaneously. These analyses thus echo those anti-Communist theories and sterile analyses of Chinese society long familiar to China scholars, fusing together the worst of Parsonian-inflected Weberianism with the most enduring of Cold War stereotypes (where Chinese Communists were deemed either completely alien to the supposed natural course of Chinese history or, alternately, completely continuous with oriental despots of old).[57] Most startlingly, perhaps, these theories not only repudiated China's socialist period but circumvented what had long been a central point in Chinese historical studies: the problem of nineteenth- and twentieth-century imperialism as a historical and historiographical challenge. Here, the tension produced by the ambiguity introduced into a purely "Chinese" history by the incorporation of the Qing empire into global capitalism (nineteenth century) relatively disappeared from theoretical view.

This moves directly, then, into the next strand of AMP recuperations, which pointed to the multilinear historical *difference* of China, both as genesis for the urgency of contemporary China's necessary convergence with global capitalism and as origin of world history in general.[58] Unlike the 1960s and 1970s Africanist scholars mentioned above, who turned to everyday life and the social reproduction of labor-power in relation to both the persistence and restructuring of local social formations, the Chinese analyses of absolute *difference* are roughly similar in trajectory to Perry Anderson's genetic approach to European history in his *Lineages of the Absolutist State*. That is, they attempt to articulate "uniqueness" as exceptionalism in Weberian terms by drawing on a culturalist-statist conceit of origins—in Anderson's case, Europe's genesis in Roman classical antiquity and the Roman empire; in the Chinese case, its origins in Confucianism and the imperial state-form. Here, China's posited exceptionalist past becomes a basis for a reconceptualization of Chinese history as the origin of all world history, thus, among other things, restoring the AMP to its position at the beginning of a global historicist sequence leading to China's contemporary rise and supposed reclaiming of its rightful centrality in the world. Meanwhile, these theories also proclaim the cultural *difference* of China as explanation not only for China's past but also for the necessity of "socialism with Chinese characteristics," or China's contemporary social and capitalist formation.[59] It is in this quasi-celebratory nationalistic vein, in fact, that Wu Dakun concludes his early 1980s essay on the AMP (and this was before the so-called rise of China): "we should . . . not be particularly afraid of the term 'Asiatic.' On the contrary. We should, in my view, intensify our study of Marx's theory of the Asiatic mode of production and endeavor to prove its correctness by China's own practice."[60] Such an approach not only obscures the restructurings of China's modern social relations under capitalist imperialism, socialism, and post-Mao capitalism but also forms the basis for a comparative historical method based in the always-already constituted national-state form. This method concludes that, because all preceding imperial formations weakened and fell (Indian, Ottoman, etc.) while the Chinese one remained stable for thousands of years and continues as a national state to this day, the AMP can be seen as a descriptor of national-imperial strength and not as a shameful deviation from Eurocentric normality. It is with this national-culturalist appropriation of AMP in the 1990s that the theory itself more or less disappeared as an explicit point of reference, only to reappear as the implicit cultural ascription that permits China to claim both continuity and transition in one breath. This dual claim rejoins China to some vulgarized version of the Hegelian dialectic of endurance by ostensibly substantiating the ideological real of our current global historical moment.

Conclusion

The above account has necessarily reduced divergent theoretical concerns to some basic common denominators. It has also collapsed a variety of discussions that were, in their specificities and at their time, potentially or initially consequential for a political and historical consideration of and in China. The point of my compressions and what I find currently significant about the general import of these new analyses is how they dovetail with certain of the now-trendy ideological strands of China studies in the United States, as well as with some of the ideological concerns of postcolonial theory. Briefly, while China studies in the United States was never completely dominated by the revolutionary paradigm of Chinese history because of the Cold War paradigm of anti-Communism, nevertheless, the repudiation of revolution in China—akin to the very end of (French) revolutionary history that inspired Hegel's theorization of the *eternal present* and its 1990s reemergence as the "end of history" in such right-Hegelian theorists as Francis Fukuyama—has facilitated the rise in the United States of particularistic theories of Chinese empire, specifically the Qing, construed as a critique of Eurocentric capitalism. In some now-trendy U.S. scholarship, China's nontransition to capitalism is no longer seen as a "failure" but as a sign of China's imperial strength and cultural resilience, of China's spectacular particularity and exceptionalism that belies the (Eurocentric) universals hitherto sought and said to define historical success. China's particularism, indeed, is now often touted as a form of potential reuniversalization in a sinocentric mode.[61] At the same time, the Manchu Qing are busily being equated with the Western imperialist powers—they were all settlers and colonizers, after all—thereby erasing differences between types of empires, modern and ancient, obscuring histories, and facilitating the empire/nation conflations mentioned above. Meanwhile, reversing decades of emphasis on the rupture of imperialism, not only is the nineteenth- and twentieth-century imperialist moment now denigrated as an unacceptable "impact of the West" theory and thus demoted to an epiphenomenal interlude in the continuous march of China's internal history, but China's commercialized noncapitalist past is held up as a form of alternative modernity—sometimes said to reach back as far as the Song dynasty (twelfth century)—an alternative that is not only particularly Chinese but also miraculously and magically suited to the contemporary demands of globalization and competition.[62]

The revaluation of national/cultural *difference* as a strategy of global cultural inclusion and the essential antihistoricity encoded in such moves facilitate the recuperation of elements of the AMP not only as a handmaiden to a nonpolitical, nonantagonistic politics of state-led modernization at whatever social cost but also as a form of global multicultural theory turning on worthiness for inclusion, which conflates rather than confronts empires/imperialism in their historical and contemporary manifestations. Finally, in these conflations and convergences, AMP becomes an all-purpose theory of the future coming of the Asian (Chinese) capitalist state and cultural nation *as such*. In the end, the AMP turns out to be precisely the ideologically real symptom of a global analytical turn that takes the culture of the state and the state of culture—not materialist political economy in all its breadth and depth—as the magical conceptual determinant of history and the arbiter of the present/future. We thus get Hegel's transience and endurance recombined into a reified ahistorical and magical fantasy of capitalism with no limits.

CHAPTER 3

The Economic as Transhistory

Temporality, the Market, and the Austrian School

The system of private property is the most important guaranty of freedom, not only for those who own property, but scarcely less for those who do not.
—FRIEDRICH A. HAYEK, *The Road to Serfdom*

Since openness is so vital to China's transition, we should determine what would contribute to China's further opening-up and liberalization. The answer is what I call the "new trinity," composed of both institutions and technology: the World Trade Organization (WTO), Permanent Normal Trade Relations (PNTR), and the Internet.
—LIU JUNNING, "The New Trinity"

In the spring 2006 issue of *Journal of Economic Perspectives*, emeritus Harvard University historian David Landes authoritatively explained that there was no industrial revolution in China's nineteenth century because "China lacked a free market and institutionalized property rights. The Chinese state was always stepping in to interfere with private enterprise—to take over certain activities, to prohibit and inhibit others, to manipulate prices, to exact bribes."[1] Landes derives his point about China in part from Kenneth Pomeranz's evidence on the parity between China and England at the end of the eighteenth century. In Landes's version of this story, the explanation for China's failure and Europe's success from their ostensible positions of parity resides in the character of the Chinese state, in particular its supposedly deficient relationship to property and the market. Taking a cue from Nobel Prize–winning economist Friedrich Hayek, whose theories extol free markets and condemn state intervention, while simultaneously mobilizing the ever-useful echoes of earlier Asiatic mode of production

(AMP) analyses of the stagnation-inducing Chinese state-cultural formation, Landes points to the (Ming and Qing) Chinese bureaucracy's misrecognition of its fundamental historical task as explanation for China's "failure." In this rendition of a transhistorical story of state and economy, the state's function is always and at all times to protect freedom, defined as private property and the market. Indeed, for Landes, just as for Hayek and his followers, any propensity toward state regulation falls into the category of what Hayek came to call the "fatal conceit."[2] As Landes has it for the Chinese case, the fatal conceit is a consistently misguided, culturally bound interventionist (and corrupt) state. No mere historical interpretation, Landes frames his argument as a warning to the contemporary Chinese state to relinquish its grip on the economy so as to let the market—and thus freedom—flourish.

Pomeranz perhaps should not be held responsible for the ways in which his work is inappropriately appropriated. Nevertheless, as suggested in the first essay in this volume, it is not so much the empirical findings as it is the consonance between Pomeranz's and Landes's epistemological assumptions and comparative method that facilitates the mobilization of a deracinated and dehistoricized "parity" as the descriptive and analytical core of a China/England (Yangzi/Manchester) comparison. In other words, the formal structure of a comparative practice assuming and establishing ahistorical equivalence cannot be treated separately from its consciousness or content.[3] In this case, the same assumptions and methods used by Pomeranz underpin Landes's comparative practice, allowing the latter to promote an alternative silver bullet explanation for China's decline. Where Pomeranz finds the accident—contingency—of coal and global conjunctures explanatory of England's rise and China's fall from a place of formal equivalence (parity), Landes find the explanation for China's failure (vs. England's success) in the form and nature of their respective states. Both versions are equally plausible or implausible, with no superior way to adjudicate other than through ideological fealty to one version of determinism over another (transhistorical technological determinism or the transhistorical relationship between state, property, and freedom). This form of determinism can only be substantiated by the piling on of ever-new and always disputed empirical evidence that may or may not add up to the desired conclusions. Thus, although Pomeranz's version of the story of

China's fall in the nineteenth century has the distinct virtue of mostly side-stepping culturalism—a hoary conceit to which Landes tightly clings—nevertheless, his comparative method produces a concept of equivalence and a myth of parity that can be analytically moved around at will, yielding equally "truthful," even if mutually irreconcilable, conclusions.

To be sure, this comparative method is standard social science combined with, in Pomeranz's case, sensitivity to longue durée details. Yet it is precisely this form that produces and reproduces historically similar perspectives on China and the world, with the continuous circular effect on scholarly practice creating an echo chamber of transhistorical repetition. Today, in sometimes vulgarized and sometimes sophisticated form, this repetitive transhistoricity—always with a twist, to make it seem fresher than it is—informs much of the renewed academic and policy interest in globalization and markets. In this echo-chamber environment, current and past gurus of market fundamentalism proliferate, while many different ghostly ancestors can be channeled to speak, as if directly, to the present obsession. Friedrich Hayek is one such (recent) ancestral wise man resuscitated to speak of markets as *the* definition of "the economic." Hayek's recent and ongoing resurrection is in part due to the fact that his historical and contemporary case is built on the designation of the transhistorical practice of market exchange as determinative of a society's development and level of freedom. He maintains, "The entrepreneurship of each person is the engine of human activity. Therefore, the economic problem is focused on explaining how each person creates and discovers the information that is relevant for the exercise of his entrepreneurship."[4] Of course, market exchange has been around since time immemorial, although the concept (and reality) of a "market economy" dates only from the mid-nineteenth century. A market economy must be seen as a different sort of historical formation than a market: a market economy requires the subordination of society to, as well as the organization of society through, the logic of the market. A market economy demands everything be commoditized, including land, labor, and money;[5] it is not merely a description of exchange and circulation, no matter how widespread. A clear distinction between markets in general and a market economy as a specific logic of sociohistorical relations would seem to be crucial to any serious account of local, national, regional, or global economies.

By the same token, it would seem necessary to recognize the apparently contradictory desire of liberal capitalism to "be(come) One across the globe *only* based on its own logic (axiomatics)" against capitalism's historical fate of being "actually destined to carry a national form."[6] Yet today, with utter disregard for historical distinctions between markets and market economies and with little attention to the historical relationship of market economies to nation-states, the magic of markets as primary determinant of (national) history is a historiographical and policy trend taken up since the 1980s in China scholarship with great fervor. This is particularly true of Song, Ming, and early Qing China scholars, as well as of post-Mao China scholars, in part because China's booming local and transregional markets flourished during those periods. Markets now are not only central to re-centering the supposed precapitalist global economy upon China (see my discussion in the first essay of this volume) but they are also central to determining the internal workings of Chinese society—Smithian (natural) and not Marxian (capitalist). Yet squaring the ideological circle requires a few magical moves. For, if contemporary orthodoxy designates markets as the measure of man, then China comes out nicely as a matter of local or regional market development, albeit only up to the nineteenth century, when it hits an impasse (essentially Pomeranz's point). And yet, if the relationship between state and market is the measure of modernizationist historical success, then China forever is left behind (this is R. Bin Wong's and in altered form Landes's point). Markets thus cut two ways and the ideological valorization of markets as such is central to both. It is central to the determination of the importance of markets as a measure of modernity in domestic terms (for the sinology crowd, for whom the socialist moment of anticapitalism is but a blip in time and an anti-argument in space, China can have been modern in the pre-Qing and post-Mao periods without ever having become capitalist); and it is central to the importance of the noninterference of the state in markets as a measure of modernizationist success (and thus the West can retain centrality for the non-sinology crowd). While the various measurings are a matter of heated dispute (see the first essay for indications), that which should be measured has been determined: it is circulation and consumption. In this version, in advance of the historical concretization of the logic of market economies by and through capitalism (globally, in its imperialist forms; locally, in its [semi]colonized forms), markets are merely a logic of circulation and consumption, conveniently abstracted and set apart from the totality of social relations; the fact of market circulation and consumption is thus treated as an independent or autonomous factor, and proffered as historically determinative. Meanwhile, the state, too, is abstracted from social relations and stands ahistorically as an enduringly generic form (see the second essay in this volume). Nothing more than the ideological hewing to contemporary market fundamentalism and the imposition of noninterventionist state wisdom on the past, these orthodoxies, while building on older culturalist and historicist ones, are bound up with the resurgence of Hayekian market theories in concert with the current financialization of capital (which goes under the name *globalization*).[7] In this regard, the contemporary link to Hayek is as thoroughly historical as it is ideological. It is a form of magic.

Hayek is one of the more famous second-generation Austrian School economists to emerge from the collapse of the Austro-Hungarian Empire, the world wars, and the takeover of Eastern Europe first by Nazism and then by Soviet Communism. A staunch anti-Marxist and anti-Communist, Hayek was an early theorist of the supposed convergence of left and right versions of totalitarianism. In the 1930s, he engaged in sharp debates about the state and markets in socialism, in the course of which he refined his theories on the ineluctable relation between freedom and the market. Focusing on the market as a tendentially perfect mechanism of distribution, he concluded that socialist (Stalinist) centralized market control was inefficient and repressive. Having languished in England in the shadow of the postwar dominance of Keynsian state interventionism, Hayek (in 1974) and his American market fundamentalist bedfellow, Milton Friedman (in 1976), each won the Nobel Prize in economics, signaling and confirming a vast ideological and practical shift in Anglo-America away from the postwar consensus on state intervention toward an emerging conviction in the self-regulating tendential equilibrium of markets (reflected and implemented in the Thatcher/Reagan revolutions). This consensus has only gotten firmer and stronger with the collapse of Communism and the transitions into market economies by the former Soviet Union, the Eastern Bloc, and China. In this ideological-historical sense, Hayek can be seen as the unconscious of a portion of today's scholarly and policy world.

Yet Hayek is more than an unconscious, as he also is very visible in Chinese scholarship and policy-making these days.[8] Since the mid-1990s, the prominent economist and one of China's leading Hayek scholars, Liu Junning, in his attempt to make explicit the supposed 1990s link to the erstwhile 1930s, never tires of asserting that "economic freedom is the mother of all freedoms," a lesson purportedly learned in China's 1930s, then subsequently forgotten through the Maoist years.[9] This transhistorical truth is concretized for Liu in the observation that the 1990s revival of liberalism in and about China (by which he means a Chicago–Austrian Friedman–Hayek version of liberalism) must be seen as marking the comeback of the prerevolutionary liberalism forcibly suppressed by Mao from the 1950s to 1980s.[10] Opportunistically conflating Hayek's market liberalism with all modern liberalisms, and China's 1930s liberalism with the liberalisms of today, Liu can claim, through a familiar sleight of hand, that free-market fundamentalists such as himself are the successors to the earlier liberals, who were heroically sacrificed on the altar of what he insistently and anachronistically calls the "Red scourge."[11] Liu's magic sleight of hand is facilitated by linguistic or vocabulary surfaces (*ziyou zhuyi* as liberalism in both eras), genealogies of scholarship (teacher-student successions), as well as opposition to the Communist Party, then and now. More important, however, it is facilitated structurally by the ideological harmony produced through the definition of "the economic" as essentially a transhistorical matter of the market, as a form of circulation/distribution, exchange, and consumption, as a phenomenon with equivalent social significance, historical effectivity, and systemic workings through the ages. In other words, Liu's magic is instantiated by defining the economic as equivalent to a historically nonspecific mode of exchange named *the market*.

These days, this transhistorical perspective has become the basis for a new orthodoxy. And yet this moment is not unique (even if its repetition is more tragic than farcical). Indeed, as economic philosopher Wang Yanan lamented already in the 1930s, this transhistory was popularized by the spread of the original Austrian School of economics from as early as the 1910s, a school of thought thence vulgarized as the common sense of the Chinese and the global economy. For Wang (and others), the Austrian influence was as pernicious as it was pervasive. I now turn to the specifics of the Austrian theories and Wang's critique, as well as to their implications for philosophical-historical problematizations of Chinese history.

Austrian School Economics

The Austrian School of economics emerged in Vienna with the publication in 1871 by its commonly recognized founder, Carl Menger (1841–1921), of his first major work, *Principles of Economics*.[12] In this treatise, Menger sketched the outlines of what came to be known as the "marginalist revolution." The hallmarks of the Menger intervention in economic theory are a focus on market distribution/consumption and a reinterpretation of the theory of value as a subjectivist rather than a productivist theory (of either a classical or a Marxian variety). In Menger's view, extended first by his student Eugen Böhm-Bawerk and then by a host of others, the basis for economics as a discipline should be found in the market operations of subjective value. Eschewing mathematical models as a type of formalism intended to impose objectivist closure on essentially subjective processes, the economists of the first generation of the Austrian School studied economics as a science of individual desire, as exhibited in the consumption, distribution, and circulation of goods in and through an unfettered marketplace, whose patterns of activity were based upon diminishing marginal utility. In this schema, the value of any given commodity is equal to the least urgent individual use to which it is applied—its marginal utility.[13]

In their focus on the individual, the Austrians resuscitated David Ricardo's "economic man"—a figure abandoned by the competing German New Historicist school in favor of the category of the national economy.[14] However, the Austrians revised "economic man" away from the classical economists' focus on self-maximizing behavior by reorienting the individual's life toward the fulfillment of desire. As value/desire are transhistorical phenomena for the Austrians, the specific social forms value takes are not relevant for their analyses. Thus, the question for them was not why a specific reality (value) came to exist in a specific form (commodity) or why this reality *appeared* ontologically grounded (in human nature/desire) and therefore ahistorical (in the market).[15] That is, their question was not about value as a historically specific form of social mediation. To the contrary, the appearance and the form were collapsed phenomenologically: commodity and value inhabit and are realized through the same locus, individual desire, and the question became how a commodity's use-value—for the Austrians, the exhaustive content of the category of value—could be reliably realized in the marketplace.[16] Their concern, thus, was not with specific forms of social relations or of domination characteristic of capitalism as a local or global systemic. Instead, the socioeconomic problem for the Austrian School was contained to how individual desires were coordinated and how subjective choices were integrated into a self-regulating system of market equilibrium in the context of imperfect knowledge and uncertainty.

To address this question, the Austrians pioneered a theory of "intertemporal" structure, visually depicted (by Böhm-Bawerk) as a bull's-eye, indicating the concentric circular time lags between the accumulation of capital and interest paid on that capital in the process of production, and between desire and its fulfillment in the market. On this view, for example, the temporal structure of production determines the value of labor;[17] thus labor's value, as a commodity like any other on the market, is realized only through its (deferred) use in consumption, while wages are considered the advance given by employers to workers before the value of their labor is actually realized. While the sociopolitical implications of this theory are in the main socially conservative and entirely antilabor, the focus on the temporality of capital realization was new at the time. It was intended to address the perceived problem in transformation between value and price that Marx supposedly had left contradictorily unexplicated in *Capital*.[18]

The main point of the Austrian School theories about the form of the economic is their historically nonspecific focus on the relationship between individuals and the market. Major questions for the Austrians thus revolved around how the market operated in the context of incomplete knowledge, how to understand the lag time in the realization of value, and how subjective valuation of value could be aggregated efficiently through the market despite uncertainty, where efficiency denoted the possibility of individual fulfillment of desire and not optimal market functionality.[19] Austrian theories hence raised the philosophical problem that Ludwig von Mises, a second-generation Austrian School economist, termed the "real present." I will come back to the philosophical import in Chinese history of transhistorical economics and the implications of its version of the temporality of the "real present." First, I turn to Wang Yanan's critique of the Austrians to illustrate how Wang figured the insufficiency of the Austrian School theory for an understanding of the Chinese present (1930s/1940s). As Wang was not concerned with the minutiae of their "scientific" procedures, those will not detain me below.[20]

Wang Yanan's Critique of the Austrians' Transhistory

Wang Yanan negatively refers to the Austrians in many of his 1930s essays on economic theory. In line with his general concern about the vulgarization of economics and its detachment from everyday life and practice, Wang was particularly disturbed by the school's antihistorical (transhistorical) premise, its reduction of economics to scientific method, its reliance upon psychology (via the mechanism of desire), and the ease of its popularization because of the apparent commonsensical nature of its descriptions of and prescriptions for the role of individual subjectivity in animating a free market. He also was concerned with the school's reactionary sociopolitical implications, its avoidance of any discussion of imperialism/colonialism, and its philosophy of the present, which amounted more to an ideology of "presentism" than to a theory of modern temporality. These were the points of departure for his critique not only of the Austrians but of global mainstream economics as well as of the adoption in China of perspectives on the economic informed by that mainstream.

In Wang's view, within economics as a contemporary discipline, there were two large trends: empiricist and metaphysical. Within the latter, there were three general types: pure science detached from reality, a discipline attached to reality but not to capitalism as such, and a discipline with relevance to capitalist countries but not to China or those similarly situated.[21] Austrian School economics fell into the first category of metaphysics. That is, in Wang's reading, with the Austrian School in the late nineteenth and early twentieth centuries, economics was rendered into pure science and detached from social practice and historicity: Wang cites one precursor, Karl Kniess, who claimed the only thing that counts for economics is how it accords with the truth of human nature. For Kniess and others of his philosophical bent, it is "something like 2+2=4: there is no temporality or spatiality to the principles."[22] This was a form of value-free ahistorical science for which Wang had nothing but contempt, as it rendered theory prior to history and in fact impervious to historical process. On this view, for Wang, the biggest problem with Chinese economists was not their acceptance of universals but rather the specific metaphysical nature of the economic universals they accepted. "Here," Wang notes, "so-called metaphysical economic theory points mainly to Austrian School economics."[23]

Because of the perceived importance of the topic, aside from his many smaller notes on the issue scattered throughout his essays of the time, Wang dedicated an entire long essay, titled "Austrian School Economics in Chinese Economics Circles," to this discussion. He begins carefully, by deconstructing and explaining the essay's title. He notes that economics has no national identity or boundary; hence the term "Chinese economics" is not meant to claim that there is such a thing as "Chinese" economics in contrast to Italian or English economics, for example (as empiricists Luigi Cossa or Robert Ingram would have it).[24] As far as Wang was concerned, capitalism imposed economic universals that were not subject to national containment. From this observation flowed three points:

1. The universals of economics and their global nature derive from the economic and global nature of reality.
2. These universals do not erase specificity. Rather, from the positive side, they are the result of the abstraction and universalizing of specificity; while from the negative side, they condemn to oblivion those specificities that cannot be abstracted or universalized.
3. The use of economics in each specific society must be tailored to that society and cannot be universalized; there is no copying from a blueprint.[25]

That is, lived specificity—or the residue that exceeds the global or the national; the specificity emerging into visibility from the abstractions of capitalism—must be the site for the excavation of historicized social meaning. This residue/excess, then, cannot be understood as the obsolescent detritus of some essential pastness ("remnants") slated to be overcome, nor as a culturalist surplus, but rather as the very stuff of social life lived in the present. It is the site of a concrete universality that, in philosopher Peter Osborne's terms, "derives less from a backward-looking historiography, than from a praxis-based phenomenology of social life."[26]

By contrast with the praxis-based version of social life advocated by Wang Yanan, the Austrians had a considerably less historicized view, one they termed "praxeological." This view was founded upon a general and a priori theory of human action. As Wang saw it, if the Austrian School rendered economics without conflict between itself and either natural science or psychology (as Böhm-Bawerk maintained)—that is, if economics was an ontology of human nature—then it was because use-value was the "central nervous system" of their doctrines. Yet, as Wang comments, "even though they define use as the source of value, they do not promote the idea that the existence or the extent of value derives from something's usefulness." In this sense, they are not a "utilitarian school" (*shaoyong xuepai*).[27] Rather, they maintain that an item's value corresponds to the urgency and importance of desire for that item: "the higher one's sense of lack or of urgency, then the higher the threshold of use, and thus the correspondingly higher threshold of value."[28] For the Austrians, the marketplace is the neutral arena in which various individuals' desires get realized as value, through the transformation of desire-value into price via competition. If competition is curtailed, desire does not get fulfilled. "In other words," Wang notes mordantly, "the measure of value of a good is not determined by the measure of production cost, but rather by the consumer. . . . In order to make this plausible, they distinguish between consumer and production goods: the former . . . directly satisfies an individual desire; the latter can indirectly satisfy that desire."[29] As he mentions later on, this differentiation makes no sense for the way people live their lives or the way society actually functions.

With the Austrians' focus on human nature in terms of need and desire, the entirety of human life becomes actually or potentially occupied by the economic; or, as Ludwig von Mises distilled the Austrian School perspective, "the economist's only responsibility is to confirm the existence of a dissatisfaction which motivates the person to act, and that the agent perceives or realizes that certain goods, be they material or immaterial, may serve him as a means."[30] Thus representing the thorough permeation of *Being* by the economic—understood as a desire responding to a *lack*—as well as the complete culturalization of human behavior in terms of consumption, life is reduced to the impulse for consumption and the satisfaction of lack through acquisition. This is, of course, a capitalist (and, differently fulfilled, a Freudian) dream; or, as Wang obliquely notes, it is the magic to which Marx's revealing analysis of the fetishism of the commodity form corresponds.[31]

In the Austrian schema, it is the "intratemporal" structure of value realization that makes the transactions between desire and consumption both possible and intelligible. As Wang comments with regard to the theory of intratemporality: "This is not wrong. Yet here, they turn the relatively small marginal utility of the future good's relation to the current good into the bridge between them. But, what relation does the measure of fulfillment of individual desire have to the length of time? If the measure of time is a year or a month and the system goes according to a standard of passing time, not some subjective feeling of the distance between times, is that then not importing an objective factor into subjective evaluations?"[32]

Beyond and connected to the logical inconsistency of the objective/subjective evaluations of time, Wang points to how the deployment of temporality, while seemingly rooted in common sense, actually "creates common sense."[33] That is, as he reminds his readers, common sense is only the most vulgarized form of normativity: it can take "all sorts of consumption desires and types" to be the natural properties of all human beings expressed in essentially analogous ways. Common sense can use the "great insight" of temporal lags in value realization to explain away why laborers' wages are small compared to capitalist profit, and/or to explain away the problems of economic crisis. Yet none of these social phenomena is natural; they are man-made.[34]

The tenor of his critiques clearly indicates Wang Yanan was interested in a historically specific approach to the problem of the economic that demanded he take on "theories that posit transhistorically what is historically determinate"[35] in the mode of immanent social critique. This mode is what historian Harry Harootunian calls a "science of criticism," through which the excavation of a lived moment forces the unveiling of ideological idealism.[36] In one sense, then, Wang's overriding philosophical and political commitment to historicization and the historically specific within the universalizing tendencies of capitalism could explain his perhaps exaggerated concern with the Austrians and their influence.[37] By the same token, writing as a Chinese and as a non-Communist Marxist, Wang was quite clear that not only had China historically not "given rise to an environment conducive to political economy" but China's subjugated position in the global economy made it imperative for Chinese economists to have a critical attitude toward classical and neoclassical political economy. Yet not just any critical attitude would do: "it is also possible," he wrote elliptically, so as to evade the pervasive Guomindang (GMD, or Nationalist Party) censorship of the time, "to select *which* critical attitude to have. And, it is because this possibility exists, that transformations will not be the result merely of China's internal social economy, but rather, of transformations in the global economic environment."[38]

Writing in the mid to late 1930s, part of the historical specificity Wang urgently wished to grasp was the nature of the crisis in China's and the world's political economy—separately and in relation to one another. Indeed, according to Wang's understanding, the whole idea of crisis was something the Austrians had no way to explain. According to him, in Austrian theory, if indeed capitalists and workers were "really producing for consumption, then the facts of crisis due to overproduction and underconsumption could not be understood at all."[39] That is, Wang took an essentially Luxembourgian/Leninist position on capitalist crisis and opined that, if the market tends toward equilibrium, as the Austrians assumed a priori, and if the free market tends toward social harmony, as they also claimed, the nature of the Great War, the Great Depression, the class struggles thereby unleashed, and the extended global economic crisis of the 1930s was unintelligible.[40] By contrast to this resistance to confronting crisis (or concealment of crisis as a problem), Wang was at particular pains to figure out what China's position in the world was and how the global crisis in its many dimensions informed, shaped, and constrained its choices in the present and future.

I more fully engage Wang's understanding of China in the 1930s in the next essay. For the moment suffice it to note that his basic diagnosis was that the country was suspended between feudalism and capitalism in what he called a hypocolonial (ci zhimindi) socioeconomic formation. This formation was concretely expressed in "comprador commerce and finance, feudal-like land property relations, as well as in the loss of control over the system of tariffs, industrial development, inner-river navigation, and a host of other aspects."[41] Under these conditions, Wang says, most Chinese economic researchers were more concerned with the fetters on the Chinese economy represented by feudal tradition than with the obstacles posed by imperialism. He writes witheringly on this point:

Thus, they specify that . . . all it takes is for China to turn itself into a capitalist nation. . . . As such, congratulating capitalism and praising capitalist economic doctrines have become the determining realities forming the major part of Chinese research on political economy. . . . These kinds of ideological reactions are not only inevitable, they are also not completely surprising: as compared to feudal society's economic formation and as compared to feudal society's ideological formation, praising the capitalist system and its theoretical articulations must, all told, be seen as a sort of progressive expression.[42]

Yet, as Wang points out, China's problems, far from being about feudal remnants, are in fact the historical product of the social relations violently established by imperialism, relations that rendered China's economic, social, and political formation what it was in the 1930s. That is, instead of taking China's formation as separate and autonomous from the global situation, as many Chinese and foreign economists were wont to do, Wang urged economists (and sociologists) to see the Chinese and the global formations in a dynamic and mutually constitutive relationship. On this view, as far as Wang was concerned, clearing away the feudal fetters simply would not produce the captialist-modernized nation for which Chinese economists wished, precisely because imperialism as a form of global structural inequality stood in the way. In addition, as Wang was clear, a simple comparative focus—China versus the West—in social scientific, value-neutral equivalence was a mere evasion of the deeply imbricated historicity of the creation of China's current formation.

Wang thus castigated the "majority" of Chinese economics researchers, who refused to take into account the "total global economic condition" so they could focus exclusively on "the difficulties of China's precapitalist economic formation."[43] Their refusal, he comments, stemmed in part from their training: Chinese economists were at best "disciple" returnees from foreign universities, mechanically applying principles learned there to the Chinese situation. In part it also derived from their ideological certainty, adopted or osmotically adapted from the Austrian School, that economics is basically the study of human nature expressed in and through the market, regardless of time and place. Because of this, as Wang recounts the majority view, Chinese economists tended to believe that what needed to be done was to change Chinese people's behavior (as exhibited in their cultural predispositions on desire and consumption, primarily) in order for the economy to change and develop accordingly.[44]

How, Wang asks incredulously, could such a "denial of economics" as exhibited in the Austrian School's metaphysical idealism spread so readily across the world and into China, such that the specificity of a historical formation is erased in the zeal for ahistorical and transhistorical analysis? For spread it had. Indeed, there was no doubt in Wang's mind that

Austrian School economics and its mutations and subspecies have spread . . . into every corner of the world (except the Soviet Union). Joseph Schumpeter, a German sympathizer,[45] has most recently lauded this spread: "the only and indeed the sole properly affirmed economics the world over is the school of marginal utility . . ." If we think his affirmation is a bit exaggerated, then look at the American, Veblen, who opposes the Austrians: ". . . this [School] will no doubt flourish in the future, even though it has no capacity to address and explain actual economic problems."[46]

In other words, as Wang surveyed the global mainstream, the Austrian School and its theory of marginal utility/consumer economics constituted the dominant trend in the minds of both its many supporters and its few critics. Beyond that, because of the vulgarization of economics, it had come to be accepted as a natural property of human beings, part of human nature.[47]

The explanation for this hegemony came down for Wang to a pervasive pure ideology concealing a historical problematic. Using felicitous wordplay (lost in [my] English translation), Wang commented: "In order to counter the economic consciousness of crisis [weiji], the Austrian School economists have turned into costumed performers playing martial arts heroes of and apologists for 'traditional morality' [weidao]."[48] Playing on the homonym wei in the terms for "crisis" and "traditional morality," Wang suggests how a historicized event—"crisis" (weiji)—can be turned by the Austrians into a performative tale about ahistorical "traditional morality" (weidao). Standing as they did on the side of the "indulgent world of finance capital," the Austrians addressed crisis as a moment—an accidental interruption, a pure contingency—in naturalized business cycles. In so doing, they promoted "consumer economics"[49] as a means of displacing the self-created crises in finance capital unto the individual consumer and unto consumption writ large. Through displacement, traditional morality could be mobilized to recall to the individual his/her primary human function: to consume. In this way, the depth and origins of capitalist crisis—in the 1930s, within and of finance capital—could be repackaged as an ontological problem of life itself: the morality of being a consuming human. Indeed, Wang notes, in the same measure as capitalist society became more preoccupied by the problem of crisis, "economists, quite ingeniously, came up with a 'spiritual therapy' cure [jingshen zhiliao], twisting research on crisis into research on economic booms [*jingqi*]."[50] In a universe where crisis becomes boom and spiritual therapy becomes economic cure, traditional morality is called upon for the resumption of the essence of human life—consumption. In this superficial performance, finance capital, the villain, is freed to dress up in costume and play the avenging hero in the tragedy *it* set in motion. (The resonances with the post-2008 financial crisis are too strong to miss!)

The circularity here is quite elegant, as is the thorough conflation of surface with depth and of performative representation with the historical real. Yet, as Wang laments, it is a far cry from addressing the problem of the current situation, as a specific form of temporality and historicity shaped by and through a more complex notion of economic crisis. Indeed, paraphrasing Jean-Jacques Rousseau, who identified France's eighteenth-century "state of crisis" (*l'état de crise*) as "the crisis of the state" (*la crise d'état*), we could say Wang was particularly concerned not to have a "crisis of the economy" be displaced unto an "economics crisis"—that is, the transposition of a materialist problem into an idealist/ideological one.[51]

In Wang's view, then, the asocial and transhistorical character of the "individual" posited by the Austrian School amounted to the denial of economics as a historically specific science of social life and social critique. He accused the Austrians of using a "plagiarizing technique" (*chaoxi jishu*) to appropriate problems from within classical economics (e.g., the difference between value and price) and turn them into pseudo-scientific procedures untethered to any particular historicity, even though, as Wang points out, the conditions of the Austrians' emergence and spread are in fact quite specific to the late nineteenth and early twentieth centuries. This period witnessed the "internal contradictions within capitalist development" becoming very apparent, through exposure and exposition in "critical economic theory" and the accumulating crises within finance capital. While critical theory (by which he means Marxism) exhorted people to "look beyond subjectivism, to open their eyes and reveal the true sources of capitalist crisis," the Austrians arrogated to themselves the "special task" of denying systemic crisis by advocating subjectivism.[52] This, as Wang makes clear, is not some value-free or neutral endeavor; indeed, it serves finance capital just as surely as if it were promoted directly by them.

Wang's immanent critique is similar in intent and structure to what Georg Lukács in approximately the same era (the post–World War I reconsolidation of finance capital in Europe and the political displacement of social crisis into anticapitalist or fascist movements) noted as the separation of the ideological from the phenomenological among classical economists and vulgar Marxists alike. Lukács condemned both types for mistaking a specific problem for a problem in its totality, for the "disruption of the dialectical unity of thought and existence."[53] He insisted (as a methodological and substantive point): "The history of a particular problem turns into the history of problems," as the "ideological and the economic problems lose their mutual exclusiveness and merge into one another."[54] That is, one must start from the totality and move to the specific and back again, rather than mistaking the specific for the totality.

In a mode of immanent critique analogous to Lukács, for Wang, who also had to consider the subjugated position of China in the global ideological-economic system, the particular problem of China was inevitably bound up with the forms characteristic of the modern world: "Various ideologies about modern capitalism filter in with the arrival of capitalist commodities. The penetration of commodities and of commodity ideology/consciousness is intimately related to one another. . . . If the arrival of commodity ideology is neither voluntary nor sovereign, those imposing the commodities violently use commodity ideology as an organizing mechanism for the imposition."[55]

Here, Wang recognizes the commodity form as simultaneously a historical materiality and a cultural-ideological effectivity—that is, as a particular totalizing type of social formation, mode of value mediation, and conceptualization in capitalism rather than as an atomized problem within an ahistorical discipline called *economics*. This recognition is central to his dissatisfaction with the relationship established in Chinese economics circles between economics, practice, and history. For Wang was quite clear that "naturalized" (*ziranhua*) and "phenomenalized" (*xianxianghua*) theories such as the Austrian School of economics, the Southwest (German) School of sociology, legal formalism, and educational behavioralism—the most "advanced" non-Marxist theories of the first half of the twentieth century—all were ideologies produced by and reflective of the commodity form. They were designed to and actually did "put people in thrall" (*yinren rumi*).[56]

Economics, Practice, and History

In the broadest as well as the most granular sense, Wang Yanan was interested in the historical concretization of particular and general social relations in China and the world under capitalism, specifically in the context of the global crisis of the 1930s. Properly understanding the economic as a practice of the everyday was the crux of this endeavor. In his historicized view, economics as a mode of inquiry and explication of increasingly complex relations within and between societies emerged only with the maturation of capitalist social relations as a dominant form in the late eighteenth century, even though the progression in political economic theory from Adam Smith through Thomas Robert Malthus and beyond was marked by the increasing detachment of economics from its roots in social practice and historical specificity. Wang writes: "Economics conforms to the demands of capitalism and it conforms to the realities of capitalism; it is from within capitalism that economics became a science. At the time of its efflorescence, its linkage to practice was extremely clear. But once it had acquired a general scientific content and was constituted as a science of research . . . its relation to practice and its link to the real gradually were obscured."[57]

Politically and philosophically frustrated by the detachment of economics from life—where economics now merely aimed to reflect and deflect the abstractions of capitalism—Wang was intent on recalling to political economy its origins in history and practice, its roots in explaining and excavating lives lived by actual people in the times and multiple places of contemporary existence under capitalism. He was interested, that is, in economics as a philosophy of the everyday, in all its variety and lived specificities.

In this regard, while Austrian School economists (including Hayek and his contemporary avatars[58]) ostensibly begin from the complexity of human action—desire, fulfillment, subjectivity—thus, apparently, from a concept of practice, nevertheless for them practice does not constitute a historicized philosophical topos. Rather, it is a hermeneutic or a form of exegesis in a psychologistic mode. For this reason, for them, on the one hand, economics had to be separated from natural sciences (which obey laws independent of thought); and yet, on the other hand, economics could constitute itself as a science organic to individual growth and thus without conflict with natural science. A transhistorical view of human nature and of market-mediated desire derived from this hermeneutic version of practice. As a major aspect of this, Austrian School economics treats each individual as autonomous—a hallmark of "methodological individualism"—and thus all sociality as deriving from the individual or from the individual psyche. This reduces the social to an aggregate of individual market desires, thereby invalidating and short-circuiting other potential understandings of sociality (political or otherwise). It also renders state regulation of the market ipso facto irrational: as the state cannot possibly know the desires of individuals, attempts to regulate represent an infringement of individual freedom (to desire, choose, consume) and a distortion of market competition and tendential equilibrium.[59] For the Austrians (as for Hayek and others), the best the state can and should do is ensure conditions for the free circulation of and competition among commodities and their corresponding desires: to ensure the growth of "organic" rather than "constructed" institutions, in their parlance.

At the same time, because practice—as human behavior, as hermeneutic—is not specific to any particular historical moment and is impervious to the interruption of events in a theoretical a priori, it floats above the fray in the frame of the transhistory of desire and subjectivity informing interactions across time and space. That is, like Hegelian metaphysical idealism, there is a claim to philosophical universalism in Austrian School economics; however, unlike Hegelianism, the founders of and successors to Austrian School methodology cling tightly to an antihistoricism that explicitly refuses to define a teleology to practice (or history). Their focus, thus, is more on process than on end-states.[60] However, the relationship between desire and need—subjectivist value and marginal utility—is theoretically construed as a constant function of an ahistorically posited human nature. Moreover, the mediator between desire and need is always-already determined to be commodity consumption, with use-value at its core. Thus, while need and desire inform one another and are apparently related dynamically, they are compartmentalized analytically, universalized across time and space, and joined only through the medium of the exchange commodity, whose use-value is subjectively realized in the market. Value is not a historically specific social mediator—a qualitatively distinct category—but use-value in general.[61]

With the huge potential scope of inquiry opened by such a perspective (transhistorical human behavior, *tout court*), the Austrian School economists, unlike Marx, claimed that their subjectivist law of value could be operationalized as an explanation of the actual workings of any market. That is, if Marx's theory of value is concerned primarily to specify value as the expression of the "inner nexus of connections of the *capitalist* social formation" rather than to find (and failing to do so) an approximation of market function (as Böhm-Bawerk and others assumed),[62] then, by contrast to Marx, the Austrians claimed to have a theory rooting value directly in and as a function of market transaction, as an explanation for how markets work, not ethically (for which they had no concern) but actually. This focus lends their theories a simultaneous apparent specificity—as practice and a timelessness—as capable of happening anywhere and anytime, carrying with it equivalent significance across time and space. That is, the Austrians, as sociologist Henri Lefebvre noted of modern philosophy more generally, in apparently rooting economics in individual and subjective practice, "have drawn closer to everyday life, but only to *discredit* it, under the pretext of giving it a new resonance."[63] By ontologizing and naturalizing it, the Austrians reduced everyday practice to a series of individual activities that could be broken down and understood sequentially and cyclically: a chronology leading from need to desire to consumption, and then all over again. Meanwhile, by stripping practice of emotive passion other than desire for consumption, desire became a mere function of need (the driving force of agentive action).[64]

In a critical vein and what Wang Yanan deplored was that Austrian theory cannot account, even in its own terms, for the fact that the "circuit from need to desire and from desire to need is constantly being interrupted or distorted. . . . Everyday life has literally been colonized."[65] As Wang derisively noted in this regard, "the so-called consumer theory, theory of desire, theory of interest and profit based on temporal gaps, along with the market signs of various 'doings' and their symbolic explanations . . . are all quite tasty and sate the appetite."[66] It is especially this type of superficiality that, he pointed out, eagerly is taken up by vulgar economists and the media, who obsessively report salaciously and breathlessly about market conditions, replete with graphic depictions of demand-side economics, all the while ignoring more germane issues. This one-sided depiction helps propel the view of the economic toward a transhistorical technocratic common sense. In its normative vulgarization, this trend facilitates a concealment of the complexity of relationships that might allow economics to become a historicized critical lens on everyday life instead of "a type of ahistorical discipline . . . performing an abstract disciplinary function."[67]

Wang Yanan's wish to rejoin the economic to the everyday promoted a view of human temporality rooted in a totality of social relations that has historical specificity rather than a hermeneutics of practice floating free of history. He grasped the simultaneity of temporalities embedded in lives lived in the arrhythmic incommensurabilities of everydayness amid capitalism's tendential global universalization and abstractions. Hence, rather than erase temporality as an issue, or reduce it to a sequence and a cycle— in Austrian terms: need, desire, consumption—or to a commensurability with superficial capitalist repetitions of circulation and distribution, Wang, in his effort to grapple with the problem of crisis and historicity (the specificity of China in and of the 1930s world) recognized the interactions and incommensurabilities between coexistent temporalities produced as a social effect and lived experience of global unevenness. In such a sense, everyday life could not be reduced to individual practice, to a hermeneutic, or to a catalog of practices. Those were merely evasions of historical logic.

Indeed, at the same time as encouraging a critical view of economics as a philosophy of everyday life, Wang advocated finding a way to decolonize life, in China and more generally. For him, colonization was tied both to the violent intrusion into and the establishment of domination over Chinese life by imperialist-capitalism. But, more generally, it was tied to the commodity form as the material and ideological violence and domination characteristic of contemporary life.[68] The difficulty of decolonization in practical terms was hence twofold: overcoming the pervasive physical presence within the state administration, universities, institutes, and other organizations of economists and advisers with a stake in continuing imperialist-capitalist domination over China's economy and production of knowledge; and, secondly, short-circuiting "the influence of comprador merchant-finance capitalist consciousness, in particular the influence of imperialist cultural policies" in their ideological forms. Wang recognized that cultural influence was historically coerced. Yet he also was fully convinced that Chinese economists, once given options, had rushed toward and embraced this consciousness of their own volition. "For this reason," he writes, "my current critique of Chinese economics circles for their attitude toward the Austrian School of economics is guided more by depression than it is by blame."[69] His depression became ever deeper, as the realization sank in that "our external weakness does not stem from the lack of sovereign economic consciousness, but from our slavishness."[70]

Social Science/Economics, Temporality, and the Present

In contrast to Wang's view of the everyday as rooted in, yet temporally incommensurate to, capitalism, the Austrians' theory of practice takes at face value what Peter Osborne calls the peculiar *dehistoricalizing* temporality of capital or capitalist sociality.[71] In aligning individual practice with the workings of the market, and in turning these into the definition of the economic as a transhistorical process and fact of life, all activities become commensurate to one another, thus equivalent across time and space. The a priori of human action adumbrates the problem of history.[72] In this respect, these two perspectives on the everyday and practice point to two different philosophies of temporality, corresponding to two different views of the relationship between the economic and the sociohistorical. On the one hand, there is the Austrians'/Ludwig von Mises's "real present" and, on the other hand, Lukácsians'/Wang Yanan's immanent present. We can understand Wang Yanan's concept of the immanent present as an attempt to recall economics to its philosophical origins in everyday life, thus as a critical lens on the possibilities for social transformation. In the same vein, it is possible to see the Austrian School version of the present, named by Ludwig von Mises "the real present," also as trying to grapple with everyday life, albeit by denying that everyday life under capitalism and in modernity is a particular form of temporality.

As we have seen, in Austrian School understanding, "the real present" is both an a priori theory of human practice—praxeology—and a hermeneutic code. In one sense, then, the real present is a form of academic genealogy, insofar as it concerns itself with the episodically continuous working out of an intellectual problem posed by the school's founder, Carl Menger, and subsequently discussed and elaborated over the course of the ensuing century and more. As economic historian Karen Vaughn puts it, "the intellectual real present . . . [is] the time in which all participants are thought to contribute to the solving of some intellectual problem."[73] More philosophically, in the sense of a hermeneutic referencing, the Heideggerian discussion of being and time (*dassein*), "the real present" can be seen as an attempt to "ground the understanding of historical time in an account of the temporality of human existence."[74] As a praxeology corresponding to the repetitive intellectual problem and the establishment of commensurability between historical and human temporality, "the real present" points to the "span of time relevant for formulating a plan and carrying out a plan."[75] Thus, in Mises's fully articulated terms, there only exists the present time of action; the past does not exist and the future, yet to come, cannot be considered. As Mises writes, "action is as such in the real present because it utilizes the instant and thus embodies its reality."[76]

This concept of the present and reality is an elaboration of Menger's late nineteenth-century perspective on individual desire and value. It also philosophically aligns with and articulates in a different realm historical philosopher Henri Bergson's interpretation of temporality as duration (*durée*), itself formulated in the shadow of Heidegger. In Bergson, duration is meant to suggest the qualitative succession of time (versus Aristotelian quantitative succession). As Bergson put it in the 1930s: "the present is arbitrarily defined as *what is*, when the present is simply *what is done*."[77] For Bergson, duration is about the indivisible flow of time—real time, as it were. (This soon was taken up by French Annales School historians, e.g., Lucien Febvre, and fully elaborated by Fernand Braudel in his late 1950s works on the longue durée.) In these iterations, temporality is encapsulated within and by human activity—it is the duration of action itself.[78]

Bergsonianism—the relationship of durational time to individual consciousness and activity—came to signify an aesthetic principle, a metaphysical interiority commensurate to an individual intuition lending concreteness to inner experience. Lukács recognized the ideological dimension of this aesthetic principle as it was expressed and elaborated in and through the narrative form and content of the bourgeois historical novel, a literary phenomenon corresponding to the advent of modern temporality.[79] This aesthetic/ideological dimension became part of Lukács's critical theorization of capitalist reification as embodied in the commodity form.[80] By the same token in the 1960s for Louis Althusser, who was also concerned with the structure of the historical present albeit not in an aesthetic dimension, the Bergsonian-inspired Annales School view of temporality as duration merely reinscribed an "ideological continuum." That is, in Althusser's view, rather than fundamentally problematize the relation between history and temporality by specifying temporality as a particular problematic of and in modernity, all the concept of duration does is reinscribe an ideological conception of time corresponding to a socially hegemonic common sense of continuous temporal flow.[81] In other words, temporality was nothing more than chronology.

Meanwhile, in the Austrians' idiom, because of its limitation to human activity in a pragmatic now—fulfillment of desire for use-value in the market of the here and now—durational time, or the real present, is constrained both by indeterminacy and by a spatialization of time: it is individually experienced and enacted, but only in the radically detemporalized sense of an atomized individual activity undertaken at and completely encompassed by a particular time and in a particular place. In this sense, the real present is pure contingency detached from any necessary historicity. If the real present is about the indeterminacy of action—in Austrian terms: the unknowability of the market, the impossibility of complete knowledge, the subjectivist realization of desire through a marginal determination of use in the market as coordinator of human activity—then all action and temporality are radically contingent as a matter of principle (that is, as a theoretical a priori). And here, contingency (indeterminacy) not only is accident—things being cast together—but the unknown/unknowable, or the absence of historical logic, a logic of historicity. This schema of contingency inscribes real time as a self-sufficient logic. Decoupled from any so-called external problems of representation (narrative and discourse) or conceptualization (semiotics and historicity), time becomes commensurate to its durational self.[82] It is pragmatic presentism; or, for historians, it is chronology combined with accidental contingency as explanatory.

Clearly dissatisfied with the ideological constriction of temporality (and thus history) to the reproduction of a normative economics, culturalism, and state, and also dissatisfied with the epistemological establishment of commensurate equivalences between past and present, China and non-China, Wang Yanan, over the course of many essays addressing a large variety of issues, worked through the problem of the temporality of the present by simultaneously taking into account the universalizing tendencies of global capitalism and the specificities of China's particular situation. The contents of this thinking—Wang's attempt to answer the pervasively posed question in China's 1930s: what is China's social formation?—are explored in part in the fourth essay in this volume. Below, I pursue Wang Yanan's more academic historico-philosophical concern with the form in which, and the ideology through which, economics/social science had been elaborated and codified in the first few decades of China's twentieth century.[83] For, according to Wang, this elaboration and codification left China suspended in time: China's time was "nonproductive,"[84] as it were. Yet, in Wang's view, the reliance in social scientific theorizing on China's supposedly ersatz or nonhistorical time was not really about China—it was not "Chinese"—but rather about how certain kinds of temporality were ideologically produced in the very magic of concepts deployed by and defined through social science and economics.

Temporality and Knowledge

Wang addressed the problem of the ideological production of temporality concretely, so as to arrive at an abstract principle. In one essay, he took up the problem as one of the categories of historical analysis: "Commerce, labor, or clans have been extant in practically every historical era, and yet in different eras, they take on different contents and aspects, they are mediated differently and play extremely different roles."[85] In other words, Wang's attention was not limited to a positivist concern with concepts and their appearance in history—commerce, labor, clans—but extended to forms of mediation and hence to differences in historical signification. This allowed him to recognize that while the twentieth century could be considered a "scientific era," that label completely obscured the unscientific and alienating aspects of the era.[86] Hence, in the social sciences, while the same concepts are applied to past and present so as to create the veneer of scientificity and regularity, all this pretense to continuity does is conceal the historical incommensurabilities between the past and the present and between coexisting presents. This produces temporality as alienating affect.

For Wang, one of the most alienating of those concealed incommensurabilities was precisely the experience of capitalism in its confrontation with, shaping of, and uneven assimilation into China's everyday life since the mid-nineteenth century. In this sense, his urgency to reclaim and refashion life—in the now and for a possible future—corresponded to a temporality of the present others already had named the "current situation" (*xianzai xing*; *xianshi xing*). It was through "the current situation" that Wang understood the present as a form of temporality within the terms of a historical problematization. That is, for him, the present was a problem of and in modernity, philosophically grasped as a conflict between the past, the present, and possible futurities in the realm of the lived everyday, as those conflicts were continually (re)produced in real life. The present for Wang did not connote a pragmatic presentism—a pure moment of practice sufficient unto itself—but rather, it connoted transformative activism aimed at changing the conditions of life. It was a process of decolonization rather than repetitive (re)colonization.

To get at this issue, Wang deemed it imperative to recognize that philosophy and economics/social science, as global forms of knowledge corresponding to the connectedness of the modern world, were linked in a coherent epistemology (*tongyi renshi*).[87] This coherence or unity (*tongyi*) did not connote absolute overlap and sameness of objects/subjects of study or realities; rather, in keeping with Marxist dialectics, it consisted simultaneously of sameness and difference. The relationship of philosophy and economics, of China and the world, was a coherent identity of levels that could be encompassed *through* history (as a product of becoming) and *as* history (in specifications of the present/future). In the first sense, as Wang notes, modern philosophy had been formed from the specificity of practice to become the premise for the study and understanding of experience, a project for which it originally depended upon the dialectically intertwined historical completions of economic/social scientific and natural scientific systems of inquiry. Yet "under the contagion of modern bourgeois philosophy"[88] these relations had been obscured: economics had become an ostensibly autonomous realm of inquiry, ruled by exclusively formulated regularities; meanwhile, philosophy also had become caught up in abstractions ruled by exclusive regularities. Because of this artificial division in forms of knowledge, only through immanent social critique—the premise that there is no normative vantage extrinsic to the critique itself—could, as Wang puts it, "the unified totality of the philosophical worldview" be completed. This possibility could only be accomplished by recalling to economics its philosophical roots in everyday life, and by recalling to philosophy its social roots in history.[89]

For Wang, in the sense of the relation of identity *as* history, philosophy and economics were categories or domains (*fanchou*) understood as structured forms of historical practice.[90] They were always political, ideological, and thus contested and conflictual. Indeed, in Wang's thinking, there is no separation between the philosophical and the historico-political, as any claimed detachment of an object of inquiry from its historicity—of a normative vantage—fell into metaphysical idealism. At the particular juncture of the 1930s in China, Wang's concern increasingly was bound up with how, in philosophy and economics as linked structured practices, the articulation of social value was becoming politically contained either to a narrow theory of remediation—reform of social problems (*shehui wenti*)—displaced to a problem of dehistoricized "culture" (see below), or retotalized through an abstracted theory of revolutionary praxis.[91] These political/philosophical alternatives toward the socioeconomic were becoming ever more rigidly divided by the late 1920s, after the revolutionary potential of the first united front had been violently suppressed by the right-wing faction of the Guomindang. The inadequacies of each side of this division were a particular source of worry for Wang.

One way in which this division increasingly was manifested in mainstream commentary was through an implicit or explicit preoccupation with "universal and proper values" (*pupian tuodang de jiazhi*) that insisted on the relative autonomy of social values from history. Rather than historicize the social and the economic mainstream, idealists tended to take society as the pregiven unitary grounds of history and critique, as the unitary truth of the grounds for remedial work, whose standards were abstracted from the historical and became universal a priori. This idealist preoccupation yielded an unyielding vantage on the philosophical problem of knowledge/truth and its relationship to historicity. Journalism and the mass media were a prime medium for the working out and popularization of this version of social values. At the same time, the mainstream concern with the relative autonomy of social values confronted a different intellectual orientation: a historical materialist concern with "historically determinant social conditions" (*yiding de lishi de shehui de tiaojian*). In contrast to the idealist mainstream, popular historical materialism insisted upon the specific historicity of social value as well as on the mutability of "the social" in relation to the economic and natural worlds.[92] To paraphrase one materialist Chinese essayist of the time, while "the social" (*shehui*) may preexist capitalism and modernity, it is only recognizable as a totality when the contradictions within capitalism make it visible. This, according to him, is the basis for a philosophy of the social and the economic as specific forms of historical temporality.[93]

Neither of these two perspectives or solutions was adequate in Wang Yanan's view. For, mainstream idealists reduced the everyday to putatively autonomous universal subjective values and maintained a preoccupation with remediation through modernizationist techniques; meanwhile, materialists tended to reduce the everyday to a realm of economic and social backwardness, a zone of irrationality to be overcome by the superior reason of collective revolution and socialism.[94] However inadequate these two versions, the perspective that most captured Wang's critical energy in the late 1930s was the conceptual relationship established between economics and culture by a certain group of scholars. Here, the economic was displaced unto culture, understood as a transhistorical given immune to history and change. As with his critical pursuit of the Austrians' transhistorical economics, Wang believed that this type of culturalist transhistory was just as dangerous because of its simplicity, vulgarity, and psychologistic palliation. He devoted much energy to critically reviewing this trend.

The Temporality of the Present and the Problem of Culture

In four essays written over several years in the late 1930s, Wang doggedly pursued an extended critique of and meditation on the "Eastern-Western culture" debates of the time. The essays include a general introduction to the problem, and then individual critiques of three representative figures (recognized then and now as major philosophers of Chinese tradition) in those debates: Liang Shuming, Qian Mu, and Zhu Qianzhi. As far as Wang was concerned, while Liang, Qian, and Zhu certainly should be considered serious scholars—Liang as a philosopher, Qian as a historian, and Zhu as an erudite polymath—their advocacies for "Eastern culture" and, indeed, their whole mode of argumentation in this realm could not be taken seriously. Or, rather, Wang defends his expenditure of large amounts of ink to address their arguments precisely because each represented a popular and serious trend in scholarship he deemed particularly pernicious, faulty, and prone to being vulgarized. Their version of culture had become a common sense that needed to be critiqued.

Wang sets the major terms of his critique in the first essay, "On Culture and Economics." In a brief introduction addressing the relationship between nature and culture, articulating a standard view of human beings conquering nature, Wang concludes by noting, "As is plain to see, so-called culture is the result of the congealing and accumulation of spiritual labor and material labor in the context of specific social relations forged by humanity."[95] In contradistinction to this basic view, Wang goes on to explain, the Southwest (German) School (a major neo-Kantian offshoot of the late nineteenth and early twentieth centuries, led by Wilhelm Wildenband and Heinrich Rickert) promoted what they call a "science of culture" (*kulturwissenschaft*), with a major focus on the relationship between culture and value (axiology). As Wang briefly explicates, for them, historical phenomena should be seen as activities of and developments from individual free will, where free will is not understood in the pure Kantian sense of intuition but rather in the neo-Kantian "scientific" sense of individual choice. However, because free will is unpredictable, social phenomena are also unpredictable, which makes general social regularities impossible to specify. In the absence of such laws, the task of the sociologist/economist is to record specifics (empiricism) held together in a system of "cultural values" (*wenhua jiazhi*). Wang does not go into further detail on this school and ends his brief discussion: "If forced to sum up their lofty views in one sentence, it would go: cultural phenomena are subjective things, they do not innately reflect any sort of developmental laws; as such, one has no choice but to mobilize a sort of extra-experiential [*chao jingnian*] set of cultural values to explain them."[96] This appeal to an extra-experiential (or outside of history) system of cultural values was further theorized by one of the major students of this school, Max Weber, in his methodological mobilization of sociological ideal types (adapted from Rickert). Even though Weber was not widely translated in 1930s and 1940s China, many of the elements comprising what became a standardized Weberian sociology were around by then.[97]

Wang Yanan's interest in the Southwest School did not reside in a history of ideas nor in a critique of cultural sociology per se. Rather, his goal was to demonstrate critically that "culture" could and should be reconnected to the economic through historical experience, without reducing any of these to pure authenticity, a purely epistemological (conceptual) problem, to some intangible ahistorical and extra-experiential values, or to pure empiricism. Rather, reconnection had to be accomplished in the broadest as well as the most granular senses possible. He demonstrated this principle not empirically but philosophically and historically, in his suggestion that it was only in the investigation of the form of social relations as the foundation of the historical that culture as a concept and as a sociologically/economically useful category (*fanchou*) of historical practice could be mobilized. In other words, for Wang, there were two large things at issue in his initial discussion of the relationship between economics and culture: in his critique of the Southwest School, he wanted to refute the idea of extra-experiential systems, whether cultural or other transhistorical systems; through that critique, he also wanted to propose a perspective that treated the temporality of the present (everyday individual experience) as irreducibly social and, thus, irreducibly historical.[98] In this sense, just as his philosophy of the economy was not limited to markets or individual desire and subjective value as ahistorical truths of human nature, his philosophy of the social was not contained by epistemologically transhistorical specifications of predetermined cultural values adduced to national time-space. For him, the problem of temporality in its relation to culture was not best understood as a principle of continuity but rather as a historically produced repetitive and urgent call to transformative action.

The mode of Wang's formulation of historical problems clearly is attributable to his Marxist philosophical commitments and training, where the history of any individual problem must be seen through the history of the totality of the problematic (as discussed earlier with regard to Lukács). In this immanent mode, it is insufficient to give a linear narrative of a conceptual becoming; instead, to get to the historical kernel or core of any particular issue, the problem in general needs to be understood in its totalized historicity. This is why each and every one of Wang's essays intimately and dialectically linked a historical dimension to a philosophical reflection to a contemporary manifestation. His method is precisely his argument and his argument is his method. Indeed, as he commented in an essay he devoted to the topic of the connections between economics/social science and philosophy, both modes of inquiry inevitably point to a certain social ideology and are expressions of a social consciousness of a particular historical moment. But, for Wang, the question of the relationship between economics/social science and philosophy was not to be posed in a mechanical base-superstructure formula (as it was for many contemporaneous orthodox Marxists in the Communist Party, whose dogmatism he deemed unproductive);[99] nor, however, was Wang's position a form of radicalized Maoism, where consciousness or voluntarism is always potentially victorious over historical conditions. Rather, for him, the question of the relationship had to be posed around and through the recognition of how all forms of knowledge are ideologies linked but not reducible to social totalities. Modern forms of knowledge could not be understood as narrowly national—containable to territorialized social formations or "cultures"—but, rather, due to the universalizing tendencies of capitalism, they always had to be thought of as global. Upon this philosophical, historical, and methodological perspective, Wang's critiques of Liang Shuming, Qian Mu, and Zhu Qianzhi focus from the start on these scholars' predetermining ascription of culture to a national container: either in the form of a national essence (Liang's ethics),[100] in the form of an attribute of an ethnic group (Qian's pre-Qin authentic Chinese tradition), or in the form of a territorialized neo-Kantian natural law (Zhu's Chinese philosophy).

Specifically, as Wang recounts, for Liang Shuming, whom he designates a leading national essence (*guocui*) scholar, Eastern culture was made equivalent to Chinese culture, which was made equivalent to an essential ethics that could be summed up in a few words. Liang's modern innovation was to adduce to the standard eight-character Confucian ethic (*ren*: humaneness; *ai*: love; *zhong*: loyalty; *xiao*: filiality; *xin*: truth; *yi*: righteousness; *he*: unity; *ping*: peace/calm) a new eight-character ethic, in the form of a phrase to be spread the world over: *rensheng xiangshang, lunli qingyi* (development of human life [produces] ethical sentiment).[101] Liang's point was to promote a view of how China could contribute to world culture through renovated ethics. Wang's critique of Liang accuses the latter of treating ethics like the Egyptian pyramids: as an unmovable supposed essence of so-called culture. Yet, because present and future societies are not and will not be mirrors of China's past, the ethics of the past cannot be the culture of the present or the future (if even it was the culture of the past, which is doubtful). More important, however, as ethics is intimately bound up with morality, which derives from individuals' social relational experiences at the level of everyday life, ethics cannot be thought as stagnant but rather must be developed by people in relation to how they live their lives in historically specific times and places. Ethics cannot be about abstractions or empty slogans, eight-character phrases or otherwise; rather, it must be about how life is lived. Hence, while Liang's desire to bequeath something "Chinese" of value to the world is nice, as Wang notes, in one sense, because China is already of the world, anything that happens in China is always-already worldly. More substantively, the only way to contribute, so far as Wang is concerned, is to devise and materially articulate from within the contemporary global/Chinese moment's constraints and possibilities a new socioeconomic system, from which could arise a new ethics. *This* could become a major contribution to and catalyst for a new world.[102]

Meanwhile, for Qian Mu, whom Wang characterizes as a leading historian, the pre-Qin Chinese tradition defined "Chineseness" as a matter of ethno-national (*minzu*) identification. This tradition, for Qian, could be posed against what he called the "Western tradition," as defined by industry and science. Qian's point in establishing this comparative equivalence was to update the late Qing "Chinese essence/Western function" (*zhongti/ xiyong*) perspective for a new day. Indeed, for Qian, the call to revive pre-Qin Chinese traditions to mix with twentieth-century Western modernization would allow the Chinese to retain their essential cultural soul.[103] Wang's critique of Qian focused mostly on the problem of his incomparable units of comparison as well as on his revival of the very moribund and ill-conceived idea of Chinese essence/Western function. On the first point, Wang cites Qian's own acknowledgment that the basis of his comparison of China and the West could perhaps be flimsy: in Qian's terminology, Chinese culture is like a marathon, one person running a long-distance race, whereas Western culture is like a relay, different people taking up the baton to run the race.[104] Even though Qian discounts this difference immediately after noting it, Wang avers that, because "China" and "the West" are not comparable units,[105] Qian's whole grounds of comparison collapse. Moreover, why should the pre-Qin period be compared to the contemporary period, either China's or Europe's, Wang asks? Indeed, as Wang notes, Qian's whole point—that Chinese culture is both "expansive" (*da*) and "enduring" (*jiu*)—really just boils down to the claim that China's pre-Qin *tianxia* (all under heaven) is pure sinocentricism (*zhongguo zhuyi*). Rather than cosmopolitan worldliness, it is mere parochialism. On the second point— essence/function—the mixing of chronologies and the imputation that China has remained stagnant whereas "the West" has not turns the whole mode of argumentation into an illogical mess. As Wang asserts in exasperation, "culture does not float in space," nor does it "stagnate in people's minds." Culture only can be constituted in social interaction.[106] Here, Qian's whole premise and method are unsalvageable, even though they may assuage some egos and provide some solace to those wishing to save something "Chinese" from the current crisis.

Finally, Zhu Qianzhi, characterized as a leading "polymath" (*baike quanshu jia*), wished to render China's equivalence to India and the West in a formalistic structuralism where each discrete entity was defined by a particular attribute: India, religious economic formation; China, philosophical economic formation; West, industrial economic formation. The point for Zhu in establishing these formalistic equivalences via neo-Kantian natural law was to participate in a global mainstream form of inquiry by typologizing cultures, so as to fix them in their proper places.[107] For Wang, Zhu's polymath nature means that he knows a smattering of everything and nothing deeply. This shallowness resolves itself in a formal structuralism that attempts to make a clean breast of all the knowledge, but ultimately it just stuffs bits of information into a structural model. Drawing upon a stage-theory of global types promoted by the German historicist Friedrich List, Zhu fills this typology with partially digested contents. Not only are the units and chronologies incomparable, then, but the ascription of "culture" to national types, and national types to historical stages (religion, philosophy, industry), simply cannot account for how the supposed national structure and the supposed national consciousness came to be and remain related through time and space.[108] In Wang's view, Zhu's argument goes completely off the rails when he equates his neo-Kantian scientific structures with Hobbesian natural law, by designating religion the "nature" of India; philosophy that of China; and industry that of "the West." This mixing and matching of incommensurate theoretical sources—in economics, German historicist-romanticism (List); in sociology, the Southwest School (Rickert); and in philosophy, neo-Kantianism—yields only incoherence. This incoherent tendency, Wang avers, is particularly dangerous, as this type of ostensibly erudite but really empty philosophical/theoretical nominalism represents a certain global mainstream, which seemed prepared to endure for some time to come.[109]

Aside from the inadequacies of the specifics of Liang's, Qian's, and Zhu's advocacies, each of these arguments was, for Wang, a slightly different version of the same fundamental philosophical error. The error was both methodological and substantive. In each theorist, the denial of sociality in its historicized forms in favor of the imposition of a predetermined conceptual formula led to a posing of equivalences fundamentally incommensurate in terms of units of comparison (why, Wang asks of each, is "China" commensurate to "the West"?) and in terms of chronology (why, Wang again queries, is China's past comparable to Europe's present?). The denial of material sociality also led to a positing of intranational equivalences that similarly made no sense: as Wang poses it, why is China's pre-Qin period equivalent to China's today, for example? These equivalences were not mere analogies, as Wang had previously criticized Ma Yinchu for magically devising (see the introduction to this volume); and thus they were not merely symptoms of lazy thinking. Rather, these equivalences made claims to a particular type of truth about the historical relationship between the economic and the cultural by relating the economic to the cultural *extrinsically* rather than *intrinsically*, ahistorically rather than through history. These pseudo-philosophies, in a manner no better than the most vulgar of the base/superstructure functionalisms for which (Stalinist) Marxism was best known, had no way to account for the establishment of a relationship between culture and the socioeconomic other than metaphysically or epiphenomenally. According to Wang, the elision of the relationship between the constitution of consciousness and the social was most characteristic of Liang's, Qian's, and Zhu's scholarly practice, and characteristic of practices connected to Chinese commentary at the time.

All three types of philosophies of "culture" suffer from the same maladies (Wang mentions other thinkers along the way, such as Lin Yutang, Chen Yinque, and so on, but he uses Liang, Qian, and Zhu as exemplars of these wider trends). The hypostasization and posited coincidence of the "national" and the "cultural" is one such malady. More fundamental still is the desire of all of these theorists to displace the contemporary economic/social crisis unto culture, thence to turn China's/the world's troubled present into an opportunity to argue for cultural renewal and remediation. This desire not only fails to address the historicity of the crisis confronting China and the world but also is purely reactive to and reflective of a form of value already thoroughly mediated and thus colonized by and through the capitalist commodity form, as material and ideological form. Indeed, the national-cultural becomes a commodified form itself, attempting to reconquer the world in its own image. And yet, as Wang well knew, the antidote to an original colonization cannot be recolonization; nor can it be a spiritual culture cure, as Liang, Qian, Zhu, and their admirers and followers advocated. Rather, any potential analysis of both the problem (crisis) and the solution required recognition of the particularity of the forms of temporality embedded in the current moment. Appeals to transhistory merely led to repetitive reproductions of the very crisis conditions for which solutions were being sought.

Temporality and Mediation

As Wang Yanan recognized, the historical problem of temporality arises only within a general historical problematic of the mediation between processes of abstraction and concrete social practice. Only capitalism raises this problem, because the form of social mediation in this historical formation is hidden and abstracted. Here, Wang's apprehension of temporality as a modern historical problematic registered what early twentieth-century philosopher Siegfried Kracauer identified as the "antinomy at the core of time": simultaneous fragmentation and universalization, a mutual incompatibility that was "insoluble."[110] For Wang, the fact of insolubility provided the challenge and necessity to explore the historical particularities of the hypocolonial situation of China in the modern world. As he saw it, the present was hard to conceptualize or even to perceive, because of the layering of temporalities and ideologies in a subjugated social-political-economic formation such as China's. Exploring the logic of the historical process of this layering occupied Wang's philosophical explorations at least up through the 1949 revolution. Indeed, as he repeatedly noted in one form or another and in essay after essay: because the historicity of the emergence of social science and economics derived from within capitalism in Europe, the difficulty of understanding their relationship to China (or any other colonized society) was compounded, not because they were European (that is, not as a matter of cultural difference) but because they were capitalist (that is, as a matter of different social formations and different histories). Moreover, so long as capitalism existed, the antinomy at the core of modern time as lived everyday experience was genuinely insoluble, in China as elsewhere, as this antinomy was a multiply layered problem that brooked no "solution," even as economists and social scientists situated in places such as China needed to grapple with the historical and conceptual implications of this insolubility in all its complexity.

Unlike for Wang, to many theorists and commentators (then and now), the insolubility of modern temporality was not acceptable. Rather than recognize this specific form and characteristic of capitalism and hence of modernity, the problem of modern temporality often has been assimilated to exclusive, and/or teleological, and/or absolute modes of investigation and resolution. As I argued in the second essay, one common "solution" has been to treat modern temporality as equivalent to scientific Hegelian time, with the state as its sole bearer, where macrohistorical disjuncture is displaced from a European core to a non-European periphery. Among other weaknesses, that view erases the politics of the everyday and with it the politics of history by replacing the political with (or constraining it to) endless state reproduction. As others have recounted, modern temporality can be viewed in the sanitized spirit of repetition supposedly indicated by Walter Benjamin's concept of "homogenous empty time." However, this view of repetitiveness can be substantiated only by turning the culturalized and spatialized would-be homogeneity of the imagined national community into the bearer of modern time. Among other problems, this vulgarization of Benjamin evacuates complexity from his highly politicized and historicized theorization of time as the conflict-ridden intertwined mixings of past, present, and future. By sanitizing and spatializing, the rereading of Benjamin evokes time as a blank slate to be filled by and in space, thus allowing the problematics of temporality to be overwritten by that of spatiality.[III] Or, then again, and as most versions of past and contemporary modernization theory have it (Marxist or capitalist), modern temporality could be reduced to the necessity of industrialized disciplinary time and hence could be seen as equivalent to a fascination with or necessity for linear and progressive time borne and produced primarily by the industrialization process itself. This goes under the name of rationalization, and it reduces time to historicist technocratic chronology. Another possibility, as we have seen with the Austrians and their consumer economic theory (most recently apotheosized in the rediscovery of Hayek), modern temporality could be reduced to the pragmatic presentism of desire, use-value, and market exchange, all of which reduce human beings to a transhistorical nature while reducing history to the workings of a transhistorical market. Finally, modern temporality can be equated with timeless culturalism, where national-cultural equivalence is established through a narrative of continuity, whose beginning and end point derive from some ascription of national-cultural essence that attaches unproblematically to racial/ethnic peoples or national states in a temporally flattened historical landscape. This has yielded arguments both on "backwardness" and on premodern "alternative modernities," depending on the perspective and valuation attached.

Wang Yanan's major targets of critique in the 1930s were the two latter versions of temporality—the Austrians' pragmatic presentism and the culturalist recuperations that flattened historical time to an eternal present; he was particularly opposed to their denial of the possibility of the social and thus the political in any form other than as preconstituted grounds for state domination, cultural reproduction, individual consumption, fulfillment of desire, and/or ground of market exchange.[112] Most troubling for him was that any discussion of the emergence of the historical conditions for the constituting of the social and the cultural—and thus of politics as a conflictual process residing outside the state—is utterly absent. In Austrian theory, this absence is attributable partially to the fact that, for the Austrian theorists, society is simply the aggregation of individual consumer preferences, as it were, where conflict is contained within and defined by (market) competition. As a corollary, the absence is also explainable in part by their elaboration of a theory of individual identity and subjective experience based upon a version of time that abolishes the past and the future in its emphasis on the present alone. This form of presentism is debilitating to politics understood as a speculative immanence, for it only recognizes a politics of what already is rather than a politics of what could be. It also establishes politics as ostensibly commensurate and bearing a durational equivalence to a preexisting sociopolitical body and cultural/individual essence.[113] This is precisely where presentism and culturalism coincide: while presentism focuses exclusively on the present and culturalism appears to abolish the present in favor of timelessness, both are suspended *in time* and *by time* in ostensibly unmediated transhistoricity.

This kind of social/political theory, as Wang wrote in the later 1940s, easily lent itself to "certain kinds of dark purposes." For a recent historical example, he notes, "political geography was transformed into a doctrine of *lebensraum* to justify the violent expansion of national territory; while anthropology was turned into a doctrine of how to dominate over people of different races." He adds, "Perhaps some say this type of appropriation was limited to fascist countries; but today, social scientists in Britain, the United States, and elsewhere . . . also are busy distorting and manipulating social science to one degree or the next. And what should we call that?"[114] Wang acknowledged that these manipulations consistently had been contested, but, by the same token, the ideologies most often mobilized for the contestations offered no real answers. Indeed, in China's 1930s and 1940s, the claim that "Eastern spiritualism" could save China (or Asia, or anyone) from the corruptions of materialism, scientism, and war was absolutely misguided. For one, there is no such thing as an unsullied "Eastern spiritualism" because the interiority of "the East" had long since disappeared, if indeed it had ever existed. Secondly, as Wang narrates, after World War I, the imperialist countries could no longer depend upon the naïveté of colonized peoples to accept their economic and social scientific ideologies and impositions. This led imperialist-colonizing countries to devise new strategies for making these ideologies and policies less apparently foreign, by adducing them to ostensibly native thought:

> England encouraged a massive increase in the construction of temples and devotion to Buddhism; Japan comprehensively took up and promoted China's Confucianism and the reading of the classics. Only from such antiscientific and antimodern forms could one derive a "scientific" explanation of the reason why, after a century or more of modernization, we have reached today's impasse and cannot yet attain a scientific research outlook or determine our own positions. This is in large part due to the cultural invasions of imperialism. Yet we also are too ignorant of the times, too likely not to recognize clearly the character of the imperialist cultural invasion; for this, we, too, must bear some of the responsibility.[115]

In other words, as far as Wang was concerned, the appeal to a parity or equivalence between native culture/native thought and Western culture/Western thought was merely a strategy for the ideological instantiation of colonized and commodified forms of mediated value and values. By the same token, social scientific concepts could not be considered commensurate to native culture or to capitalist societies; even less could they be considered commensurate to some "hybrid" form. In Wang's view, the historicity of the encounters could not be understood as a mere mixing but needed to be apprehended as a complex and violent insoluble historical process without end.

In view of these incommensurabilities, for Wang, the genuine vocation of social science/economics, instead of attempting to establish equivalences and parities through a "sociological calm" bearing innocent witness to the violence of the production of capitalist unevenness,[116] instead had to assist in understanding the most highly contested and yet the most hidden and the ugliest parts of quotidian life: the specific forms of mediation producing the specific forms of temporality through and in which every-day people lived their everyday lives. If that challenge were taken up, then the social science/economics practiced in the mainstream of the 1930s and 1940s in China as elsewhere soon would be shown to be useless, since its standard was most often not "truth or falsehood, but rather if it serves capitalism or not."[117] In this sense, even the broadest sociological, eco-nomic, and political scientific studies as practiced in the mainstream were inadequate to or unable to account for the actuality of the unevenness of the contemporary global formation and for the specific position of China within it. As Wang stated unequivocally: "In this era of ours, the develop-ment of communications and cultural exchanges in the whole world have made it possible to narrow the world to one society; nevertheless, this one big society is comprised of the social formations of many different his-torical eras forced into close proximity and coexistence. Moreover, there is a tendential necessity for these to continue to coexist. This fact poses blazingly clear irrefutable evidence for the incommensurability to reality of even the broad theories of economics, political science, sociology, and so on."[118]

In the face of this actuality, the responsibility of Chinese economists (or any economist) was not the mechanical application of "advanced" social sci-entific theory, nor the elaboration of a supposed "native" approach. Rather, it was to understand the regularities of social science/economics as modes of inquiry to specify China's social formation within the global capitalist sys-tem so as to properly grasp the present and hence possible futures. Wang averred that this required "us to bravely engage in the study of ourselves," not as a form of nativist narcissism but as a form of political and social transformation.[119] This engagement could not be based upon an attitude of "study for the sake of studying," nor upon the vulgarization or magic of con-cepts. While both these attitudes existed in China in abundance, neither was what was urgently needed.[120] Instead, the engagement needed to be based upon real-world investigations informed by dialectically produced concepts. It was only in the process of investigation that concepts adequate to social actuality could be elaborated.

In the late 1940s and early 1950s, as the Communist victory became first likely and then was secured, Wang—ever the non-Communist Marxist (until the late 1950s forced his hand)—increasingly turned his attention to the construction of socialism. While he never left behind his concerns with philosophy and mostly resisted Chinese Communist Party dogmatism, in the post-1949 period he added to his philosophical considerations a broad concern with the specificity of China's socialist construction, as an urgent question of politics, educational necessity, and social transformation.[121]

CHAPTER 4

The Economic as Lived Experience

Semicolonialism and China

Contemporaneity is never "given" but must always be constructed to express what matters.

—ÉRIC ALLIEZ, "What Is—or What Is Not—Contemporary French Philosophy, Today?"

One of the more interesting analyses of semicolonialism in the pre-1949 period in China was by Wang Yanan, a non-Communist Marxist economist and sociologist.[1] For Wang, the point of specifying and analyzing semicolonialism was not for the purpose of creating a revolutionary social unity (as it was for Mao, for example); rather, it was intended to find a way to rejoin the abstractions of Marxism and capitalism as global systems of thought and practice to the specificities of China's current social formation. The current formation (of the late nineteenth century through the 1930s and 1940s) was what Wang (and others) called "the semicolonial socio-economic formation." In Wang's view, and unlike other theorizations, this formation was characterized by the specific ways in which the commodity form as a material and ideological form had imposed itself upon and been articulated to China's preexisting social relations (themselves in flux and possessing their own logic).[2] In a manner more analytical than most of his contemporaries who also used the term *semicolonial*, Wang's emphasis on the commodity form in his theorization intended to link China's modern socioeconomic history to the global history of capitalism, thus to root conceptually the everyday lives of ordinary Chinese—in all their temporal and material unevenness and contradiction—in larger historico-philosophical apprehensions of economics and society.

Taking a cue from Wang's discussion, this essay explores the fraught question of semicolonialism as it appeared in the 1930s and reappeared in the 1980s and 1990s. I wish to consider the concept in its materialist historico-philosophical mode, as an analysis *not* of the exceptionalism (culturally hybrid or otherwise) but rather of the lived specificity of China's participation in the global capitalist economy. In this sense, the argument here is *not* that semicolonialism as a concept should be revived in either a descriptive or analytical mode. To the contrary, the argument is that, by re-embedding semicolonialism in its proper philosophical mode—as a global analysis from the perspective of a historically specific Chinese reality—it will be possible to see it as the name given to imperialist capitalism as lived in China in the 1930s: it is what some would call China's "colonial modernity" or what I would call just modernity (as all modernity is colonial).[3] When semicolonialism became codified as revolutionary strategy through the later 1930s and 1940s in Mao's historical and practical analytical usage and thence became the incantatory descriptive historical periodization of pre-revolutionary China, and then when it reemerged in the 1980s and 1990s as a description of a historical distortion or an embraceable Chinese (cultural) hybridity, this is when the analytical-conceptual purchase of semicolonialism as a lived experience of modernity in China was transformed into a pure ideology of (historical or cultural) exceptionalism and difference. It became a magic concept.

Temporality and Semicolonialism

As a primarily descriptive category of historicist stages, semicolonialism derives most clearly from V. I. Lenin's usage in his 1916 pamphlet, *Imperialism, the Highest Stage of Capitalism*,[4] in which it indicates a way station to full colonization. This definition of the semicolonial foretells the modern passage or transition of all non-Western peoples either into complete colonization by capitalist imperialism (most likely) or, through revolution, into national sovereignty and independence (the path to be sought). Indeed, the Baku conference of September 1920 (the First Congress of the Peoples of the East), convened by the nascent internationalist wing of the new Soviet state (the Comintern), was informed by Lenin's formulation: at Baku, semicolonial countries were seated with colonial ones as part of the same global bloc and were made to speak to the same global problem of national subjugation/national liberation. The support of the Comintern for national liberation projects in colonial and semicolonial countries just recently had been adopted in the course of the sharp debates between M. N. Roy and Lenin on the National and Colonial Questions during the Second Congress of the Communist International in summer 1920, to which Baku was a follow-up.[5] In this sense, at the time, this formulation was a global revolutionary imperative. However, it also was intended as a historico-philosophical analytic: as a way to think about the global and local nature of national liberation projects and the necessity of class coalitions among nonsovereign peoples in light of the projected Bolshevik victory in the Russian civil war (then ongoing) and the violent capitalist restorations in postwar Europe (also then ongoing).

Through the 1920s, as national and global social, political, cultural, and economic disintegrations became more acute, and hence, as the field of the social itself became more contested in political theory and practice, the concept of semicolonialism also underwent a transformation. New articulations and theorizations increasingly focused not only on the problem of national-state sovereignty in the global arena, nor merely on a descriptive condition of an inevitable historical transition from partial to full colonization, but on the historical-analytical problem of social formation and/or mode of production. These included uneven economic structures globally as articulated to unequal internal social relations of production, as well as the everyday cultural conditions produced in the micro- and macro-interactions of capitalism with received cultures in different localities. Thus, if Lenin's (and, after 1927, Stalin's) emphasis on modern colonialism/semicolonialism focused on the *nationally* constitutive role of uneven global power as a matter of the state, subsequent local rearticulations and reconceptualizations added a concurrent concern with uneven social relations at the local level that, while not separable from the global/nation-state arena, were nevertheless not reducible to it.[6] This refocusing helped contribute to widespread research on the specific socioeconomic, political, and cultural processes structuring life at the level of the lived quotidian. As discussed in previous essays in this volume, in China, these researches helped kick off the social history debate and the agrarian economy debate of the 1930s. Semicolonialism, transformed from being a merely descriptive concept of a historical transition to nation-statism, now became an analytical mode of specifying the temporal asymmetry of everyday life, or what Henri Lefebvre called in a different context "desynchronization."[7] It provided an analytical optic on the problem of the incommensurate constitutive temporalities of modern social formations at global, regional, national, and local levels simultaneously.

As semicolonialism became a way to figure this simultaneity in temporal terms, it also became necessary to understand how temporal asymmetry was established historically.[8] For this, semifeudalism came to be most closely allied with semicolonialism in the specification of modern China's condition.[9] Also a heavily contested concept, feudalism and hence semifeudalism were used to refer to different things by different scholars/political factions. Guomindang (GMD, or Nationalist Party) theorists of the 1930s, such as Tao Xisheng, used the term *fengjian shili* (feudal forces) as a concept that revolved around the problem of the remnants (*canyu*) of feudalism in the *political* arena. In Tao's usage, this was meant as a uniquely Chinese politico-cultural asymmetry established between a putative advanced political economy of the urban/global in confrontation with the agrarian backwardness assumed to be still dominantly represented in the central state form (despotic or semidespotic). Here, "remnants" were a social-political problem to be rectified by superior social rationalization undertaken through the rationalization of the state. This rationalization would bring the asymmetries into alignment, it was suggested. Meanwhile, Communist theorists used the terms *feudalism* and *semifeudalism* to define the socioeconomic relations characterized by the overlapping and mutually reinforcing surpluses (*guosheng; shengyu*) demanded by the two types of socioeconomic and political exploitation then dominating Chinese social relations: the precapitalist/feudal (extra-economic) appropriation and the imperialist-capitalist (surplus value) appropriation of surplus.[10] In this sense, and taking into account differences in usage, the combination of semicolonialism and semifeudalism (the "two semis") was articulated around problems of residue, surplus, and excess as problems of the lived experience of ordinary Chinese in a global age of imperialist capitalism.

Semicolonialism and Incompletion

Substantially following Lenin, many Chinese in the 1930s saw semicolonialism as a temporary political condition marked by the partial autonomy of the national state, circumscribed by unequal treaties and territorially constrained by "concessions" to imperialist powers. For example, in 1937 Chen Hongjin, summarizing the most commonsensical view, specified the parameters and special characteristics of semicolonialism in a popular pamphlet:

> In general, semicolonial countries have a colonial character. Precapital-ist social relations are dominant [*zhan youshi*] in their social formations, and imperialism is in the leading position [*zhan tongzhi diwei*] in their national politics, economics, and societies. Yet, aside from these general characteristics, semicolonial countries also have their particularities. . . . These can be encapsulated in the following six points:
>
> 1. The transitional nature of semicolonialism;
> 2. Formal political sovereignty;
> 3. The importance for imperialism of capital export;
> 4. The demand for national unification and the establishment of state capitalism;
> 5. The vacillation between dictatorial and democratic politics;
> 6. The role played by the rejection of global capitalism by semicolonial revolutions.[11]

In further explanation, Chen clarified that the transitional nature (*guoduxing*) of semicolonialism was attributable to semicolonial spaces being a rem-nant of the imperialist struggle to partition the globe. Here, he named Iran, Iraq, Afghanistan, Siam, the South American nations, Egypt, and Mexico as the major semicolonial countries of the time, each characterized by a different albeit cognate form of remainder.[12] This globally remnant char-acter, according to Chen, informs not only the international situation of the named *national peoples* (as semisovereign) but also the future of the global sphere itself, as transitional either to a world of national-state equivalence or to imperialist consolidation (as far as Chen was concerned, both of these outcomes were plausible). In this sense, the resolution to semico-lonial situations would decide whether semicolonies would become full colonies—thus allowing imperialist capitalism to extend its temporal and spatial dominion completely over the globe—or whether semicolonial peoples would become independent within sovereign nation-states, thus contributing to the further differentiation of global space and time at the level of the national state (with or without capitalism as the socioeconomic form). Whatever the outcome, still in the balance in 1937, Chen insisted that a semicolony was not and could not be an enduring or autonomous formation; rather, it was a temporary or transitional one, constituted by and a remnant of modern imperialism's contemporary inability to complete or spatially consolidate itself, as it were.[13]

Chen's commonsensical version of incompleteness—the one most common in China at the time—was not the only possible one. Indeed, it is possible to see incompletion through what Slavoj Žižek calls "the logic of systemic or structural totalities."[14] It is in this idiom that Wang Yanan designated not political sovereignty as the most important aspect of the semicolonial condition but the social relations of production he, and others in that era, named comprador-bureaucratic capitalism. As discussed in the third essay, the major constituent historical marker of this social formation for Wang was the violent intrusion of the commodity form as material and ideological effectivity and its restructuring of Chinese socioeconomic and ideological relations. Conceiving of imperialist capitalism as an extended global historical moment of tendential unity necessarily characterized by the constant reproduction of incompletion (unevenness) at any given level, Wang saw semicolonialism not as a "transitional" form of incompletion (although he did see semifeudalism as transitional between the landlord economy and an economy more fully saturated by capitalist social relations), nor as an exceptional form of Chinese socioeconomics (that is, it was Chinese but not exceptional). Rather, for him, semicolonialism was a form of ongoing global primitive capital accumulation carried out in the context of an overall crisis in global capitalism.[15] In other words, for Wang, semicolonialism was not a problem of remnants in an already constituted global realm of imperialist capitalism emanating from a Euro-American/Japanese center, as with Chen Hongjin's and cognate conceptualizations. To the contrary, semicolonialism was a problem of a locally instantiated global formation characterized by a surplus (*shengyu*) exceeding or escaping the tendential move toward capitalist totalization and real capitalist subsumption.

In this idiom, Wang commented upon the relationship of China's feudal form to other versions of feudalism in world history: "Other feudal formations were erected upon the basis of feudal land relations, where land was not alienable and where labor's relationship to the land rendered it unfree. The foundations of Chinese feudalism, however, were built upon a landlord economy, where land was generally alienable and where labor was generally free to move. Where there is free exchange between land and labor or labor power, there is the basic premise for the development of a capitalist commodity economy" (40). In this light, Wang continues, the Trotskyites and bourgeois economists, who emphasized that China's semifeudal, semicolonial economy was a commodity economy built atop an incipiently indigenous capitalist economy, were partially correct, even if one had to disregard what he called "the reactionary services they have rendered on behalf of imperialism, compradors, and feudal landlords" (40). Bracketing for the moment the political implications of such a position in the fraught political context of the time, and looking at the situation from the perspective of alienable land, free labor, and a well-developed market, Wang conceded that China's economy from the Song dynasty onward could indeed appear to be an incipiently capitalist economy, whose sprouts somehow were blocked. And yet, he argues,

> the kind of freedom that emerged from this not only is quite distant from the kind of freedom demanded by capitalism. In its very essence [*zai benzhi shang*], one could even say that it was not the kind of freedom demanded by capitalism at all. For this reason, its progressiveness is contained within feudalism at best, and cannot be encapsulated within capitalism. It is thus progressive only within feudalism and remains feudal; under that external appearance of freedom are hidden all sorts of obstacles to the development of the reality of capitalism. (41–42)

It is thus beneath the appearance of "free land and labor"—which, in any case, he notes, have been fetishized in bourgeois economics as atomized attributes rather than structural aspects of a total socioeconomic formation—that Wang seeks the affinities and structural correspondences between China's historical feudalism and its semicolonial, semifeudal instantiation.

The key to these affinities resides in the "comprador-bureaucratic class" (*maiban guanliao jieji*), which he (unlike his compatriots of the time or since) designates as a *structurally necessary element* of China's interactions with and articulation to global capitalism.[16] This structural necessity did not vitiate for Wang the utmost importance of struggles over political ideologies and state power. However, his recognition of such a structural element did prevent him from displacing the historicized and politicized products of China's particular situation completely unto the global sphere of imperialism, even while it also prevented him from mischaracterizing China's preimperialist economy as bearing the sprouts of capitalism. Hence, while recognizing the integral role of capitalist imperialism in producing China's modern socioeconomic formation, Wang insisted that this formation could not be reduced either to its global or its local aspects.[17] It is for this reason that Wang, unlike many 1930s CCP theorists or GMD economists, rejected the notion that there were neatly demarcated foreign and Chinese economic sectors in spatially distinct realms. He also did not accept the Trotskyite position that there was no point in distinguishing between foreign and Chinese economic sectors at all. Wang Yanan—as ever, unconcerned with CCP, GMD, or Trotskyite orthodoxies instrumentalized as revolutionary or counterrevolutionary practices—argued instead that the particular historical formation of capitalism in its semicolonial form had demanded structural revisions *in capitalism itself* at the same time as it forced structural revisions in China's relations of production/social formation. That is, refusing to hold "capitalism" stable, Wang outlined a complex dialectic between the global capitalist system and its encounter with the geographically uneven indigenous economies in China. With this complex dialectic and historical incommensurability, Wang argued, "capitalist economics can assist only to a certain degree in the understanding of China's economy" (43).

Indeed, as he specified:

> With the deepening of the semicolonial situation, even our "comprador" economists have progressively lost the vitality of the reformist wealth and power [*fuqiang*] economics of several decades ago; like fanning dying embers in the current situation, they occasionally spout a few phrases about [economic] construction that have nothing to do with the real situation in order to animate the scene. This explains how deeply we have fallen into the poison of consumer economic theory [i.e., Austrian economics], which has continuously submerged our understanding of our own economy in a dense fog of magic. (44)

That is, according to Wang, the "consumer economic theory" pioneered by the Austrians and taken up by Chinese economists (as discussed in the third essay in this volume) failed to comprehend the particular structural totality of a local economy in a determinate global historical context. In such a light, neither the "mechanical instrumentalism" of Stalinist economics nor the "opportunism" of what Wang called "vulgar mainstream econo-

mists" was sufficient to produce a real understanding of China's semicolonial situation. This is because China's economy could not be "managed as
if it were a capitalist commodity economy," a position perversely arrived at
by mainstream economists through their dismissal of the historical particularity of the modern situation and through their use of "citations from the
classics to explain that China has already been a commodified society [for a
long time]" (46). As Wang Yanan earlier lamented in the latter vein: "During the May Fourth Movement, I recall there was some national essence
journal that published some major essay praising Confucius. In this essay,
they took the several phrases from the Analects—e.g., 'Let the producers be
many and the consumers few'—. . . to indicate a Confucian concept of the
economy and thus to produce Confucius as a 'major economic thinker.'
Even though this type of argument is on the wane, nevertheless . . . it can
be seen to persist."[18]

According to Wang, instead of this kind of faux analogizing through ci-
tationalism, "a method that merely succeeded in concealing China's current
situation in a purported historical continuity," and instead of this attempt to
build commensurability between China's past and its present, when there
was none to be built—the culturally essentialist position he so deplored
(see my discussion in the third essay)—it was necessary to recognize that
"feudal relations have been compradorized [*maiban hua le*], and [that] the
activities of comprador capital also exhibit the special characteristics of
feudal exploitation" (48). This recognition, in turn, required a recognition
that not only is "China's economy constantly under the influence of the . . .
situation of the global capitalist economy; . . . but, by the same token, the
global economy is also directly or indirectly influenced by the Chinese
economic situation" (50). Only with such a dual recognition would it be
possible "to expose the real mutual relations between economies" (50).

And yet he cautioned that China's economic history could not be understood through the narrativization of stages leading to capitalism through the
mechanical use of "critical economic categories." (Here, he was essentially
refuting the utility of the social history debates in clarifying economic historical matters, even though he acknowledged that the "critical economists"
who had participated in the debates were more progressive than mainstream academic or state economists [46–47].) As he noted, that type of
narrativization started from the premise of "what the development of capitalism would be, rather than explicate where capitalism came from" (46).

That is, it was far too teleological. By contrast, to understand a semicolonial society such as China's, it was particularly important, Wang thought, to research capitalism's derivation and not its deviant or distorted path of nondevelopment. In this regard, Wang wrote, "evidently, the residual elements of the traditional economy are being restructured by the capitalist commodity economy, and at the same time, they constantly act as a series of constraints upon the elements of the capitalist economy, either by contesting or adapting to them" (52–53). This dialectic of interaction led Wang to see semicolonialism in China not as a spatially or temporally (exceptionally) *Chinese* transitional moment but as a distinct historical moment of primitive capital accumulation on a global and local scale simultaneously (what David Harvey might call a moment in the intensification of capital accumulation[19]). This was an accumulation effected not under the direction of an independently constituted or constitutive Chinese national bourgeoisie, but rather under the constituted and constitutive class of "comprador-capitalists," a class that corresponded to and was created by the structurally necessary alteration of global capitalism in its semicolonial form.

In this sense, semicolonialism as primitive capital accumulation at a particular moment in global capitalist expansion could not be understood through a chronologically conceived confrontation expressed as a transition from "primitive accumulation" (*yuanshi jilei*) to capital accumulation (*ziben jilei*) proper, as if these were separable temporalities or spatialities of activity that mutually excluded one another. Rather, in keeping with Marx's concept of primitive capital accumulation understood as the basic condition of possibility for the continuous movement of capital around the globe,[20] Wang's concept of primitive capital accumulation articulated the excess of feudal exploitation (its extra-economic dimension) to the surplus value demanded by capitalism as the historical socioeconomic form of the semicolonial social relations of China's current situation. And China was not the sole constituent of these global relations of articulated excess/surplus. Rather, China's social relations, while obviously shaped by and lived through China's unique history and situation, were part of a larger global trend of primitive capital accumulation, which constrained while informing the particular possible directions of social transformation, in China as elsewhere.

In short, Wang's conceptualization of the semicolonial did not reduce the so-called feudal elements of the Chinese economy to a past temporality that corresponded to an endlessly reproduced spatial/territorial locatedness and boundedness comprised of archaic residues. Nor was the semifeudal and semicolonial a uniquely Chinese form of national incompletion (whether understood as political or economic incompletion or as the global incompletion of imperialist capitalism). Even less did Wang reduce the urban/global to a concept of the modern that corresponded to either an ahistorical cultural essence ("Western genius") or a historicist standard of scientificity divorced from a structural totality or constrained by a presumed universal and historicist unidirectionality to historical development. Rather, he recognized these spheres of local and global space-time as mutually productive of the unevenness of a historical moment understood as a simultaneously local and global formation dominantly characterized by the restructuration of *both* capitalism and China through the never-ending and ongoing process of primitive capital accumulation at all available scales simultaneously. In this sense, for Wang and with regard to contemporary global social relations, capitalism and feudalism were co-temporal and mutually productive of one another, thus yielding the semicolonial economic formation. Indeed, it was precisely this structural totality that characterized modernity as a lived everyday of imperialist capitalism exceeding the constraints of its local and global instantiations. In this sense, semicolonialism (just as modernity) was understood as a global necessity, as a regime of formal (not real) subsumption.[21]

Clearly, Wang's concept of incompletion (where "completion" does not exist) is far different from the incompletion that connotes a fundamental lag or lack, a "backwardness" to be filled with an inevitable content waiting to arrive. (In other words, his is not a form of modernization convergence theory as universal history or as a pure ideology.) Rather, for him, incompletion was the never-ending condition of primitive capital accumulation on a world scale that would, if possible, be locked into place by imperialist capitalism so as to retain China (and other locations) as an open field of continuous surplus exploitation and appropriation in the process of unequal exchange and capital accumulation on a global scale.

Semicolonialism and Revolutionary Necessity

In 1932 Zhang Wentian, at the time recently returned from Moscow and an important member of the Chinese Communist Party (CCP) as its propaganda minister, wrote a scathing rebuttal to Ren Shu (aka Ren Xu), a Sichuan-based Trotskyite who had previously worked with the Central Peasant Bureau prior to the 1927 GMD counterrevolution.[22] Ren had argued—in keeping with Trotskyist positions at the time—that China should be considered a fully capitalist society whose feudal relations were no longer relevant because of the domination of its economy through the invasion of commodities from abroad. In rebuttal, Zhang, upholding the CCP orthodoxy of the time, argued that

> in China, imperialists use political and economic indebtedness as well as the indemnities paid by China after military defeats in order to monopolize China's economic resources, achieve their spheres of influence, and render the regional landlords and warlords, as well as capitalists, into their own tools. In order to monopolize and control China's economic resources, they must establish their banks, factories, tools of communication, and commercial mechanisms. They rely upon these (we won't even mention here the extra-economic methods) to sell their commodities, extract China's natural resources, and enslave China's industrial and peasant masses.[23]

This form of "enslavement," Zhang continued, was designed not to transform China into a sovereign economic entity but rather to "destroy the productive forces of the colonies and semicolonies, not develop these forces."[24] In this sense, the rapid growth of the commodity economy in the rural areas was a symbol not of Chinese economic productivity and the transformation of feudal relations into capitalist ones but rather of "the strengthening of landlords', merchants', and usurers' exploitation of the Chinese masses, [which] has created a huge amount of bankruptcy and unemployment as well as unprecedented famine and starvation."[25] In this orthodox party view, semicolonialism and semifeudalism were forms of the failure of Chinese social and political relations to be transformed from a traditional to a more fully modern type.

Subsequent to Zhang's and other party members' specifications through the social history debates of the historical parameters of the two semis, the CCP came to accept the two semis as their basic historical narrative of the current situation. In addition, at approximately the same time as Wang Yanan, and yet unwilling to settle philosophically on unevenness and incompletion as an insoluble analytic, Mao Zedong, who was responsible both for the further theorization of semicolonialism and its codification as revolutionary strategy, wrote in December 1935: "One of the main political and economic characteristics of a semicolonial country is the weakness of its national bourgeoisie." This weakness, he pointed out, was a major manifestation of "China's uneven political and economic development [that] has given rise to the uneven development of the revolution." In Mao's view, it would be the task of revolutionary strategy and activity to change the revolutionary situation "from a state of unevenness to a certain degree of evenness . . . [and from] a localized one into a nationwide one."[26]

In other words, for Mao, semicolonialism was a type of specific nationally contained multiclass formation to which a united front form of revolutionary tactics (*cilüe*) could broadly correspond; moreover, semicolonialism was the temporally uneven dimension of the current situation, understood as a tendentially unified but dispersed social and historical struggle narrativized as "revolutionary." That is, the semicolonial was a tactical and ever-changing temporalized spatial conflict in a revolutionary mode, whose contemporary historical-tactical object was the seizure of state power and its imposition over a particular territory (China) in the strategic pursuit of socialism (global). In this sense, this conflict was part not only of a struggle for the state and its rearticulated relationship to the nation but also a revolutionary struggle against capitalism, whose dimensions were always-already global. As an effort to specify a socialist revolutionary praxis in an uneven national and global terrain, Mao's theory of semicolonialism was of crucial analytical importance.

At the same time, semicolonialism for Mao pertained to a national historical narrative periodization, whose temporal transcendence was to be the object of the Chinese people's revolutionary practice. In this historicist idiom—more widely recognized, perhaps, from the famous 1939 textbook titled "The Chinese Revolution and the Chinese Communist Party"[27]—Mao deployed the concept of semicolonialism to indicate the parameters of China's specific current situation in revolutionary terms; this was a condition to be overcome through revolutionary activity led by the CCP. That is, for Mao, it was absolutely necessary to grasp fully the current moment, along with its past, in order to grasp the possibilities for action in the present.[28] His particular invocation of semicolonialism in this text comes with his comment that "it is certainly not the purpose of the imperialist powers invading China to transform feudal China into capitalist China. On the contrary, their purpose is to transform China into their own semicolony or colony."[29] (We can see how he mobilizes here Zhang Wentian's prior theorization.) The remainder of the work deploys the concept in the specific sense just indicated: that the object of all genuine revolutionary practice—and particularly that led by the CCP—would need to take on the dual task of toppling feudalism and imperialist capitalism simultaneously. In other words, for Mao semicolonialism was a logic of revolutionary necessity in the idiom of a historical imperative actualized through a united front of progressive social classes. The historical imperative was informed both by a global situation—the antifascist war, of which China's war of resistance against Japan was one component—and a local situation of capitalist collusion with feudal forces (landlords, etc.). It was a historical stage to be overcome.

In this sense if, for Lenin, for example, semicolonialism as a concept was the unstable product of his pre-1914 concentration on the analysis of capitalism in Russia as confronted with his wartime (Great War) and postwar focus on the problem of global imperialism,[30] then for Mao, semicolonialism as a concept was already a consolidated historicist stage of history. It was an established historical period for certain non-Western countries, such as China, which, in the midst of the extended global capitalist and political moment of crisis, whose death throes were signaled by the rise of fascism and the global spread of antifascist war, were also beset by local contradictions demanding revolutionary solutions. This historical period was characterized by the growth and development of national and global unevenness simultaneously, a simultaneity that yielded not only revolutionary necessity but also national and global unevenness in revolutionary consciousness. In this sense, semicolonialism for Mao was a historical argument about the necessary tactical revolutionary overcoming of unevenness as a strategy first of national revolution and, next, of global revolution.

However, in Maoist circles and in Maoist China, semicolonialism soon became an incantation. It was dogmatized in Chinese scholarly production during the Maoist years as an all-purpose descriptive term of blocked transitions (to capitalism/socialism). Its specific revolutionary purchase was blunted by being turned into a cliché, and its potential analytical problematizations of history as simultaneously global and national were dropped. It is in relation to this dogmatization that contemporary debates on semicolonialism were joined by academic historians in the 1980s and 1990s.

They were joined, however, not to complicate or resuscitate the analytical utility of the concept, nor to better understand to what these concepts pertained as they came into being historically, but rather in the service of the repudiation of revolution and its naming as a historical aberration so as to reassert China's national historical and cultural uniqueness.

Semicolonialism and the Scientifically Displaced Temporality of Transition

In recent decades, the problem of contradictory temporalities of historical experience has been reconceived as a problem of national historical obstacles to be eliminated and radical cultural particularities to be burnished and exported rather than as the very stuff and process of historical struggle and of historicity themselves. That is, while contradictions famously were instrumentalized by Mao and the Maoist CCP as revolutionary strategy, nevertheless, philosophically and often also as a matter of practice, never-ending and yet always-changing contradictions were seen as the site of the very historical itself. These days history seems to happen elsewhere and is supposed to proceed more harmoniously. Indeed, on a dominant contemporary academic and media view, China has emerged from the now-condemned anachronism of revolution and socialism, which can be cast out of historical and national time and recast as remnants of a particularistic time informed by the persistence of feudalism in the political sphere (the version much touted by those such as Qin Hui and Roderick Mac-Farquhar, albeit differently).[31] In this perspective, China of the 1990s can thence be figured as returning to an originary modern transition to capitalism felicitously located as immanent in the 1930s semicolonial (hybrid cultural) formation, subsequently blocked as China was hijacked first by the Japanese and then by socialist revolution. Here, the Maoist period is seen as an aberration, or to use François Furet's destructive notion, as a dérapage, or brief parenthesis opened in an otherwise inertial trend of history that goes toward a predetermined end.[32]

In this incipient climate of revolutionary ambivalence and soon repudiation, by the late 1980s and 1990s, after a half century of appearing as talismanic incantation, the semicolonial and semifeudal characterization that had authorized and analytically underpinned the revolution and its major historical tasks and agents since the 1930s was not immune to interrogation.[33]

The initial moments of the debate on the two semis emerged just prior to and then coterminous with the theory of the "primary stage of socialism" promoted at the 1987 Thirteenth Party Congress by then-Party Secretary, Zhao Ziyang. The "primary stage" was essentially a backtracking theory of Chinese history; it promoted not a leap into socialism but an era characterized by a slower accumulation of national wealth that would endure potentially for a century or more before another assault on socialism could be made. First in newspapers and later in academic journals, this new theory spawned controversy over China's choice in the 1940s to take a socialist rather than (quasi-)capitalist path. Specifically, the aborted path through the "new democratic stage" of the revolution—embarked upon in 1950 and then summarily abandoned by the middle of that decade—was condemned as voluntaristic and historically ungrounded. Soon enough, the "choice" problem led to a questioning of the whole "two semis" designation.

The first to reopen the question of the semis formulation in academic circles was historian Wang Jinglu, in an essay published in 1986 in the venerable *Lishi yanjiu* [Researches on history]—a journal that had recently been rehabilitated after being shut down during the Cultural Revolution.[34] Wang construed "semifeudalism" as a progressive stage beyond feudalism, thus not as an appropriate target of revolution but rather an appropriate place for China to have developed its own unique economic path—neither socialist nor capitalist. A rejoinder to Wang was published by historian Li Shiyue in the same journal in 1988—after the "primary stage" theory debate had been joined.[35] Li's text took Wang to task for his notion that semifeudalism indicated progress. That is, according to Li, semifeudalism had to be considered not uniquely (culturally) Chinese and progressive but exceptionally (historically) Chinese and stagnant. Subsequently, from 1989 through 1998, the debate proceeded in various other journals, including *Jindaishi yanjiu* [Researches in modern Chinese history], *Xueshu yanjiu* [Scholarly researches], and *Makesi zhuyi yanjiu* [Researches in Marxism], all major scholarly journals rehabilitated after the Cultural Revolution and publishing scholarly works again in the fields of history and philosophy. In the wake of the events of 1989, the link between the semis and the "primary stage" theory became less overtly the point of departure, although a repudiation of revolutionary necessity and the history of revolution became commonplace.[36] In place of abstract theorization, historian Chen Jinlong pedantically traced the origins of the terms *semi-*

colonialism and *semifeudalism*, so as to demonstrate that they were foreign imports and thus not necessarily suited to the Chinese situation.[37] A response was published by Zhang Qinghai, who disputed whether "semicolonial" indicated the problem of social formation (Chen believed it did; Zhang maintained it did not) or whether it is only "semifeudal" that had that significance.[38]

Whatever the technicalities of the case, Zhang's comment at the end of his essay summarily undermined the semis as history: "This author believes that 'semi' [*ban*] is merely an empty word and has no real meaning; it is not like a method that would make the colonial question into a problem of social formation. Thus, in historiography, it is perhaps more scientific to not use the 'semi' prefix. . . . But this author also believes that whether or not one uses 'semi' is not a question of principle and that it is not necessary to seek unanimity on the issue."[39] Thus effacing a half century of historical practice and discourse on revolutionary necessity—precisely as a problem of principle—the use of "semi" was dismissed, reduced to an individual choice rather than a potent historical analytic or party-approved incantation, perhaps subject to refinement and further specification.

These and cognate interrogations authorized historians if not to repudiate outright the "two semis" formulation in its minimal aspect as nominalism then at least to evacuate the concept;[40] it became, by virtue of this evacuation, reconstrued through the lens of a different form of transitional time: to argue for an essential historicist continuity between the 1930s and the 1990s, with the revolutionary period dropped out of the equation or put into the Furet-like brief parenthesis. In this vein, one participant in the decade's debates, historian Ma Min, called China's "two semis" society of the 1930s a "lopsided" structural totality that resulted from "the confrontation between the universalization of modern capitalism and the narrow tracks of feudal society." For Ma, therefore, "semi" was most properly understood as a "special transitional social formation" (*yizhong tesu de guodu xingtai shehui*) that accounts for "the bizarre contradictions that arose and developed from the structure and movement of modern Chinese society [and that] all revolve around the combination of its continuous transition to capitalism and its ultimate inability to complete this transition." Ma goes on to explain that transition must be understood as a historical process that "leads from the partial to the complete qualitative transformation of society."[41] And, whereas some transitions have been "spontaneous" (the

Euro-American variety), others have been "coerced."[42] Japan and Russia are examples of those that completed the latter (coerced) process, while China and India are examples of those that have yet to complete any process. Japan and Russia, Ma concludes, powerfully demonstrate that "if one can correctly take up the challenge, without losing time and wasting the opportunity, and if one relies upon the power of the state to promote reform and to boldly transplant capitalist modes of production, then less advanced nations are completely capable of realizing social transformation and leaping into the ranks of advanced industrialized nations."[43] Needless to say, those who did not take up the challenge correctly remained mired in transition, or worse, stagnated and regressed. On this account, China failed the historical test because of its inability to complete either a spontaneous or coerced transition to capitalism.

Here, transition is not a contingent historical situation without a telos— as in Wang's account—but rather unidirectional and teleologically indicated: anything other than the correct path (capitalism) toward so-called completion is deviant and historically aberrant. In Ma's estimation, the "semi" condition yielded neither historical regression nor progress, a stagnant situation from which the socialist state was born and which it, too, failed to overcome, thus sending China into a further half century of fruitless searching, not for the correctly mandated transition to capitalism but rather for a historically anachronistic and ultimately futile transition to socialism. For Ma, the failure to complete the capitalist transition either before or out of the semi condition confirms the correctness of the post– Mao Deng/Zhao theory of the "primary stage of socialism," which assigns China to a special stage of transitional development intended to get the nation off its distorted historical track back onto a normal (*zhengchang*) path of development.[44]

Partially refuting the logic, although joining in Ma's assessment of the significance of semi as a blocked transitional formation newly invigorated by the primary stage theory, Nie Xiwen rejoined that both "semis" had their advanced and regressive aspects, as any transitional social formation would have. Indeed, as Nie points out, the very definition of a "transitional formation" presupposes both residues of older (outmoded) formations and sprouts of newer (progressive) ones.[45] As Nie recounts, it was in fact precisely out of the recognition of the combined unity of regression and progress ("transition") that the historic Third Plenum of the Thirteenth Party

Congress (November 1987) fashioned the "primary stage" theory. As Nie cites the conclusion on this question adopted by the Congress: "Because our socialism emerged from the womb of a semicolonial, semifeudal society, the level of our productive forces greatly lagged behind that of advanced capitalist countries. This determined that we have to go through a relatively lengthy primary stage period in order to realize what many other countries have achieved under capitalism in industrialization: commodification, socialization of production, and modernization."[46]

A strong displacement of contingent historicity unto a scientific teleology of stages characterized by universal processes of transition from one to the next marks both Ma's and Nie's commentaries. Indeed, both rely for intelligibility upon a normalization of the concept of transition as a universal, unilinear, and necessary normative transition to capitalism, where the revolution and Maoism can only appear as aberrations. This normalization rejects transition as a socially immanent process or historically contingent one. For, the state, whose form and function comprised an important object of revolutionary struggle during Mao's time, turns out not to have been the appropriate object of struggle at all; rather, the state was apparently sufficient unto itself to secure China's needs, if only Mao and the revolutionaries had left it to its proper technocratic devices. In this reinstalling of the state at the center of history—rather than as the object of historical struggle—these theories of transition are utterly unlike Mao's earlier theory of new democracy (despite their occasional rhetorical bows toward a lamented aborted path of new democratic politics).

Indeed, Mao's new democracy, as articulated in the late 1940s and early 1950s, was an attempt to deal with the problem of China's devastated domestic economic and relatively isolated global situation with a theory of the immanence of social conflict in the historical determination of state form and the directionality of historical development themselves. That is, "new democracy" in Mao's version was a contingency mandating not pure capital accumulation (by the state) but rather conflicting and contradictory struggles inherited from the immediate past (the war, the GMD period, etc.). Hence, through the early to mid-1950s, "transition" in Mao's sense was certainly acknowledged as a temporal-spatial necessity to consolidate some version of the socialist project through the aegis of an unstable state intent on shaping history rather than merely presiding over it; however, it was not a taken-for-granted unidirectional dynamic of history whose form could be known in advance. By contrast, more contemporary theories of transition assume an untheorized transhistorical state that is not a product of the historical process but rather resides above it. While this state bears a superficial resemblance to the Leninist revolutionary state, Lenin's version, philosophically and historically, was the product of class struggle, historical conflict, and a philosophy based in principles of contradiction. These days, the Chinese state is no doubt a form of Leninist bureaucratic state, yet it more closely resembles not the philosophical theorization of the state in Lenin but rather the actual Soviet state under Stalin. During Mao's time, the state *was* one of the primary arenas of transitionary struggle—it was what the transition was about! Today, the state is taken as the sine qua non of a wished-for and never completed process of transition that stands ahistorically above the stuff of struggle itself.[47] One could almost venture the suggestion that the current version of the state, as an ideology of historical centrality, bears a strong resemblance to that state posited in the once-discredited Asiatic mode of production theory, as discussed in the second essay in this book. This becomes an even stronger linkage with the more recent subsequent mutations of party-state theory into the "Three Represents" and the newest theory of "Harmonious Society," where the state is said to be one with the people and not the product or representation of social struggle at all.

It is upon the premise of a transhistorical state unitary with society that the "primary stage of socialism" theory (which scientifically secures history through the state), in its link via a transitional formation to the "semi" formulation, provides the historico-ideological bridge over which the 1930s and the 1990s can be spatio-temporally reconnected as an apparently continuous historical process. That is, by purposefully dropping the socialist period out of historical consideration, the proper tasks of the Chinese nation-state can be said to be the accumulation of capital and wealth rather than the revolutionary upending of social exploitation and domination. Meanwhile, the CCP can be seen to embody that state, not as a matter of historical contingency but as the rightful essence of China qua enduring cultural entity. In this vein, current appeals to transition produce a mode of global and intranational historical comparability based upon the well-known Weberian method that secures comparability between two (or more) already constituted commensurate entities. Just as the state (and the nation-state) is central to the theories of "primary stage" and of "transition," while remaining untheorized in their historicist teleological implications, the category of the modern (*jindai* or *xiandai*) is also central to these articulations but reduced to a straightforward acceptance of historicist capitalist-style modernization (*jindaihua* or *xiandaihua*) as its exhaustive content. Thus are contemporaneity—in Éric Alliez's sense, which forms the epigraph to this essay—and historicity displaced. This displacement serves to reaffirm national-global continuity as temporal universality through the recuperative gesture of science secured by and to the state. As discussed in the first essay, this type of approach merely helps affirm a supposed universal transhistorical and comparable desire named modernization/capitalism, while reducing the historically contingent concept of "transition" to a magic concept of historicist teleology and naturalized transhistorical temporality.

Semicolonialism as Comparison

In his introduction to a book about 1990s China, Shanghai cultural theorist Wang Xiaoming observed that current paradigms are wholly inadequate to an investigation of contemporary Chinese society. He writes:

> How can we state anything clearly about contemporary China by using mechanical binary concepts alone? It [China] is clearly not a capitalist nation, but it is also quite clear that it is no longer the socialist nation it was previously; it is just in the process of forming a "market" that is not "planned," but this really has little to do with a capitalist market of "free competition"; it is in the process of importing Western technology, management systems, cultural products, and values systems, but it would be quite difficult for it to "transform" itself into some type of "modern" Western nation in any foreseeable future.

From this series of negative determinations, Wang observes that "it is really impossible to know how to define today's China, as it conforms in not one respect to any theoretical model, whether one already well known to us, or a newer one imported from Euro-America."[48] Wang's observation echoes left-Guomindang theorist Tao Xisheng's question of late 1928 that was at the heart of the social history controversy of the ensuing years. Tao queried at that time: "What kind of society is China's anyway [*zhongguo daodi shi shenma shehui*]?"[49] As Arif Dirlik has noted in his discussion of the controversy, the investigations into Chinese history undertaken by Tao, among many others, in an attempt to answer this question "resulted in the rather unfortunate description of a major portion of Chinese history as transitional"[50]—transitional, that is, from an imperfect model of feudalism to an unfulfilled model of capitalism. While Wang Xiaoming resists the temptation to exceptionalize contemporary China or to scientifically displace China's contemporary situation unto a ready-made concept of "transition," the question he raises, in its resonance with Tao's, is indicative of how the 1990s can sometimes appear as if it were a repetition of the 1930s. Indeed, seemingly similar experiences of historical and social dislocation in the 1990s have led to a seemingly repetitive posing of the same questions as those of the 1930s. Repetitiveness poses problems in thinking about comparisons between the 1930s decade and the 1990s.

As we have seen, many scholars simply conceal the problem of repetition or comparison under the pseudo-answer provided by transition as a narrative of national continuity. With this answer, scholars have found themselves in the peculiar conundrum of revisiting the problem of social specification first opened in the 1930s while simultaneously upholding the designation of China as transitional in the current period. This depressingly endless transitionism is upheld by eliding the very revolutionary years that supposedly did nothing to correctly bring the social formation and mode of production into a harmonious correspondence. Indeed, the Maoist period is usually now seen as having precipitated an untenable *noncorrespondence* between social relations and productive forces and, equally importantly, a *noncorrespondence* between China and the global capitalist economy. Because of the Maoist emphasis on transforming the relations of production ahead of developing the productive forces, the "primary stage of socialism" is now required to modernize the forces, it is said.[51] This apprehension of the problem leads to the denegation and even repudiation of the self-understanding of the revolutionary period as a historical attempt to come to terms with contradictions within and between the Chinese social and global formations of the 1930s–1940s in the context of crisis, whether financial panic or total war. That is, the very point of the revolution in its own terms was to challenge the primacy of forces of production through the insistent transformation of productive relations so as to place the leading classes (the peasant-proletariat alliance) in charge of the productive forces themselves. The current apprehension thus displaces the revolutionary period and the whole project of socialism, treating it as an Other to Chinese history proper.

Tao Xisheng's along with the contemporary insistence on a transitional formation—of 2,000 years' or 100–150 years' duration, respectively—could remind us of French theorist Étienne Balibar's attempt to argue for the necessity to conceive a social formation in transition as governed by a transitional mode of production, where the formation and mode in "normal" circumstances would be conceived as mutually reproductive internal effectivities of a single expressive structure.[52] Balibar elucidates that in a transitional social formation, relations of production and productive forces do not correspond. Theories of China's endless transition could be said to conform to Balibar's formulation. Yet, as Barry Hindess and Paul Q. Hirst elaborate in their critique of Balibar, in *any* mode of production (properly so called), the relations and forces of production must be related in the mode of *noncorrespondence*, because "each moment of reproduction is also a moment of dissolution of the structure of the mode of production; the concept of a transitional mode of production is also the concept of its suppression."[53] In other words, *all* modes of production, if one is to take the theory seriously, are "transitional" insofar as there are always elements of the past and the future in the present formation, which will inform the direction of the next mode. Thus, "transition" actually names nothing at all other than a banal truism of all historical moments.

The point here is twofold: by insisting on the necessity of endless "transition," the specificities and unevennesses of the lived experiences of any contemporary moment can be politically justified as the historically necessary cost to be paid for social/national completion (the full arrival, as it were, at some other mode). This is precisely what some contemporary theorists and policy wonks in and outside China maintain: that the sacrifices of, for example, the peasantry and the old working classes must be tolerated and endured to enable the nation to progress in the proper direction. (This is the Chinese liberal/neoliberal intellectual position, *tout court*.) Secondly, then, in the contemporary case, the resort to "transition" under the "primary stage" theory as a phony state–Marxist alibi for capitalism constitutes both a political and a quasi-theoretical effort to turn the "irrational" preoccupation and policy of the Mao years on transforming relations of production before the productive forces were fully developed into a more "rational" policy of building the productive forces in a context defined by the supposedly exceptional *noncorrespondence* of the two. This theory closely mirrors the formal-idealist conception of the structure of the economy, which is exactly one of the most problematic aspects of Balibar's theory, or of any theory of a transitional mode of production or transitional time. That is, if the directionality of "transition" is assumed (i.e., to be considered "normal," all transitions must move toward capitalism, or at least toward the development of the productive forces), there is no room for contingent human activity (e.g., revolution), as all activity must be properly geared toward the developmentalist goal. This is capitalist and vulgar Marxist modernization as pure ideology, with "transition" as its bloody handmaiden. For this, the supraclass state is essential as a theoretical as well as practical bulwark against the crushing social conflicts that such transitional normativity requires.

By contrast to these contemporary evocations of "transitionism," as we have seen, among at least some 1930s theorists of semicolonialism there was an explicit commitment to a dialectical understanding of national/social becoming and global transformation that endowed those theories with an expansive concept of history: Chinese history as a particular problematic embedded in a global theory of capitalist crisis. Semicolonialism appeared as an extended conjunctural moment during which the commodification of labor power was achieved through the violence of the primitive accumulation of capital in its imperialist form and its partial collusion with the state as well as with the comprador-bourgeoisie. As Wu Qingyou wrote in 1937 with regard to distinguishing semicolonialism from Kautskian theories of ultra-imperialism (and by extension, from Sun Yatsen's concept of hypocolonialism [*ci zhimindi*][54]):

> The points of departure for theories of organized capitalism and of ultra-imperialism are logically connected. They both consider that it is possible to draw a boundary around the nation and to develop capitalism within those boundaries. When they analyze developmental trends within capitalism, they isolate particular key aspects of it. They do not understand that within the developmental process of capitalism itself are expressed interlocking contradictions, which are the result of uneven development. Unevenness itself, as a process of capitalism, thus includes the sum total of the mode of production and its anarchic char-

acter. This type of unevenness does not weaken in the imperialist era, but rather strengthens.[55]

Here, then, *noncorrespondence* in global terms—that is, unevenness—is precisely the condition of possibility for capitalism's ongoing strength, *not* an obstacle to its development.

In short, the thorny issue dealt with in many semicolonialism theories in the 1930s was the question of the role played by imperialism in the dissolution of China's old relations of production (whether those were called "feudal" or not) in their relationship to the state and in the articulation of China's productive capacity to the global economy.[56] It was, hence, precisely the issue of the relations of production—*not* the enhancement of the productive forces—that was of primary concern at the time. It is no coincidence that it was precisely this issue that was taken up by Mao Zedong, for, as Mao clearly recognized, it was *not* the purpose of capitalism to transform relations and forces of production; rather, it was the purpose of capitalism to lock relations in place, to further the extractive and exploitative capacity of capitalist accumulation. On this Mao and Wang Yanan agreed fully. Moreover, it was the problem of the relations of production—specifically Chinese, but only when globally contextualized and understood—that provided the basis of an analysis of historical experience that could yield concepts adequate to reality. It was in this context that Wang, for his part, and Mao, for his, came to determine the analytical ambit of semicolonialism as a lived experience of socioeconomic life in China from the late nineteenth century to the revolutionary years. For Mao, this recognition was the premise for the fomenting of a revolutionary unity; for Wang, it was an analytical point of departure for the reconnecting of Chinese reality to the abstractions of global capitalism as a system of thought and lived experience.

Conversely, today's reduction of the concept of semicolonialism to the status of aborted transition to capitalism proposes that the rectification of the imbalance in Chinese socioeconomic life requires a commitment to a normative tipping of history toward a sociopolitical elite that allies itself with the state and with forces of global capitalism in the restructuring of the Chinese nation as a fully commodified labor force and consumer society. In the 1930s, this social element was called, accurately, the "comprador-bureaucratic class"; today, much less antagonistically, it could be called, in Wang Xiaoming's ironic terms, the stratum of "successful personages" (*chenggong renshi*).[57] "China-in-transition" hence is offered in the 1990s as a seemingly commensurate comparative object, in formal terms, to "semicolonial China" in the 1930s, of course with the major difference that now, China has a fully sovereign national state. By contrast, my argument is that China in the 1930s and China in the 1990s should more appropriately be seen as incommensurabilities that are at best a packaging device for a comparative practice that conceals the ongoing production and reproduction of global and domestic unevennesses consequent upon accelerating transformations within capitalism both inside and outside China. The current re/production of capitalism at a global scale mystifies the internal social consequences of the commodification of labor power through violent state-sanctioned primitive accumulation of capital that, among other things, has led to the categorization of a large portion of the (rural and urban) Chinese population as either "redundant" (people) or "surplus" (labor). Wang Yanan long ago commented with regard to this kind of categorization: surplus labor can only be considered "surplus" when social distribution is unequal and ill conceived; otherwise, it is just the reserve army of labor needed by capital to depress wages and control workers.[58]

Conclusion

Many versions of the theory of "semi" in the 1930s at the very least recognized the temporal disjunctures consequent upon the shared embeddedness of all within a global capitalism, itself in the process of being reoriented around new forms of class structures and new modes of capital accumulation occasioned by and through the global expansion and collapse of the financial system and its attendant crises, including the rise of fascism globally. As Wang Yanan wrote of this process in his book on economic principles, only by considering the historicity and specificity of the commodity form as a combined ideological, material, and sociopolitical formation could one understand, for example, the historical nature of commercial capital under the conditions of war (which brings commerce into a prominence and social effectivity it perhaps hitherto had not possessed) or, for another example, could one grasp the particular nature of rural economics through the process of the gap between rural and urban processes of valorization.[59] In other words, for Wang, counting quantities of things produced (as empiricist practice would have it) was simply insufficient to address the more pressing historical question of the specific and variable forms that value takes at particular times or that the valorization process takes at various moments. In his view, by the 1930s and 1940s, the uneven process of valorization—through which the value of rural commodities was being subordinated to both the global and the urban economies and the value of rural labor power was being depressed by the collapse of industrial and financial capital, thus provoking an agrarian crisis—required historically rooted research into the commodity form and its attendant social relations, not merely into specific commodities and their quantities in circulation, consumption, or distribution. This was the kind of research, Wang noted, that would allow social scientists and economists not only to define China's social formation as semicolonial and semifeudal but, far more important than the category designation, such research would enable them to find solutions to the precise modes of the uneven articulation of rural and urban economies in a specific national and global historical context. This approach would, perforce, require a thorough understanding of the varying geographically uneven conditions for the selling of labor power, the reproduction of labor, as well as the dominant, rising, and residual ideological premises for the production of socioeconomic value and cultural values.[60]

All of this combined—taken not as a question of the "nationalization" of economic studies in a culturalist vein nor as a pure reproduction of endless transition but rather as a question of the real conditions of possibility for socioeconomic transformation in a capitalist world system at war and in economic crisis[61]—had to form the basic approach to economic study and the study of the economy in China. In other words, a theoretical emphasis on the commodity form, value/valorization, and the social relations of production, Wang believed, would give a far better material and conceptual grounding for empirical work and hence a far better sense of possible future directions, without either meekly surrendering to a capitalist inevitability or blindly leaping into a socialist utopia. Indeed, as he wrote scathingly in late 1949, on the eve of Communist victory, about the Guomindang's proposed economic plans, their emphasis on a "national economy" was no different in form from the nineteenth-century *yangwu* (Westernization) movement. Both used the centralized bureaucracy to retain feudal relations while building modern industry on top; both intended to sacrifice the rural areas in favor of the cities while using the cities to suppress rural areas as a way to preserve the rural as a site for the primitive accumulation of capital, reproduction of labor power, and labor exploitation on a national scale; and both preserved imperialist-capitalist relations and the comprador class to prop up their own economic and political power.[62] For Wang, the promise of the defeat of the GMD—already on the horizon by the time of the publication of his critique—was the promise that the process of value-creation and value-production would take center stage in economic policy and research, and along with these foci, there would come the necessary emphasis on the social relations of production. Some of this was attempted in the post-1949 era (only to be undone after Mao's death); and some of this remained an entirely failed experiment in social transformation. In 1949 Wang believed the experiment worth undertaking.

By contrast, in the 1990s, the wide and implicit acceptance of the inevitability of capitalism, as discussed here through the analytical mutation of semicolonialism into a theory of perpetual transition and blocked forms of enhancing productive forces, presents little in the way of a critique of either capitalism or contemporary globalization. It is, rather, a form of conceptual recolonization. The type of global and intranational comparison articulated in this recolonized form is precisely that secured through the social-scientific certainties discussed in the first and third essays of this volume. It reanimates the ideas of "backwardness" and "catching up" as the ultimate goals of economic growth and development, while reinscribing the premises of modernization theory back into the heart of economic theory and practice. It was precisely against this form of comparative practice and theory that many in the 1930s wrote their critiques.

Finally, then, the 1990s names the 1930s as its originary moment and organizes that era as its historical point of departure even as the contemporary resort to transition as a national narrative conceit locates its inevitability and necessity within the failure of the Chinese socialist project. By contrast, my endeavor in presenting the 1930s and 1990s raising and reanimation of semicolonialism through the problematic of comparability based upon the principle of *incommensurability* rather than on claims to continuity can help elucidate how the open-ended futural historical immanence that was the basis of 1930s theorizing came to be absolutized in the 1990s as a historicism designated the transition to capitalism.

CHAPTER 5

The Economic as Culture and the Culture
of the Economic

Filming Shanghai

Contradictions are our hope!
—BERTOLT BRECHT, "The Film, the Novel, and Epic Theater"

In his introduction to an anthology on Chinese film, Yingjin Zhang proposes that a proper archaeology of knowledge about prerevolutionary Chinese cinema—proper, in the sense that it would dispense with the overpoliticization that has generally contained this type of film study to its leftist manifestations—would enable one to "understand better the persistent nature of certain types of *mentalités*." As he explains: "The revisiting of cinema and urban culture in Republican Shanghai . . . encourages a rethinking of China's changing film culture in the new *fin de siècle*."[1] Among other things, Zhang's archaeology is intended to link Republican-era Shanghai (1920s/1930s) to present-day Shanghai (1990s/2000s) through an exhumation of noncontradictory continuities in meaning and signification supposedly long masked by the ruptural orthodoxies of leftism. To make this argument, Zhang mobilizes the tired notion of "mentalité" to restore cultural propriety to its proprietary place.

The problem with mentalité, as Jacques Rancière notes in commenting on François Furet's book on the French Revolution, is that the type of antirevolutionary account that relies upon such a notion is premised upon the conviction that "the historical actors live in the illusion of creating the future by combatting something that, in fact, is already in the past." Rancière continues: "And the Revolution is the generic name of this illusion, of this false present of the event that is the conjunction of a misapprehension and a utopia: the misapprehension of the past character of what one believes to be present, the utopia of making the future present. The Revolution is the illusion of making the Revolution, born from ignorance of the Revolution already made."[2] In other words, the illusion is that the revolution *was* a revolution, illusory because the event can be dissolved by the historian into a scientific precision that demonstrates the revolution to have been unnecessary, since the state against which it was waged died long before the revolution ostensibly killed it. In this retrospective abolishing of the revolutionary event, those who thought they lived and acted in a revolutionary present are relegated to a nonexistent temporality and an insignificant one. Thus is the lived temporality of historical actors flattened into scientific time, crowding out politics "by prematurely imposing," in Peter Osborne's words, "the perspective of a future which absolutizes existing relations to the past."[3]

Lived histories in this fashion can be figured as endlessly particular and timelessly continuous, reenacting the same cultural values over and over again, interrupted only by aberrant historicities imposed by misguided ("leftist") historians. As Rancière goes on to note in his account of the retrospective rewriting of the French Revolution, in Jules Michelet's hands, the revolution can be absorbed seamlessly into the realm of "mentalités": assimilated into that utopian present projected from and into a timeless past and future consisting of "uninterrupted discourse" that territorializes meaning by "leaving no spoken word . . . without a place."[4] With Michelet, then, lived temporality is doomed to endless reproduction as a form of spatio-cultural coherence and normative desire: the event's potential ruptural significance domesticated, the heretical voices raised in its making efficiently contained to their proper places. Thus, again, is the propriety of place restored to a class-specific form of sociocultural property: the masses who rose in the revolution were historically mistaken, as history belongs to the properly classed bourgeois historian and scholar. Thence is "mentalité" linked to a reaffirmation of homogeneous localities and class-specific cultures in a tight nexus of mutually reinforcing sociological and cultural reproduction. Mentalité is that which wraps or entraps peoples in the timelessness of culture and place, apolitically deflecting and deferring history. This is one form of "liberation," albeit an idealist liberation from the historical contingency of the past. Rancière's account of Furet and Michelet succinctly reveals that the scholarly resort to mentalités is a compensatory gesture that dehistoricizes and depoliticizes by effecting displacements that leave us with an attenuated spatio-cultural tautology: "*the place is what gives a place.*"[5] It becomes an important way of making possible claims of temporal continuities tied to bounded culturalist essences.

As we have seen in the previous chapters, such a procedure informs and suffuses the Weberian method of comparison that displaces the global historical rupture of capitalism unto an ahistorically spatially differentiated world and misplaces ideas in all sorts of ways. In this reading, Zhang Yingjin's perhaps casual evocation of mentalité can be considered an important gesture insofar as it efficiently and succinctly reflects a growing trend in today's scholarly and Chinese state-ideological world that similarly conspires to establish a direct link between China's 1930s and 1990s, with the revolution understood as an unnecessary and thus historically aberrant event. As suggested in the previous essays, this link works on one level to displace an uneven dynamic temporal relationship between politics and history in favor of a universal global diachrony embodied by the state and the pure ideology of economic development/modernization. Yet, on another level and in the realm of culture, it proposes a static spatio-temporal mentalité—an ahistorical set of cultural values—as the basis for comparability. This methodological presupposition authorizes an erasure that reflects a more profound desire than one simply to recuperate lost voices from the suppressions promoted by the (valorized) revolutionary-leftist/(unvalorized) popular culture–bourgeois binary hitherto dominating histories of Chinese film (and of Shanghai studies more generally). For, as confining as that older binary is and as necessary as it is to seek new analytic frameworks derived from a more complex conceptualization of history/culture, Zhang's project and those like it merely seek to substitute a utopian futurity—that Michelet-style restoration of every voice to its proper place—for a contingent and tortured past process of political and economic struggle.[6] This futurity renders that struggle and all its contradictions into a mirage conjured by a massive historico-ideological hoax.

In this essay, I foreground some problems raised by willed displacements/misplacements in film by working through some explicit and implicit comparisons made between China's 1930s and 1940s and the 1990s in two films about Shanghai.[7] As we saw in the fourth essay, the 1990s historiographical debates on the concept of semicolonialism recuperate albeit significantly transform aspects of the originary 1930s and 1940s debates on the social relations of revolution and human emancipatory potential; the 1990s version depoliticizes the earlier debates by reading semicolonialism through the lens of today's preoccupation with (inevitable) transition to capitalist-style modernization and the hybrid social-cultural forms that facilitate and authenticate such transitions. Indeed, the contemporary consensus labeling of China's current moment as a "transitional social formation" (*zhuanxing shehui xingtai*) or a "transitional period" (*zhuanxing shiqi* or *guodu shiqi*)— codified in official doctrine as the "primary stage of socialism"—effectively evacuates the possible critical or conflictual dimensions from semicolonialism, dimensions of great concern to 1930s theorists, who most often used the term to analytically name the nature of global and national unevenness and the forms of activity required for its overcoming. Semicolonialism is thus displaced from the global and national social processes in which the concept was originally embedded and from which it originally emanated as a historical problematic, and is relocated and misplaced to the level of the continuous national state and its securing of the cultural values that might guarantee "transition" to economic efficiency.

In a corollary to that discussion, I next consider two films—Zheng Junli's *Crows and Sparrows* (*Wuya yu maque*, 1948–49; hereafter, *Crows*) and Peng Xiaolian's *Once Upon a Time in Shanghai* (*Shanghai jishi*, 1998; hereafter, *Shanghai*)—both of which emplot the city of Shanghai as a site of revolution and liberation. I explore the ways in which Peng's contemporary enactment of Shanghai's modernity proceeds with ostensibly direct reference to its prerevolutionary other through appeals to the city as a stable place embodied in bourgeois mentalité, whose lure is inscribed in a past to which the present inevitably returns. In this vision, Shanghai and its past resemble a form of what Marx called a "self-valorizing value," a closed circuit of reproduction representing a stable exchange between value and place, past and present.[8] In *Shanghai*, that is, the city is construed via a past episode of sociopolitical imbalance (the 1940s); and it is liberated (in the 1990s) when the ruptural and aberrant decades of socialism are disappeared and the city is able to return to its supposedly original values (of bourgeois cosmopolitanism). As counterpoint, I explore how Zheng Junli's prerevolutionary filmic enactment of Shanghai in *Crows* constructs an urban lifeworld through an account of a historical experience of modernity figured through what Harry Harootunian has called "everydayness."[9] In this version, Shanghai is construed as an uneven space of production— economic, historical, cultural, social—and not as an endlessly reproduced place; meanwhile, the city's late 1940s sociopolitical upheavals are figured as moments of intense struggle in the context of total crisis. Liberation in *Crows* is thus an open-ended opportunity to create anew the practices of the everyday by imagining a history and a futurity that has not yet been and yet still could be: the 1940s is not an era whose end is foretold by the imposition of managerial control in the 1990s and a teleology of "transition" but rather an era whose resolution is in an ongoing process of sociohistorical becoming and dialectical political struggle.

Placing Shanghai in History

Any cursory viewing of Zheng Junli's *Crows and Sparrows* and Peng Xiaolian's *Once Upon a Time in Shanghai* immediately reveals that they are polar opposites of one another—notwithstanding the fact that the latter appropriates the former through extensive cinematic quotation. At the material level, the conditions of the production of each film could not be more different. Zheng's film was produced on a shoestring budget, mostly underground and through subterfuge in an effort to evade the radar of Guomindang (GMD, or Nationalist Party) censors, who would have objected violently to Zheng's stringent critiques of a regime in its death throes. Indeed, *Crows* was only postproduced and released upon the capture of Shanghai by the People's Liberation Army (PLA) in 1949 and after.[10] By contrast, Peng's film was commissioned by the Chinese Communist Party (CCP) as an official commemoration of the fiftieth anniversary of their liberation of Shanghai from GMD control; she was given a huge budget as well as massive cultural, political, and technical assistance to filmically reconstruct late 1940s Shanghai.[11] Supported by the Shanghai Film Studio, *Shanghai* was the winner of a major prize for best dramatic film in 1998, and, as the studio's director, Zhu Yongde, later wrote about the film's appeal: "the unique perspective selected by *Shanghai jishi* allows this film, which describes the liberation of Shanghai, to distance itself from the conventions of revolutionary historical topics; it thus has a charm all its own."[12]

Shanghai is a beautiful, coherent, technically accomplished and monumental tribute to its sponsors and to the historical moment they wished Peng to commemorate. However, it turns out that that moment is the present, not the past. That the present is more at issue than the past is initially revealed through the bookending of the film in glowing scenes of contemporary Shanghai, presented through the return of the protagonist, Shaobai, to the city after a fifty-year absence. The opening sequence situates the viewer in the safe place of an already constituted present viewed through the windows of an airplane circling the skyscraper-strewn, LED-lit skyline of Pudong/downtown Shanghai. After lingering briefly but dramatically in the airspace over the city, the film moves smoothly to a linearly rendered narrative of Shaobai's past in the city during the crucial final years (late 1948 through early 1950) when the CCP/PLA was wresting political and economic control of the city from the GMD. The main characters in the historical narrative—Shaobai and his lover, Li Huirong—are both offspring of the "national bourgeoisie": their parents are co-owners of a textile factory that has patriotically resumed productive activities amid the chaos of the city after the defeat of Japan. The narrative follows three main strands: the attempts by Shaobai to rescue the textile factory from inflationary disaster; his concurrent attempts to convince Huirong to leave Shanghai with him, as the city becomes increasingly dangerous; and the course taken by Huirong's conflicted and simultaneous loyalties to Shaobai, the factory/her parents' class position, and the CCP, which she serves as an underground operative, for which her family background and privileged social status provide cover. The privileged social background combined with Huirong's correct (Communist) politics also provide cover for the filmmaker—Peng Xiaolian—to depict many scenes of the alluring bourgeois lifestyles of the 1930s and 1940s Shanghai elite, those lifestyles diligently replicated in 1990s commodity-driven Shanghai, without betraying any hint of contradiction between the lifestyle and the politics.

Despite the intimacy of the story—which soon devolves into a series of melodramatic romances (Shaobai's with Huirong; Huirong's with the CCP; Shanghai's with the bourgeoisie)—the narrative of the city in the 1940s is carefully contained, sealed off, as it were (to use Zhang Ailing's phrase), from the protagonist's present (1998) by the nightmarish sequence of events that is the reason for both the protagonist's flight from China in early 1950 and his return from abroad in 1998. Indeed, that which might materially link the past to the present is nowhere presented or represented, other than obliquely in the modernized prospects of the current-day metropolis and in Shaobai's frozen memories. Thus, the end of the film—which returns to the beginning, when Shaobai has arrived in Shanghai after the fifty-year interval—has Shaobai strolling along the late 1990s Bund, gazing over to the new Pudong district, with the Oriental Pearl TV tower looming large in the night. Pausing to admire the now-iconic scene of the city's 1990s resurgence, Shaobai remarks that his lost love, Huirong, who was killed in February 1950 by a counterrevolutionary during the GMD's final attempt to destabilize the city, "will always be young and smiling" despite the passage of time. Another detail: Shaobai, who is returning in 1998 from the United States to remember his forever young and smiling lover and to enjoy the new Shanghai, was also returning to Shanghai in 1948 from the United States in order to marry Huirong. He has, then, always been an outsider to Shanghai, absent from its history of becoming. For him the city must always be frozen in time, with the "new Shanghai/China" promised in the revolutionary 1948–50 now realized, in his absence, albeit in the spirit of the very class he embodies and against which the revolution had been waged.

According to the film, Shaobai can only render his past into Shanghai's (absent) history because he has been away from the events' aftermath. Shanghai has now become his ideal city: the young, smiling lover of his eternal, hitherto unconsummated longing. This idealization and distance are marked by an apparent spatio-temporal continuity, as present-day Shanghai effortlessly metamorphoses into a latter-day Shanghai, and vice versa, a spatial continuity that allows Shaobai/the filmmaker to return to the exact same place by inscribing it with an unchanging meaning (the frozen-in-time young and smiling face of his lover; the bourgeois comforts to which he is entitled). In *Shanghai*, therefore, it appears that we are to understand that the condition of remembering/rendering pasts into history is the complete occlusion of the passage of conflictual historical time in favor of a rendition of history as nostalgia and smooth continuity.[13] Relatedly, we are to understand Shanghai as a stable place that can only be fully appreciated/apprehended from the overarching perspective of a completed present, whose teleological realization of the transition from the past is produced in and through the returnee's fantasies of a romance reflected in Shanghai's alluring iridescence. In this fashion, Shanghai appears as a place and space of endlessly reproduced romantic longing/desire, a space where cultural and economic value are at one with place. Put differently, Shanghai can be seen as an emblematic modern trope and site for what German fascist theorist Carl Schmitt called "political romanticism," as realized through a type of "subjectivism" directed "not to concepts and philosophical systems, but rather to a kind of lyrical paraphrase of [individual] experience."[14]

Zheng Junli's 1948 film presents an utterly different aspect: that of a revolutionary everyday being produced slowly, painstakingly, and painfully from the materials at hand. These turn out to be a four-story house inhabited by a selection of Shanghai citizens, whose positions in the socioeconomic-cultural hierarchy of urban life are differentially marked but commonly characterized by marginality from an economic and political center, however in collapse that center may be. In the steadily worsening socioeconomic-political conditions of late 1940s Shanghai, all of the solidities that might make up a routinized lifeworld—tins of (American) evaporated milk, gold jewelry, residences, property, professions, work, identities, money, relationships—almost literally melt into air in the process of their historicization and valorization (that is, in their realization as use and exchange value). Value is not solid but entirely unstable. Overdetermined as this process might be because of the literally exponential inflation of the last desperate weeks and months of the GMD's rule, Zheng's film nevertheless understands that "liberation" from these conditions needs to be lived and thus construed as a topos of everydayness: that is, it must be understood in intimate relationship to particular histories, for which there is no escape or idealized return as such. In other words, value cannot be rediscovered as if it already existed and somehow got misplaced; value must constantly be created anew. Thus, unlike in Peng's Shanghai, the present in Crows is anchored neither in a teleological narrative of revolutionary liberation by the party, nor in a desired return of Shanghai to its proper bourgeois roots; nor is it presented as a nostalgia for a history/politics that could have been and now finally is; nor in a sense of an eternally stable spatiality whose essential return is always-already foretold. Rather, inherent in the present of Crows is, in Harootunian's words, the "coexistence of different forms of economic life [that] came to signal an experience that was both modern and distinct."[15] It was from this coexistence that revolutionary urban values along with the value of revolution were to be forged as a lifeworld.

To be sure, one could see Crows as a transparent urban ethnology that catalogs "friends" or potential "friends" and "enemies" with reference to a stable center of the revolution according to strict Maoist criteria.[16] Indeed, each character, or cluster of characters, can easily be read as representing a recognizable urban (class/political) type of the 1930s and 1940s—intellectual, teacher, petty bourgeois peddler, rural migrant laborer/servant, GMD official/landlord, bourgeois modern girl/mistress/wife, and so on—and with the exceptions of the official/landlord and his mistress/wife, each of them is a potential revolutionary friend who must first recognize and then actualize his/her true social relationship to the collective. At this level, the film can easily be deconstructed schematically as an anatomy of the coming into being of an urban revolutionary consciousness—the formation of the urban revolutionary united front collective called the "masses"—in a linear time marked by the rumored progress of the PLA toward Nanjing/Shanghai, where the tendential unity of the masses is provided by the (party-led) revolutionary movement itself.

However, while the utopian conceit of the film is no doubt that the everyday disjunctness represented by the initially conflictual relations among the house's inhabitants can be overcome through collective action, nevertheless, what the resulting unity might be or do is less clear. For even though the film begins and ends in the tendentially unifying space of the same house, the *meaning* of that house is utterly transformed by the conclusion, and the meaning at which we arrive at the film's end has not been foreclosed by the putative unity of a revolutionary center. Thus, the return of the house to its rightful owner, Mr. Kong, from whom it had been seized after the war by Mr. Hou ("Monkey"), who had hidden his prior collaboration with the Japanese in order to gain his position in the GMD, is figured not as a return to the past, nor as a return to a stable place/space of private property, nor even as a blinding recognition of the revolutionary task in the present. Rather, the return of the house forms the pretext and premise for an open-ended new beginning. Indeed, because the return has been effected not by Mr. Kong alone, nor by state legal fiat, but by the transformation of atomized citizens—the residents and accidental neighbors—into a collective, this is no return to a previous regime of private property. In fact, the house—as ostensibly stable place, not to mention as private property—has by the end of the film been transformed into a potentially revolutionary space, with its internal relationships utterly reconfigured into a "friendly" collective of urban subalterns intent on claiming mastery over their lives. The insistent dynamic of everydayness as history imposes no closure on either the residents or the house. Here, then, the meanings of return—of Shaobai to Shanghai after a fifty-year absence in Peng's film, and of the house to Mr. Kong in *Crows*—could not be more differently construed.

In the process of tracking the reconfiguration of the sociality of the house—which is the produced space and not merely the inert place of the contingent conditions of possibility for the social itself—it is interesting to note that Shanghai is never represented as an urban totality or national microcosm in *Crows*. Rather, Shanghai is a series of lived spaces, or produced spaces, of life. Far from an arbitrary choice of location, of course, Shanghai nevertheless is not made to fetishistically stand as a self-contained entity or a self-valorizing value whose meaning is only proper to itself.[17] It is not semicolonialism as a hybrid given of a cosmopolitan present but semicolonialism as a lived temporality of modern unevenness. *This* Shanghai cannot be viewed and encompassed at a glance from an airplane!

The majority of the action in *Crows* occurs in "Hou's residence" (the monkey house, as it were)—as it is identified in the opening shot of the film, which comes after a credit sequence projected upon photographic stills of Shanghai's densely built alleyways (*lilong*) (now torn down and built over in favor of megamodernized malls or replicas of themselves as shopping centers with "authentic" flavor[18]). The single-family home has been cut up into any number of individually occupied rooms, some with small families living crowded together in one room. Mr. Hou collects rent on all the rooms and occupies the top floor, consisting of two rooms. Sometimes the action is depicted in one continuous shot and sometimes through editing—from one space of this residence to another: top to bottom, bottom to top, roof, courtyard, entranceway—where different lives take shape, lives that increasingly are brought into historical relationship with one another not by the mere fact of proximity but by the impending sale of the house, which problematizes all the lives in a similar way in relation to history/commodities/property. While all the individual lived spaces are contained within the house itself, the ceaselessly produced unevenness of that space is immediately presented as *the* historical problem at issue.

In other words, rather than, as in Peng's film, unevenness being understood as the static given center, in *Crows* unevenness is provided a dynamic history, or, rather, it is *the* dynamic of history itself. The endlessly produced unevenness—attributable to capital/property as processes of creating and uncreating social relations—is underscored by the occasional moves away from those densely lived spaces. Yet the forays into the city by the inhabitants of the house do not so much trace a unified metropolitan space as they are intimately tied to the fragmentary ways in which each inhabitant experiences the larger city, and how each of these experiences contributes to the ongoing production of individual and social unevenness. The teacher, Mr. Hua, goes to his school, where he reluctantly gets caught up in a political movement against the school's newly imposed principal, for which he eventually gets arrested by the GMD/their gang sponsors. Meanwhile, the peddlers, Mr. and Mrs. Xiao (Little Broadcast and his wife), go to the marketplace, where they attempt to maneuver through the minefields of inflation; or they go to the gates of the bank, where they unsuccessfully attempt to capitalize on the instability of the official gold market. Mrs. Hua, the teacher's wife, goes to various uncaring and imposing government offices in her effort to retrieve her arrested and imprisoned husband, just as Mr. Kong, the former house owner dispossessed by the crafty Mr. Hou, and who now inhabits one of the more provisional spaces under the stairs in the house, ventures to the newspaper office, where he resignedly participates in the creation of disinformation on behalf of the GMD censors. Meanwhile, Mr. Hou proceeds to his office at the Ministry of Defense, where he uses his official position to manipulate markets in rice, money, and gold, while his mistress/wife remains in the house, trapped by her status—she must *act* the landlady part as she is aggressively manipulated by Mr. Hou and manipulates everyone else.

Through all of this coming and going, Shanghai is represented only in fragments, through trajectories that are tied together by the needs of each inhabitant's life. The fragments, however, are not merely individuated parts of an "urban 'text'" written blindly or from a bird's-eye view, as Michel de Certeau would have it.[19] Rather, the trajectories overlap, unifying as they disaggregate the temporalities of lives in crisis. Thus, one of the most interesting dynamics of *Crows* is how these trajectories figure the immanence of temporality that provides the structure for the film.

Productive and Reproductive Economies

The most dramatic turning point in *Crows*—and one of its most famous sequences—is the climactic queuing for gold at the bank by Little Broadcast and his wife (a scene reprised almost frame for frame in Peng's film, albeit to little dramatic effect). In one sense, the drama of this moment in *Crows* is purely visual: it comes as a startling contrast to the minutiae of everyday struggles that make up most of the film. The sheer size of the framing, which takes in the monumentality of the bank, the forces that control it, the crowds that besiege it, all underscored by the violently heavy rainfall, come as a visual surprise after so much small-scale intimacy. This contrast between monumentality and the everyday is underpinned by the insistent distinction made throughout the film between capitalist and simple repro-ductive economies, which coexist while producing different temporalities of lived experience.

In *Crows*, the capitalist economy that is underwritten by the GMD and its gangs is ardently figured as "theft," the premise of which is none other than primitive accumulation based upon pure expropriation. It is based, in other words, upon a prior act, violent and bloody, whose historicity must be erased for the arrangement to be normalized in the present as property. This is clearest in Hou's relation to the house, which he has expropriated from Mr. Kong all the while hiding his wartime collaborations with the Japanese; it is also evident in the accounts of Hou's attempts to corner the rice market and in the GMD's/gangs' manipulations of the price of gold. As for the house, the insistent memory of Mr. Kong and the other resi-dents blocks Hou's efforts to impose forgetting as the normalization of his property rights. By contrast, this forgetting is crucial to the nostalgia of Peng's film, where the origins of the modernized present in corruption and the privatization of public/party property are buried by bourgeois normal-ity and the cultural continuity of place. In *Crows*, Hou's life is structured temporally by the instability of its premise (the imminent collapse of the GMD/the historicity of the prior theft); temperamentally by his continuous sneaky efforts to disguise his theft as rightful, legal property; and spatially by the trajectories he traces between the house, Nanjing (offscreen, and the nominal capital of the GMD's Republic), and the Ministry of Defense office in Shanghai, which doubles as his illegal rice exchange's company head-quarters. Thus, in temporal terms, Hou attempts to erase the memory of expropriation/the historicity of his own becoming; while in spatial terms, he attempts to normalize his status by inscribing it in his personal and spatial connection to centers of political and economic power. However, the supposed linear temporality of capital and/or its assumed ahistoricity as secured by the legality of the state refuses to resolve itself: its contradictions and its bloody origins, as Marx put it, are continually exposed through historicization, in the film understood not merely as memory but as the coming into being of a social collectivity not ruled by the values of property or thieving state legality but by a sense of the value of social and historical (if not legal) justice.

Meanwhile, the location of an economy of simple reproduction—Little Broadcast's peddler or petty bourgeois economy—in such a structure is what exposes the contradictions in the coexistent temporalities of life under capital's own attempt at ahistorical narrativization. Specifically, as Little Broadcast prepares to go to the bank to queue for gold, he first has a daydream in which he calculates in simple reproductive fashion how his "capital" of one ingot of gold will soon yield two; and two, four; and four, eight; and eight, sixteen; and so on, until his chair breaks beneath him and wakes him from his reverie. In this and the subsequent scenes, the extant and coexistent gap between a capitalist economy of theft and a reproductive economy of use-value is alluded to. To be sure, Little Broadcast's dreams, if brought to successful fruition, could not end with mere reproduction—as Marx writes of the process, "although this reproduction is a mere repetition . . . this mere repetition, or continuity, imposes on the process certain new characterstics."[20] Indeed, Little Broadcast's intent all along is to buy the house in order to prevent his family's eviction from it upon its proposed sale by Hou. Little Broadcast's dreams of simple reproduction yielding property are dashed, however, because *his* capital (*benqian*) melts into thin air through government-manipulated market machinations that render his money/goods worthless—"balanced away," as he says. Little Broadcast's benqian (capital as money for exchange) cannot become *ziben* (capital, in the capitalist sense of producing a profit).

It is at the bank, in the scene of monumentality, that he and his wife realize their error and the hopelessness of their dreams. For, crucial to the inadequacy of Little Broadcast's reproductive dream is his tragic misrecognition of the bank: a citadel of ziben capital—monopoly, industrial, finance, bureaucratic, here it matters not what type—the bank is certainly not and can never be a site for the realization of simple reproductive dreams beginning with benqian capital. The bank is there to reproduce ziben capital, not benqian capital. Yet it is precisely the simultaneous unity and disjuncture between the temporalities of these two modes of life/production that provide the film's motor: the dream/ideology that the two are potentially synonymous has to be exposed. At the same time, historically, it is the crisis in both types of temporality that yields the utopian potential for a new economy of the revolutionary everyday, where desire and value(s) would be unified.

This is figured most clearly in the scene where the maid steals penicillin from Mr. Hou's room, to give to the teacher Mr. Hua's daughter, ill with pneumonia and at death's door. The maid had previously overheard a telephone conversation in which Mr. Hou's mistress had mentioned their hoarded stash of "pe-ni-si-lin"—a series of sounds that had no language significance or meaning to her at the time. The hoard, we know, was clearly illegally obtained; it is locked in the wardrobe along with the jewelry in Mr. Hou's living room, ready to be sold on the black market, when the going gets really rough and when its scarcity jacks up the price appropriately. The doctor who has been summoned to treat the child solemnly pronounces, also in the maid's hearing, that only the hard-to-find and horridly expensive "pe-ni-si-lin" can save the child's life. Mrs. Hua is distraught, knowing that her arrested husband cannot help her and that she has no possibility of obtaining the precious medicine on her own. Putting two and two together, the maid decides spontaneously to take the "pe-ni-si-lin" from Mr. Hou's mistress. Here, it is very clear that this theft is not equivalent to the theft that stands at the origins of capital/property. Medicine is the public right of all those who need it; it cannot be treated as property in any system of justice that takes everyday life as its point of departure. It cannot be used to produce or reproduce wealth/capital; it can only be used to produce health. Its use-value is its only value; the desire for it and its value are entirely unified. (And indeed, the child recovers with the miraculously "found" pe-ni-si-lin.)

In Peng's film, by contrast, we are to understand that the crisis of late 1940s Shanghai/China is containable within the realm of the proper management of industrial capital (ziben), where "normal" life—the bourgeois life of Shaobai, Huirong, and their set—is continuously disrupted by the machinations of the GMD and their corrupt henchmen. This view not only leaves capitalism and bourgeois life unproblematized and unhistoricized but leaves the impression that the crisis is a crisis in management rather than a politico-economic struggle over the meaning of the future (that is, whose capital [ziben]?). It also leaves open the distinct possibility that the CCP can be the steward and guide of capital (ziben) in China. For, in *Shang-*

hai, capital as a social relation has no history and the disruption of its re-production and accumulation merely requires documentation and propi-tious management for a return to normal functioning. Indeed, in the late 1940s setting of Peng's film, Shaobai's curious reaction to his/Huirong's dif-ficulties with their factory is to ally himself more closely with the American consulate in Shanghai, in the conviction that if only the Americans knew the true situation in China, they would cease providing support for the GMD and instead support the supposed apolitical, independently minded and capitalist-friendly national bourgeoisie, such as himself. In contrast, then, to *Crows*, where all forms of information are untrustworthy, in Peng's film, there is a touching belief in the possibility and effectivity of apolitical truth: if only the truth—which somehow can be accessed transparently—were known, it could be acted upon properly.

Through the escalating violence of 1949–50, Shaobai takes pictures of the events in the streets to document the moment. The following exchange between him and Huirong is critical to understanding the film's logic here:

HR: "Do you believe that the Chinese Communist Party can build a new China?"

SB: "I'm just an objective observer, a journalist; while I trust that the Communist Party is doing the right thing, I cannot be their mouth-piece, as then, who would believe me?"

. . . .

SB: "We are common people; we should just live our own lives [*guo ziji de rizi*]."

Shaobai's is the quintessential voice of liberalism, whose only desire is to return to the normalcy of an idealized *status quo ante* by denying the structures that rendered such a status quo problematic to begin with. His is by far the most persuasive voice in the film. This voice, which avers that journalists are in pure pursuit of objective truth, wishes only to docu-ment, without ostensible judgment or ideological position. In this voice, the logic of liberation turns out to be a desire to liberate bourgeois men-talité/capitalist strength from the chaos of crisis and ideology. Through Shaobai's own rendering of his past/desire into Shanghai's history/present, then, Shanghai comes to stand as the iconic expression and reflection of a present figured as a return to the normal living of "our" lives, where each life can be lived individually, untroubled by political chaos, struggle, or social contradiction. This illusion of an individual life that can be lived untrammeled by politics is the quintessential voice of the bourgeois liberal.

Shanghai in Transition or Crisis?

In *Crows*, rather than the metropolis serving as a universalizing space unto itself, the fragmentation of the city serves to underscore the contingent temporalities or even the residual temporalities of the urban in late 1940s China out of which a new (revolutionary) collective everyday would need to be fashioned. Indeed, the proposed return to normalcy with the reclaiming of the house at the end of the film is no reinscription of Mr. Kong's former socioeconomic status (as property owner). Rather, it signals the inauguration of a new time of politics and life. As the residents of the house gather around, the penultimate shot focuses on Mr. Kong's photograph being hung in the upper level of the house to replace the sneering photo of Mr. Hou, who has fled to Taiwan with the GMD, escaping the advancing troops of the CCP's People's Liberation Army and leaving behind his ill-gained property unrealized as monetary value. The replacement of Mr. Hou by Mr. Kong is not, however, to be understood as a static replacement of one owner for another in a universal regime of property. It signifies, rather, the transformation of a former property regime (private, individual) into a new regime of collectivity. Here, the ineluctable historicity of the everyday is affirmed: the individuals living their lives collectively under one roof come together in a ritual celebration of the spring festival, a celebration that *this year* (1949) represents a break from the ritualized past and leads elsewhere. That is, the celebration is certainly a performed ritual, albeit now it is one with an open-ended futurity that does not promise the certainty of repetition but rather the possibility of transformation. In this sense, the return of the house to its "rightful" owner—Mr. Kong—is also the transformation of property into the collective ownership of the "people," whose right to a roof over their heads is confirmed. In short, the victory of the organic spirit of capital is not yet enshrined over the critical spirit of the street.[21]

In Peng's film, while the posited desire for return is surely not a desire to return to the chaos of 1948–50, it just as surely is a desire to return to a class-specific utopian futurity foretold in the past (the 1930s, prior to the war and revolutionary aberration that temporarily erased the bourgeoisie as the dominant political class). This utopian (class) futurity is secured through a teleologically understood history of capitalist modernization, finally now being fulfilled in the present under the aegis of the Communist Party, which has awakened properly to its historical task (which turns out to be *not* socialism but party-led capitalism). It is the bourgeois dream of each living his/her own life, without politics and without contradiction—where politics and contradiction are contained within the state, leaving people to fashion their individual lives themselves through journalistic and market activity. This bourgeois dream figuration dovetails remarkably well with Zhang Yingjin's call for a return to spatial continuities through an investigation of mentalité—as if bourgeois dreams were the only possible mode of thought. It also resonates completely with current CCP desires to depoliticize everyday life and return it to a "normalcy" of the pursuit of private and individual gain/property, leaving politics in the hands of a supra-state party. Indeed, it is in this evocation that history/politics is neatly erased in Peng's film through an ideology of historicist continuity, where spatial stability and temporal linearity merge into a perhaps persuasively closed circuit of reproduction and repetition that mirrors and reflects capital's own dehistoricized liberatory narrative of itself. The displacements effected by Peng's film thus appear as displacements of a series of multifaceted crises unto a linearly construed notion of transition: 1948–50 can be seen, by looking at it properly, as a transition not to Maoism or socialism but to the party-led neoliberal 1990s, it turns out.

In *Crows*, by contrast, this moment (1948–49)—still ongoing at the time of the making of the film, thus not retrospectively totalized—is understood as a cataclysmic crisis that yields an opportunity to reconstruct and reimagine the lifeworlds of historical agents. Indeed, on the one hand, Zheng's film is clear that, having passed through the crisis of world war and civil war, there can be no return to an original point because life has been irremediably transformed; yet, on the other hand, this transformation works itself out not in the time of the state or in ahistorical cultural or utopian (bourgeois) class time but through a temporality of lives lived in collision with forces beyond individual control: conflictual and contradictory temporalities that must be worked out in the present continuously. This, then, is history as unceasing conflict in an everyday that is necessarily politicized through participation and struggle in the moment, rather than through the reproduction and repetition of class certainty, property, and profit. Rituals remain; routines are lived in daily rhythm—the children running to the roof to sing and play is one such routine to which Zheng returns often in the film—but those repetitions and routines do not foreclose history; rather, they are its condition of transformative possibility. By contrast, in Peng's film, it is precisely the displacement of crisis unto a national politics understood as primarily about the state management and control of capitalist transition that depoliticizes the everyday and evacuates it of historical significance. This echoes well the contemporary calls in China for depoliticization of society in the name of modernization and a culture of technocratic management and limitless capital accumulation. Here, one could say that the crisis of Zheng's 1930s and 1940s semicolonial Shanghai is transformed into the 1990s transition to capitalism of Peng's Shanghai.

Conclusion

These films both take up problems of the historicity of a place/space. In comparing them, the problems articulated through contemporary theories of transition and those taken up through postcolonial theories of alternative modernity can be connected. Indeed, the 1990s revaluation of semicolonialism in China (discussed in the fourth essay), which yields a narrative of failed transition and blocked history of the 1930s now being fulfilled in the 1990s and 2000s, proceeded just as semicolonialism was being discovered in English-language scholarship to identify something akin to an alternative modernity for China or, at least, for Shanghai and its environs. This coincidental convergence is not fortuitous, for it is precisely through a displacement of history and politics that semicolonialism can be transmuted into a blocked transition (to bourgeois modernity); a similar sort of displacement configures semicolonialism into a wished-for alternative form of hybrid modernity—or, modernity with Chinese characteristics. Peng's film figures both these problems explicitly.

The convergence of the two—semicolonialism as blocked transition *and* as alternative modernity—seems to be founded upon an implicitly shared sense of the nation-state as a hitherto failed historical project. In today's China, that failed project is usually said to inhere in the failure of the Mao years to properly recognize the historical task, which turns out not to have been social revolution but capitalist modernization underpinned by a bourgeois (or national capitalist) mentalité of accumulation and global normality. This position, or historical adjudication, displaces the complexities of the global and national conjunctural moments of the 1930s and 1940s unto the 1990s, when the posthistorical promise of Chinese socialism was repudiated and the future promise of capitalist global normality embraced. It refashions that crisis into a version of proper and proprietary history: space is the endless reproduction of place and the continuous repetitiously accumulating time of capital.

The spirit of the genuine Chinese state, then, is the guarantor of commercialization, cultural continuity, and individual life (however repressive it might be); this state is the state of the post-Mao present. And now China's commercialized noncapitalist past—that Smithian market economy discussed in the first essay—is held up as a model that is particularly Chinese (that is, culturally so) and "alternative" to Eurocentric capitalist modernity. It is also, miraculously, figured as particularly suited to the demands of contemporary globalization and depoliticized (that is, market-centered) social life. Here, we can see how historical incommensurability is recuperated as a transhistorical ideology and method of comparability eternally fixing desire for an apolitical, nonantagonistic path of state-led transition to modernization with Chinese characteristics as its essential foundation. The comparison of the two films on Shanghai visually and culturally present the value of these values while underscoring the distance traveled from the 1930s and 1940s to the 1990s. These are not continuous eras; they may not even be comparable. Rather, they may merely enact the nature of repetition, now as tragedy and farce simultaneously.

Afterword

"Partisan writing" is not an act of sectarianism, but a token of basic honesty
towards the reader.
—DANIEL BENSAÏD, *An Impatient Life*

In 2004 a group of influential Chinese economists felt secure enough in
the ideological turn of Chinese society up to that point to form the Chinese Hayek Society. Dedicated to the proposition that any and all state
intervention in the economy is the "road to serfdom," as Hayek had famously termed it in 1944 and as Chinese were well familiar with after
the late 1990s translation of that work, the Chinese Hayek Society held
its seventh annual conference in 2012, with papers ranging from attacks
on state-owned enterprises to defenses of the full privatization of land
in the rural areas, along with a host of more esoteric topics. While the
society does not appear to be a big player in policy or academia, its existence is symbolically important. Indeed, these days, the force of almost
two decades' critique of state dominance of the economy, the global wave
of austerity hysteria, and recent World Bank reports on marketization and
the Chinese economy are likely to push China farther down the road to
market fetishism than anyone might have thought possible after the 2008
global financial downturn. And yet this Chinese "Hayekian" moment will
possess certain characteristics particular to this historical juncture at this
location. For, contemporary Hayek-in-China cannot be about the total
withdrawal of the Chinese state from the economy or from society; it will
most likely have been about the more thorough merging of the state with
the economy, albeit not as its centralized commandist director (as under
Mao), nor as its puppet master, but in the guise of its censorial comprador.
Indeed, while Mao is surely turning in his grave over what his successors

have made of socialism in China, Hayek is likely turning in his grave as well, albeit in a less public place.

Friedrich Hayek was an Austrian-born economist who made his major career in the United Kingdom. Although not the progenitor of what is known as Austrian School economics (see the third essay), Hayek is surely one of the most famous of that school's students (having won a Nobel Prize in 1974). His ideas have again gained a vital importance and hearing in most discussions on economics today, in China and globally. As Liu Junning, one of China's earliest post-Mao Hayekians and a well-placed economist in the Chinese think-tank hierarchy today, supposedly noted a few years back, "Even the prime minister of China has Hayek's works on his bookshelf." Or, as another firm Hayekian, Wang Ruolin, a former vice secretary at the economics institute of the state's premier think tank, the Chinese Academy of Social Sciences, and the author of one of the first books on "the socialist market economy," proclaimed, and here I paraphrase, it is only with more thorough financial marketization and property privatization that China will be able to transform its society into an enduring global economic powerhouse.[1] Why Hayek and market fundamentalism appeal to serious intellectuals today, beyond a knee-jerk affirmation of the abstract notion of "freedom," is a mystery to me. At a political-ideological level, clearly the appeal of Hayek is part of a furious attempt to tame and discredit any attraction to socialism or alternatives to capitalism. But, intellectually? There must be more to it than that. This book can be considered an extended effort to try to work out my puzzlement.

I have proposed that it is only by going back to the extended 1930s, when the first Chinese critique of the Austrian School was written—as it turns out by none other than Wang Ruolin's father, Wang Yanan—that we can begin to reconstruct a plausible approach to that and related questions. As I have argued, it was precisely in the 1930s, understood broadly, that many systemic and systematic thinkings about the global/the world and related conceptual apparatuses were elaborated and engaged. Many of the questions raised then, in the context of multiple ongoing crises in global capitalism, were "repeated" in the context of the collapse of socialist economics and China's reengagement with global capitalism in the 1980s and 1990s. While oscillating back and forth between eras has facilitated my building of a series of historical problematics and thematics, I am quite certain that I have not come close to answering the questions posed, then or now. Yet my insistence about the necessity to think and consistently re-think our categories of historical inquiry is motivated by the ways in which these categories always were and have become ever more inadequate to the complexity and abstraction of lives lived differentially and unevenly within the structures of global capital. The tropes of repetition, magic, and pure ideology help me make that point.

As has become ever more evident, the optimistic theories of "global-ization" and "transnationalism" about world peace proffered with the end of the Cold War (1990s) have foundered—as they were destined to do—upon the dystopic realities of their fantastical desires for one world, what once upon a time in China was called *datong*, a Buddhist-inspired striving for one-worldism. This datong desire has recently been revived in anachro-nistic mode by various ideologues of the Chinese state and its intellectual ventriloquists to give voice to a wished-for social harmony in one of the most unequal societies in the world and in the context of the production of unprecedentedly unequal social relations globally, to which China is be-coming ever more central. In the most basic sense, then, to what does "the global" or "the world" refer? Can datong really encompass today's world? Can *tianxia* (all under heaven), another one of those Chinese conceptual formations that is being anachronistically revived to live another day, be anything other than a bid for a new sinocentric world? Or, is the global/the world merely a spatial-temporal disposition that pertains to the capitalist formation specific to our commonly lived current moment? How do we think that disposition, in its multiple lived complexities?

In a less sinocentric mode, many theorists within the scholarly com-munity have resorted to a reanimation of the concept or descriptive term of cosmopolitanism to deal with the professed and proclaimed (bourgeois, managerial?) one-worldism of the modern past, the present, and a utopian future. And yet, how is this evocation of the cosmopolitan connected to an earlier interwar moment (the 1920s and 1930s), which overnight, as it were, turned certain cities (Shanghai, Berlin, Bombay, Tokyo, San Francisco, Mexico City) into sites for bourgeois *and* revolutionary racial and cultural mixing, but also turned those sites into the locations of urban-based un-equal and uneven production and reproduction of global capitalist power in its imperialist and colonial forms? That is, have we merely resumed an urban bourgeois cosmopolitan quest with our evocations of "the world" and "the global'" now that revolution and communism are vanquished? Indeed, what characterizes these revenant versions of cosmopolitanism is how they have been evacuated of any materialist analysis of social conditionality. If cosmopolitanism is now (and always has been, as a theory) about world culture without politics, have we merely rejoined the 1930s to the 1990s as a matter of global circulatory desire and congenial cultural activity (thus turning a blind eye to the politics of culture and cultural politics)? Or, alternatively, to what extent are our current and past appeals to the cosmopolitan just excuses for the urban among us to be conceptually disconnected from rural hinterlands, even as those hinterlands are more mercilessly exploited than ever before? If the appeal to cosmopolitanism does not draw from that 1930s/1990s historical genealogy, one could of course go back to Immanuel Kant, the great-grand-daddy of cosmopolitan theorizing. But then one would have to grapple with the fact that Kant's pioneering vision was forever marred by a blinding racist and Eurocentric conceit, bequeathed to and taken up by subsequent theorists, including Max Weber and others, who wished to displace the emergent divisions of capitalism in Germany/Europe unto a global geographical spatial-cultural-racial divide. Does one resuscitate or rescue Kant for our current cosmopolitan project by erasing his racist Eurocentrism? Or does one, following David Harvey, recognize that Kant's racism and culturalism, and thus the very concept of cosmopolitanism to which he gave animate intellectual life, mire him in an abstracted and alienated reason, any resuscitation of which is doomed to reproduce the deficiencies of the concept itself?

From my current vantage, the growth over the past decades of a pervasive naturalized (purportedly apolitical) culturalism in politics, history, and social life strikes me as a dangerous form of pure ideology.[2] Posed by states, "globalizing" university administrators, scholars, media, and many in the general public and everyday life as an antidote to the conflicts of (geo-)politics and thus as a bromide prescription for settling transnational, translocal, transidentity understanding, the return of and to "culture" as natural identitarian difference appears to appeal to a manufactured desire to erase the fundamental structural political and economic contradictions unleashed by limitless capitalism in favor of a contained liberal accommodation. Where previously, knowledge and activity were imbued by the contingent ideology of Cold War political impasses (the binaries of modern/tradition, Communism/capitalism, male/female, and so on were characteristic of such contingent and mutable Cold War thinking), all of which represented a pervasive colonization of the world by unsatisfactory and insufficient explanatories, today, the feel-good fuzziness of the multicultural global cosmopolite as adequate to historical and contemporary understanding is a pure ideology that helps undermine more thoroughly than ever possibilities for various politics of solidarity based in a conflictual apprehension of global structure. It seems that at every moment these would-be solidarities pop into view as potentials, they have been overwhelmed by culturalisms—as an organizational form of already existing heterogeneities—that proclaim such solidarities impossible.

This book is a highly personal rumination on these topics. It takes up themes—global and world history; Marxist and anti-Marxist categories of historical conceptualization; social science, economics, and positivism; film, culture, and history—that have preoccupied me since I began thinking and writing about history almost three decades ago. My formulations of the questions that animate me perhaps are beholden more to my own idiosyncratic notion of historicity than they are to the disciplinarity of history. And yet I would like to propose that this version of historicity—repetition, magic, pure ideology—is in fact a hallmark, a sine qua non of our discipline. By the same token, the topics I have chosen to ruminate upon are linked to my particular engagement with modern Chinese history. Yet this volume can hardly be counted a book of "Chinese history" as such. It is not meant to be one. "China" for me is (and always has been) a way to think about larger historical problematics.

Theodor Adorno once wrote of Richard Wagner that "in Wagner, for the first time, the bourgeois imagination disavows the impulse toward escape and resigns itself to a situation that Wagner himself conceived as worthy of death."[3] This disavowal and resignation finds its emblematic musical expression in Wagner's late 1850s opera, *Tristan und Isolde*, where the opening chord, famously known as the "Tristan chord," moves through the four-hour-long opera only ever partially resolved—gaining, in Brian Magee's words, a "resolution-yet-not-resolution."[4] As Magee points out, "Only at one point is all discord resolved, and that is on the final chord of the work; and that of course is the end of everything. . . . The rest is silence."[5] Could it be that the "yet-not" is not necessarily the end of everything? Nor is it a false "promise of reconciliation" with the existing social order, as Adorno would have it? End or reconciliation? Perhaps it is neither. But rather, as

Jacques Attali suggests, maybe the "yet-not" is the tentative heralding of a utopian moment of what he calls composition: a silence that is the uncommodified noise of politics.[6] Wagner could or would not transcend the political tension between *Tristan*'s official ideological project, a project that proclaims, in Slavoj Žižek's words, "love as an act of radical transgression that suspends all sociosymbolic links";[7] nevertheless, Wagner's musical prophecy of dissonance with his "yet-not" resolved Tristan chord may be a good place to end my essentially pessimistic discussion of the impossibility of politics in China and the world today. That impossibility could be understood in terms of the absence of silence, that absence of noise that might herald a meaningful uncommodified politics.

Is there still a yet-not? In China, as with much of the world today, all appears to be *noise* and reification. I consider this book a yet-not resolved chord, a modest protest against the repetitive pervasiveness of noise in our lives.

NOTES

Introduction

Epigraph: Karl Marx, *The Eighteenth Brumaire of Louis Bonaparte* (New York: International Publishers, 1994).

1 Wang Yanan is known in China—if he is known at all outside Xiamen and his native Hubei—as the translator of seminal texts in political economy. His renditions (with Guo Dali) of Adam Smith, David Ricardo, Karl Marx (*Capital*, vols. 1, 2, and 3), and a host of others were until recently considered standard translations of these classic texts (all the works since have been retranslated several times). Born in Hubei Province in 1901, by the early 1920s, Wang attended Wuhan Zhonghua University, where he studied sociology and economics in the education department. In the late 1920s and 1930s, he studied in Japan and traveled to Europe, coming to Marxism at that time. He did not join the Chinese Communist Party until 1957, when he was imminently to be denounced as a "rightist" and hastily enrolled in a bid to protect himself. As the long-time president of Xiamen University in Fujian—appointed to that post by Mao Zedong in 1950—Wang's philosophical work soon gave way to pedagogical issues. Wang died in 1969. His final illness was apparently precipitated by the Cultural Revolutionary struggles at his university campus. His reputation was restored in the early 1980s, and his collected works were edited and published by a specially convened collective at Xiamen University, albeit just in time for the turn away from Marxist political economy in China's Dengist era. He is now remembered in Xiamen as a martyr, while his economic philosophy is rarely considered at all, clearly deemed outdated and too Marxist for contemporary times. The Wang Yanan Institute at Xiamen University, for example, is entirely given to research into econometrics; no one there does research on Wang or on economic-intellectual-historical issues.

2 These nine essays were reprinted in 1981 as part of a larger anthology of Wang's work, published in connection with his political rehabilitation. Citations throughout are from the 1981 edition.

3 Wang Yanan, "Jingji kexue lun" [On economics], in *Wang Yanan Jingji Sixiangshi lunwen ji* (*WYNJJ*), ed. Xiamen Daxue jingji yanjiusuo (Shanghai: Renmin chubanshe, 1981), 1. Translations are mine unless otherwise noted.

4 "Jingjixue yu zhexue" [Economics and philosophy], in *WYNJJ*, 59–71.

5 See his extended critique in "Zhongguo jingji xuejie de Audili xuepai jingji xue" [Austrian School economics in China's economics circles], in *WYNJJ*, 148–71. See also the third essay in this book.

6 Ma Yinchu (1882–1982) had degrees in economics from Yale and Columbia; in 1916 he was invited by Cai Yuanpei to head up the Beijing University economics department. After a stint with the Nationalists (GMD), whom he criticized and by whom he was imprisoned, Ma decided to remain in China after 1949. President of Beijing University after 1951, he became infamous in 1957 for proposing population control to Mao Zedong. This led to his condemnation as a "rightist" for demographic Malthusianism. He died shortly after his political rehabilitation in the 1980s and is remembered as a hero and martyr in China and abroad.

7 Prior to Wang and Guo's translation of Adam Smith, under the title *Guofu Lun* [On national wealth], there existed an earlier translation by Yan Fu, titled *Yuanfu* [The origin of wealth]. For the consistent conflation in Chinese scholarship of the two translations, see Hu Peizao, "Dang bian *Yuanfu* yu *Guofu Lun*" [Let's distinguish *Yuanfu* from *Guofu Lun*], *Xueshu Yuekan* [Academic monthly] 9 (2012): n.p.

8 Ma Yinchu, *Zhongguo jingji gaizao* [Tranformation of the Chinese economy] (Shanghai: Shangwu yinshuguan, 1935).

9 This is a direct reference to Sun Zhongshan's ill-advised notion that because the Chinese people were a "loose plate of sand," one could create a politics and a social ethic *ex nihilio*, as it were. Ma's use of the term clearly is intended to echo albeit alter Sun's idea. Mao, of course, famously declared China's peasants "blank paper" upon which any narrative could be written.

10 Wang, "Jingji kexue lun," 5. In the 1950s, Wang also critiqued Ma's demographic theories, although not for Malthusianism but from the standpoint of Ma's distortions of the relationship of "surplus population" to "the economic" in a broad sense. Unlike Ma, Wang understood "surplus population" as the result of capitalist primitive accumulation and its related social structure. See Wang Yanan, *Makexi zhuyi de renkou lilun yu Zhongguo renkou wenti* [Marxist population theory and China's demographic problems] (Beijing: Kexue chubanshe, 1956), 2, 19. This issue will be further elaborated in my forthcoming monograph on Wang and his interlocutors.

11 In Ma's case, this ideological magic underpinned the egregious analogizing forming the basis of his reform proposals: that China's desperate social unrest and economic problems of the 1930s could be seen as analogous to Wang Mang's (45 BCE–23 AD) Han-era social unrest and economic problems. Since the unrest had led to the Wang Mang Institutional Reforms (Wang Mang gaizhi), it followed for Ma that learning from this ancient ancestor would allow China to select the proper reformist institutional path to resolve

the problems presented in the 1930s. Wang found this analogical method completely flawed. In a different essay, Wang accused Japanese scholars of this kind of analogical ahistoricity; in particular, he sarcastically noted the Japanese propensity to attribute eighteenth-century French physiocratic thought to the more general European fascination at the time with the Chinese classics and Chinese society (*chinoiserie*), allegedly pointing to China as an origin of one of Europe's most influential economic theories. This, too, Wang found laughable. See Wang Yanan, "Zhengzhi jingjixue zai zhongguo" [Political economy in China], in *WYNJJ*, 117–47, esp. 118.

12 For the relation between abstractions and concrete historical content, see Massimiliano Tomba, *Marx's Temporalities*, trans. Peter D. Thomas and Sara R. Farris (Chicago: Haymarket Books, 2013), 119–21.

13 Wang, "Jingji kexue lun," 5.

14 Marx, *The Eighteenth Brumaire of Louis Bonaparte.*

15 For example, Isabella Weber, a PhD candidate at Cambridge University, is currently involved in a research project intended to dissect the economic conceptual roots of the socialist market economy of the 1980s, an excavation that goes back to the socialist calculation debates of the 1920s and 1930s.

16 Tomba, *Marx's Temporalities*, 38.

17 Karl Marx, "Preface to the First Edition," in *Capital*, vol. 1, trans. Ben Fowkes (New York: Penguin, 1990), 91.

18 For a useful discussion, from which my summary is derived, see Peter Pels, "Introduction: Magic and Modernity," in *Magic and Modernity: Interfaces of Revelation and Concealment*, ed. Birgit Meyer and Peter Pels (Stanford, CA: Stanford University Press, 2003), 1–38.

19 Jean Baudrillard, *For a Critique of the Political Economy of the Sign*, trans. Charles Levin (St. Louis, MO: Telos Press, 1981), 143, 146.

20 Henri Lefebvre, *Critique of Everyday Life*, vol. 2, *Foundations for a Sociology of the Everyday*, trans. John Moore (London: Verso, 2002), 289.

21 Daniel Bensaïd, *Marx for Our Times: Adventures and Misadventures of a Critique*, trans. Gregory Elliott (London: Verso, 2002), 89.

22 Henri Lefebvre, *Critique of Everyday Life*, vol. 1, *Introduction* (London: Verso, 2000), 21. Regarding the centrality of ambiguity, Lefebvre notes, "*ambiguity* is a category of everyday life, and perhaps an essential category" (18).

23 Henri Lefebvre, "The Theory of Moments," in *Critique of Everyday Life*, 2:340–58.

24 Peter Osborne, *The Politics of Time: Modernity and Avant-Garde* (London: Verso, 1995).

25 This relation of the quotidian to objectification has been noted by many anthropologists, with specific reference to Marcel Mauss's signature book, *A General Theory of Magic* (London: Routledge and Kegan Paul, 1972).

26 Marilyn Ivy, *Discourses of the Vanishing* (Chicago: University of Chicago Press, 1995), 178.

27 Reinhart Koselleck, *The Practice of Conceptual History: Timing History, Spacing Concepts*, trans. Todd Samuel Presner et al. (Stanford, CA: Stanford University Press, 2002), 20–21, 22.

28 Arif Dirlik, *Revolution and History: Origins of Marxist Historiography in China* (Berkeley: University of California Press, 1978).

29 In this sense, they were not merely about the invention of social scientific disciplinarity, as a new trend in China studies has recently discovered. Indeed, while the disciplinarity of social science is no doubt important, there is a historicity beyond it that needs to be explored.

30 There was a trend not long ago in the China field, emanating from the People's Republic of China (PRC) and Hong Kong, to recover valuable economic thinking from the Chinese ancients. This trend made possible such titles as "Confucianism and Economic Ethics" or "A Brief Discussion of the Modern Transformation of Confucian Ethics into an Economic System." The first is included in the anthology *Zhongguo jinxiandai jingji lunli de bianqian* [The changes in China's modern economic ethics], ed. Liu Xiaofeng and Lin Liwei (Hong Kong: Hong Kong University Press, 1998); the second is included in a companion anthology edited by the same two scholars, titled *Jingji lunli yu jinxiandai zhongguo shehui* [Economic ethics and modern Chinese society] (Hong Kong: Hong Kong University Press, 1998). There are many others, and they follow upon the "discovery" of Confucian-style capitalism, pioneered in Singapore and popularized by Chinese-born American sinologists such as Yu Yingshi and Du Weiming. See the third essay in this book for Wang Yanan's critique of an analogous trend in 1930s China. By the same token, Tamara Chin's recent masterpiece deals with "the economic" not as an artifact of social scientificity but as a form of imaginative literary representation. See her *Savage Exchange: Han Imperialism, Chinese Literary Style, and the Economic Imagination* (Cambridge, MA: Harvard University Press, 2014).

31 As a frequent translator from Chinese to English, I am not unaware of the problems in translation as a mode of rendering equivalence. My point here is to raise translation as a philosophical-historical problem, not a technical one.

32 James Clifford, "Prologue," in *Routes: Travel and Translation in the Late Twentieth Century* (Cambridge, MA: Harvard University Press, 1997), 11.

33 John Kraniauskas, "Transculturation and the Work of Translation," *Traces: A Multilingual Journal of Cultural Theory*, no. 1 (2000): 101.

34 Roberto Schwarz, *Misplaced Ideas: Essays on Brazilian Culture* (London: Verso, 1992), 19–32.

35 Koselleck's version of the relationship between conceptual and social history leaves a residue of the social outside the conceptual. See the various essays in Koselleck, *The Practice of Conceptual History*.

36 In the 1930s, Wang Yanan wrote several critiques of the "Eastern spirit/Western materialism" positions espoused by Liang Shuming, Lin Yutang, and others. See the discussion in third essay in this book.

37 Wang increasingly used the more Leninist/Maoist term *semicolonized* (*ban zhimindi*) in the 1940s. *Hypocolonized* (*ci zhimindi*) comes from Sun Zhongshan.

38 Roberto Schwarz, "Beware of Alien Ideologies," in *Misplaced Ideas*, 36. I thank Barbara Weinstein for clarifying some issues in Schwarz for me.

39 Wang, "Jingji kexue lun," 5–6.

40 Lefebvre, *Critique of Everyday Life*, 1:96.

41 I have been the fortunate recipient of a generous grant from the Institute for New Economic Thinking (in NYC) for this newer project. It is now in process.

Chapter 1. The Economic, China, World History

Epigraph: Walter Benjamin, "Conversations with Brecht" in *Understanding Brecht*, trans. Anna Bostock, 105–21 (London: Verso, 1998).

1 For a recent exploration of modernization as discourse in the Chinese historical case, see Pan Guangzhe, "Xiangxiang 'xiandai hua': 1930 niandai Zhongguo sixiangjie de jiepou" [The imaginary of "modernization": An anatomy of the 1930s Chinese intellectual world], *Xin Shixue* [New history journal] 1, no. 5 (2005): 85–124. The Hegelian version of the argument has been common in the China field at least since Prasenjit Duara's *Rescuing History from the Nation: Questioning Narratives of Modern China* (Chicago: University of Chicago Press, 1996).

2 Giovanni Arrighi, *Adam Smith in Beijing: Lineages of the Twenty-First Century* (London: Verso, 2007).

3 For a critique of the names of history, see Jacques Rancière, *The Names of History: On the Poetics of Knowledge*, trans. Hassan Melehy (Minneapolis: University of Minnesota Press, 1994). The *Journal of Agrarian Change* (July 2015) takes up a number of these conceptual concerns. Clearly, some critical scholars are now engaged in an effort to reconceptualize categories. I thank Yan Hairong for alerting me to the special issue, although I lament it came too late for me to include substantively here. See Carlos Oya, Jingzhong Ye, and Qian Forrest Zhang, eds., "Agrarian Change in Contemporary China," special issue, *Journal of Agrarian Change* 15, no. 3 (July 2015).

4 I do not enter here the huge contemporary debate over whether China's Maoist state was primarily engaged in the primitive accumulation of capital as a method of industrial modernization; or, that is, whether the Maoist state was a capitalist state. These kinds of debates tend to conflate socialism and capitalism by diminishing the political challenge posed by socialism to the capitalist world.

5 Since Adam Smith, analysis of the economy is often broken into three pairings (land-rent, capital-profit, labor-wages) that form the central pivots of

economic behavior. In textbooks, these are called "the trinity." Wang Yanan translated this as *sanwei yiti shuo*. For a concise introduction and explication of Gramscian hegemony in its relation to language and concepts, see Peter Ives, *Language and Hegemony in Gramsci* (Ann Arbor, MI: Pluto Press, 2004).

6 Antonio Gramsci, *Selections from Cultural Writings*, ed. David Forgacs and Geoffrey Nowell-Smith, trans. William Boelhower (Cambridge, MA: Harvard University Press, 1985), 183–84.

7 Slavoj Žižek, *The Sublime Object of Ideology* (London: Verso, 1989), 19–21.

8 Osborne, *Politics of Time*, 21–22.

9 For a recent forum in the AHR on the dominance of this structure, see Manu Goswami's contribution. She notes, "One of the characteristics of a genuinely critical framework is the ability to think itself, to locate its own categories and concepts in the social and historical context of its emergence" ("Remembering the Future," *American Historical Review* 113, no. 2 [2008]: 422). It is precisely the failure of this kind of historicizing reflexivity that turns the contemporary "revisions" of the China field into a complicit rather than a critical endeavor.

10 Masao Miyoshi, "Ivory Tower in Escrow," and Bruce Cumings, "Boundary Displacement: The State, the Foundations, and Area Studies during and after the Cold War," in *Learning Places: The Afterlives of Area Studies*, edited by Masao Miyoshi and Harry Harootunian (Durham, NC: Duke University Press, 2002), 19–60, 261–302. For a cogent reflection on these trends in Taiwan, see Chen Guangxing and Qian Yongxiang, "Quanchouhua zhi xia Taiwan de xueshu shengcan" [The production of scholarship in Taiwan under globalization], *Dushu* 2 (February 2005): 56–66.

11 Andre Gunder-Frank, *Re-Orient: Global Economy in the Asian Age* (Berkeley: University of California Press, 1998).

12 Patrick Manning, "Asia and Europe in the World Economy: Introduction," *American Historical Review* 107, no. 2 (2002): 420.

13 Manning, "Asia and Europe," 422.

14 More than two decades ago Joan Scott criticized "women's history" for a focus on inclusion, which changed nothing in mainstream narratives. Although Scott contained her critique to a linguistic, semiotic, and discursive mode (all inadequate to the task she set), she nevertheless pinpointed a crucial problem. See Joan Scott, "Gender: A Useful Category of Historical Analysis," *American Historical Review* 91, no. 5 (1986): 1053–75.

15 See Pierre Vilar, "Marxist History, a History in the Making: Towards a Dialogue with Althusser," in *Althusser: A Critical Reader*, ed. Gregory Elliott (Oxford: Blackwell, 1994), 41. See also Ellen Meiskins Wood, *Empire of Capital* (London: Verso, 2003).

16 Huang sneers at Pomeranz for not using original data, relying upon secondary sources, and selectively emphasizing congenial parts of an argu-

ment, among other things. Philip Huang, "Development or Involution in Eighteenth-Century Britain and China?," review of *The Great Divergence: China, Europe, and the Making of the Modern World Economy*, by Kenneth Pomeranz, *Journal of Asian Studies* 61, no. 2 (2002): 517. Pomeranz accuses Huang of distorting the arguments of *The Great Divergence*, chastises Huang for misplacing decimal points, and mocks him for making other statistical errors. Kenneth Pomeranz, "Beyond the East-West Binary," *Journal of Asian Studies* 61, no. 2 (2002): 539, 542.

17   For a different type of discussion of the Huang/Pomeranz debate, see Alexander Day, "Review: Philip Huang, *The Peasant Family and Rural Development in the Yangzi Delta, 1350–1988*." I cannot discern where this was published, but it is available under Alexander Day's name at the following URL, accessed May 15, 2015: http://www.academia.edu/9409110/Review _Philip_Huang_The_Peasant_Family_and_Rural_Development_in_the _Yangzi_Delta_1350-1988. See also Daniel Little, "The Involution Debate: New Perspectives on China's Rural Economic History," accessed May 2015, http://www-personal.umd.umich.edu/~delittle/new%20perspectives%20 short%20journal%20version.htm.

18   Huang's version of Chinese economic history has been adduced enthusiastically to the Chinese national state project of dreaming. Critiques of Huang have long pointed out that what he calls uniquely Chinese involution is in fact the norm for most precapitalist economies. For a recent critical analysis of Huang's complicity with the Chinese state desires, see Yan Hairong and Chen Yiyuan, "Agrarian Capitalization without Capitalism? Capitalist Dynamics from Above and Below in China," *Journal of Agrarian Change* 15, no. 3 (July 2015): 366–92.

19   As Huang notes in articles published in China, the comparability thesis for the eighteenth century merely fuels nationalist pride over China's hitherto neglected parity with England. See Philip Huang [Huang Zongzhi], "Da fencha: Ouzhou, Zhongguo ji xiandai shijie jingji de fazhan" [The great divergence: Europe and China in the development of the modern global economy], *Lishi yanjiu* [Researches on history] 4 (2002): 3–48; Philip Huang, "Beilun shehui yu xiandai chuantong" [Social theory of paradoxes and modernity's tradition], *Dushu* 2 (2005): 3–14.

20   Dirlik, *Revolution and History*.

21   See Robert Cole, "To Save the Village" (PhD diss., New York University, forthcoming). Cole documents the conceptual, ideological, and empirical problems that emerged in specifying what constituted the "agrarian crisis" of the 1930s in China and the world.

22   The 1940s social scientist Wang Yanan notes that the basis for classical economics, "economic man," was not only insufficient for an adequate analysis of capitalist society but even less adequate for precapitalist ones. Wang Yanan, "Zhengzhi jingjixue shang de ren" [Man in political economics],

in *Wang Yanan Jingji sixiangshi lunwenji* [Collected essays on economic thought of Wang Yanan], ed. Xiamen daxue jingji yanjiusuo (Shanghai: Renmin chubanshe, 1980), 8–22. For more on Wang, see the third and fourth essays in this volume.

23 There are exceptions. For an exemplary one, see Walter Johnson, *River of Dark Dreams: Slavery and Empire in the Cotton Kingdom* (Cambridge, MA: Harvard University Press, 2013).

24 A 2015 book by Qin Hui, *Zouchu dizhi* [Out of imperial autocracy], a collection of essays from the last decade or so, proposes some "theoretical" interventions into the problem of modern Chinese economic history, although it hews completely to a rigid conceptual positivism that is inimical to ideological reflexivity. In this vein, Qin takes "systems" as the a priori mode of historical explanation and comparison, privileging political over material systems as social sites of conflict and historicity. The book was no sooner published in late 2015 than it disappeared from the shelves. I have been unable to ascertain who originally published the book; the articles that comprise the book are still available individually.

25 At a 2005 conference in Taipei, where I presented an early version of this argument, Ken Pomeranz and Gail Hershatter—both in the best of humor—defended this approach in methodological terms, as these are the conventions of economic history. That is true. My point is certainly not that Pomeranz is a bad social scientist. He is a very good one, in my opinion. I merely wish to point out that there are axial moments in history that demand reflexivity and a deep historical engagement with the concepts and methods we use to pursue our inquiries. Just for starters, the Smith–Marx moment was one; the global 1930s was another; and our current moment (approximately 1970s to today) is yet another. Thus, I am calling not only for good social science but good history that recognizes that the economic cannot be treated transhistorically.

26 Behind the 1970s Japanese economic debate was Japan's own 1930s agrarian history debate. See Katsuhiko Endo, "The Science of Capital: The Uses and Abuses of Human Sciences in Interwar Japan" (PhD diss., New York University, 2004). My recuperation of the Japanese debates as the unconscious to the Chinese ones is not in the realm of magic. It is rooted in the kinds of inquiry into modern Chinese history (formerly in the United States and now in the PRC) that compel an implicit or explicit comparative perspective between China and Japan, even as the centrality of Japan to the framing of the Chinese problematic seems to have been submerged and rearticulated more recently by the focus on combatting Eurocentrism and recentering an autonomous "Asia." This new focus has produced its own problems. For a critical view of the rediscovery of Asia, see Koyasu Nobukuni, "Riben jindai de dongya xushi" [Narrating Asia in modern Japan], trans. Zhao Jinghua, *Shijing* [Horizons], no. 14 (2004): 2–75. As Koyasu points out, "the Asian

sphere" can be constituted as an object of inquiry *only after* global capitalism has constituted the world as a totality. See also his *Dongya lun: Riben xiandai sixiang pipan* [The discourse of Asia: A critique of modern Japanese thought], trans. Zhao Jinghua (Jilin: Jilin renmin chubanshe, 2004). In addition, see the series of discussions on Asia through the 1990s published in the journal *Dushu* [Readings], some of which are collected in *Yazhou de bing li* [Asia's pathology], ed. *Dushu* Jingxuan [*Dushu* editorial board] (Beijing: Sanlian chubanshe, 2007).

27 Debates in the early 1970s between Robert Brenner and Christopher Hill—the later part of a much larger set of debates on European economic history—took up the question of internal or external sources of social-economic change, and specifically the problem of "transition" from feudalism to capitalism. The issues, never resolved, have continued to be central to many discussions of modern economic history, European and not.

28 Sydney Crawcour, "The Tokugawa Period and Japan's Preparation for Modern Economic Growth," *Journal of Japanese Studies* 1, no. 1 (1974): 114.

29 Susan B. Hanley and Kozo Yamamura, "A Quiet Transformation in Tokugawa Economic History," *Journal of Asian Studies* 30, no. 2 (1971): 377.

30 Thomas Smith, *The Agrarian Origins of Modern Japan* (Stanford, CA: Stanford University Press, 1959).

31 At the 2005 Taipei meeting, Pomeranz insisted that his focus on accident was a focus on contingency. But contingency is not the same as accident.

32 See Michael Perelman, *The Invention of Capitalism: Classical Political Economy and the Secret History of Primitive Accumulation* (Durham, NC: Duke University Press, 2000); Samir Amin, *Eurocentrism* (London: Zed Books, 1989).

Chapter 2. The Economic and the State

1 Wang Yanan, "Zhongguo shehui jingjishi gang: Xulun" [An outline of China's socioeconomic history: Preface], in *Wang Yanan wenji* [Selected works of Wang Yanan] (Fuzhou : Fujian jiaoyu chubanshe, 1987–89), 4:14. This essay was originally published in book form by Shanghai's Shenghuo shudian in March 1937.

2 For a related but ultimately rather different approach to the same question, see Lin Chun, "Marxism and the Politics of Positioning China in World History," *Inter-Asia Cultural Studies* 13, no. 3 (2012): 438–66.

3 Tu Chenglin, "The Asiatic Mode of Production in World History Perspective: From a Universal to a Particularistic View of History," *Social Sciences in China* 35, no. 2 (2014): 5–25. I thank Robert Cole for bringing this to my attention. For an utterly different resurrection of AMP, this time in the interest of reburying it, see Lin Chun, *China and Global Capitalism: Reflections on Marxism, History, and Contemporary Politics* (New York: Palgrave Macmillan, 2013), chapter 1.

4 Stephen P. Dunn, *The Fall and Rise of the Asiatic Mode of Production* (London: Routledge and Kegan Paul, 1982).

5 Dirlik, *Revolution and History*, chapter 3.

6 For the sprouts debate, see Arif Dirlik, "Chinese Historians and the Marxist Concept of Capitalism: A Critical Examination," *Modern China* 8, no. 1 (January 1982): 105–32.

7 For a collection of Chinese discussions of the AMP in the 1980s, see the anthology edited by Timothy Brook, *The Asiatic Mode of Production in China* (New York: M. E. Sharpe, 1989). Brook, in his introduction, casts these essays in the light of the reemergence of social science in 1980s China; below, I cast them in the light of a reemergence of a non-Marxist world historical paradigm.

8 For an indication of the latter, see the collection of essays published from 1996 to 2005 in the journal *Dushu* [Readings], anthologized in *Yazhou de bing li* [Asia's pathology], edited by *Dushu* editorial board (Beijing: Sanlian Chubanshe, 2007). Many of these are critical considerations of "orientalism" and/or Asianism; some are attempts to reconceptualize "Asia" for the contemporary moment and China's rise. This latter trend has been more prominent since the advocacies of the Taiwanese scholar Ch'en Kuang-hsin for "Asia as method." See also Lü Xingyu, *Xiangcun yu geming: Zhongguo xin ziyou zhuyi pipan sanshu* [The villages and revolution: Three essays on the critique of Chinese neoliberalism] (Shanghai: Huadong shida chubanshe, 2012), for her tracing of the revival of AMP categories in recent Chinese studies of rural China. Her critique of Qin Hui is of particular interest. See also Lin Chun, *China and Global Capitalism*.

9 The cover of the *Economist* for May 4, 2013, with Xi Jinping in Qianlong-era imperial garb is emblematic. Thanks to Hu Minghui for directing my attention to that image.

10 One major example of this increasingly vacuous comparative empire trend can be found in Jane Burbank and Fred Cooper, *Empires in World History: Power and the Politics of Difference* (Princeton, NJ: Princeton University Press, 2010). For a similar critique of Burbank and Cooper, see Richard Drayton, "Empire and Other Scales of Domination and Inequality: Towards an Intersectional *longue durée* Global History" (paper prepared for CFP: The Future of Atlantic, Transnational, and World History, University of Pittsburgh, May 1–3, 2014). As Drayton writes unsparingly, Cooper and Burbank "mistake regimes based on brutal inequalities for cosmopolitan utopias" and their "extraordinarily loose definition of 'empire' . . . ends up conflating twentieth-century forms with ancient and medieval polities" (4–5). I thank Prof. Drayton for providing me a copy of this unpublished paper, which I cite with permission.

11 Jim Hevia, *Cherishing Men from Afar* (Durham, NC: Duke University Press, 1995).

12 Frank Dikotter's corpus of work suffers from this problem; the earlier work is broadly characteristic of "new Qing history," although there is a lot of variation in that field; the Manchu-centered parts of it are now under nationalist attack in China as being anti-Chinese (that is, anti-sinic).

13 Ke Changji, "Ancient Chinese Society and the Asiatic Mode of Production," *Lanzhou daxue xuebao* [Journal of Lanzhou University] 3 (1983): 16–25; Zhao Lisheng, "The Well-Field System in Relation to the Asiatic Mode of Production," in *The Asiatic Mode of Production in China*, ed. Timothy Brook (New York: M. E. Sharpe, 1989), 65–84.

14 Karl Marx, *Grundrisse: Foundations of the Critique of Political Economy*, trans. with a foreword by Martin Nicolaus (New York: Penguin, 1993), 489.

15 Marx, *Grundrisse*, 489.

16 I thank Lin Chun for suggesting I clarify some of these issues.

17 Ronald Meek, *Social Science and the Ignoble Savage* (Cambridge: Cambridge University Press, 1976).

18 These component parts are derived from Marx, *Grundrisse* and *Capital*, vol. 3. In the text, I will note by G and C, 3 plus page number where the specifics can be found. All citations are to the following editions: *Grundrisse*, trans. with a foreword by Martin Nicolaus (New York: Penguin, 1993); *Capital*, vol. 3, trans. David Fernbach (New York: Penguin, 1991).

19 This latter issue gave rise in the course of the 1920s and 1930s debates to a good number of difficulties in specifying the class relations of the AMP, as appropriation of surplus has nothing but seemingly arbitrary ways of happening. For contours of the 1920s and 1930s debates, see Du Weizhi, "A Criticism of Research on Ancient China," *Dushu zazhi* 1, nos. 2–3 (1932): n.p.; Guo Moruo, *Zhongguo gudai shehui yanjiu* [Research on ancient Chinese society] (Beijing: Renmin chubanshe, 1972); and He Ganzhi, *Zhongguo shehui xingzhi wenti lunzhan* [The debate on Chinese social history] (Shanghai: Sanlian chubanshe, 1939). There are many others.

20 I thank Lin Chun for the wonderful turn of phrase "phony Marxist state."

21 Wang Yanan, in the fourth chapter of his 1948 book *Zhongguo guanliao zhengzhi yanjiu* [Research into China's bureaucratic polity], has a long summary of this dispute; it is part of his refutation of the AMP, as well as a building block for his own theory of the Chinese state. This work was originally published by Shidai wenhua chubanshe and republished in 2010 by Shangwu yinshuguan. For more discussion of Wang and his theory of the state, see my "Compradors: The Mediating Middle of Capitalism in Twentieth-Century China and the World," in *Marxisms in Asia*, ed. Joyce Liu and Viren Murthy (New York: Routledge, forthcoming).

22 See Dirlik, *Revolution and History*, for the Chinese debates; for these issues in European history, see T. H. Aston and C. H. E. Philpin, eds., *The Brenner Debate: Agrarian Class Structure and Economic Development in Pre-industrial Europe* (Cambridge: Cambridge University Press, 1987).

23 Osborne, *Politics of Time*, chapter 3.

24 Mark Elvin, *The Pattern of the Chinese Past: A Social and Economic Inter-pretation* (Stanford, CA: Stanford University Press, 1973); Philip Huang, *The Peasant Family and Rural Development in the Yangzi Delta, 1350–1988* (Stanford, CA: Stanford University Press, 1990); Hill Gates, *China's Motor: A Thousand Years of Petty Capitalism* (Ithaca, NY: Cornell University Press, 1996).

25 Dorothy Ko, *Teachers of the Inner Chambers: Women and Culture in Seventeenth-Century China* (Stanford, CA: Stanford University Press, 1994); Susan Mann, *Precious Records: Women in China's Long Eighteenth Century* (Stanford, CA: Stanford University Press, 1997).

26 See Georg Lukács, "Reification and the Consciousness of the Proletariat" (1923), in *History and Class Consciousness: Studies in Marxist Dialetics*, trans. Rodney Livingstone (Cambridge, MA: MIT Press, 1971), 83–222. For an illuminating discussion, see Moishe Postone, "Lukács and the Dialectical Critique of Capitalism" (paper delivered at the NYU Social Theory Workshop, April 5, 2002). The emphasis on the historically *necessary* reification is some-what different from Slavoj Žižek's explanation of the merely homological, not necessary, relationship between ideology and history, in his *Sublime Object of Ideology*, 11–84.

27 It was in this sense that Lukács rediscovered Hegel in the 1930s. See Martin Jay, *Marxism and Totality: The Adventures of a Concept from Lukács to Haber-mas* (Berkeley: University of California Press, 1986).

28 Umberto Melotti, *Marx and the Third World*, trans. Pat Ransford (Atlantic Highlands, NJ: Humanities Press, 1977). This book became available in Chinese in 1980, translated by Gao Sian. Melotti, an Italian Marxist, was attempting to explore the historical antecedents to underdevelopment in the Third World. Melotti is often credited for reanimating the discussions on the AMP in China in the post-Mao period. For a thorough critique of Melotti at the time of the book's availability in Chinese, see Lin Guangquan, "The Asiatic Mode of Production and Ancient Chinese Society: A Criticism of Umberto Melotti's Distortion of Chinese History in His Book 'Marx and the Third World,'" *Chinese Law and Government* 22, no. 2 (1989): 47–70, trans. V. Young from a 1981 essay originally published in *Lishi yanjiu* [Re-searches on history]. For the impact of Melotti's work on Chinese intellectual circles of the 1980s, see Lin Chun, *Transformations in Chinese Socialism* (Durham, NC: Duke University Press, 2006), 309. For the continuing relevance of Melotti in Chinese economic debates, see Li Yining, *Economic Reform and Development in China* (Cambridge: Cambridge University Press, 2012), 205.

29 Timothy Bewes, *Reification; or, The Anxiety of Late Capitalism* (New York: Verso, 2002), 68.

30 "Good-Bye to Revolution" is the title of one of the most celebrated Chinese rethinkings of twentieth-century Chinese history in the post-Mao period, by

two of China's leading philosophers. Li Zehou and Liu Zaifu, *Gaobie geming* [Good-bye to revolution] (Hong Kong: Cosmos Books, 1995).

31 The Japanese Marxist oriental scholar Akizawa Shuji, among others, argued this position forcefully. I thank Osamu Nakano for discussions on Akizawa.

32 On Liu Xiaobo, see Barry Sautman and Yan Hairong, "The 'Right Dissident': Liu Xiaobo and the 2010 Nobel Peace Prize," *positions: east asia cultures critique* 19, no. 2 (2011): 581–613.

33 M. Godes, *Diskussia ob aziatskom sposobe proizvodstva* [A discussion of the Asiatic mode of production] (Moscow and Leningrad: Gosudarstvennoe sotsialno-ekonomicheskoe izdatelstvo, 1931). For a discussion of Godes's views in the context of the 1930s debates in the Soviet Union on the AMP, see Dunn, *The Fall and Rise of the Asiatic Mode of Production*, chapter 1.

34 At the same time, these debates also provided some crucial politico-intellectual justifications for the final routing of the Trotskyists in the USSR, as well as for the renewed specification, after the 1927 counterrevolutionary debacle in China, of the nature of the Chinese Revolution as a bourgeois-democratic revolution led by the proletarian and peasant classes in cooperation with the national bourgeoisie. This specificity will be important in what follows.

35 Anne M. Bailey and Josep R. Llobera, "Introduction," in *The Asiatic Mode of Production: Science and Politics*, ed. Anne M. Bailey and Josep R. Llobera (London: Routledge and Kegan Paul, 1981), 51, 52.

36 As Bewes points out in *Reification*, capitalist demystification is more properly understood as radically secularizing—"the effect of which, paradoxically, is a deistic as much as an atheistic conception of a God who is absent from human experience. Thus is reiterated a conception of a world abandoned to a set of already existing ontological and epistemological categories. Reification is a process of radical secularization in this sense" (69).

37 Most philosophically informed theories of globalization proceed from the assumption that real subsumption has been achieved globally. Taking a cue from Gilles Deleuze and Félix Guattari, they either explicitly or implicitly rework Marx's distinction between formal and real subsumption into settled historical fact. In particular, see Michael Hardt and Antonio Negri, *Empire* (Cambridge, MA: Harvard University Press, 2000), whose argument is further clarified in Antonio Negri and Danilo Zolo, "Empire and the Multitude: A Dialogue on the New Order of Globalization," *Radical Philosophy* 120 (July/August 2003): 23–37. See also Jason Read, *The Micro-Politics of Capital: Marx and the Prehistory of the Present* (Albany: State University of New York Press, 2003).

38 Justin Rosenberg, *The Follies of Globalisation Theory* (London: Verso, 2002), 14. He adds that this renaturalization results in a *reduction* of the explanatory claims of theory (14–15).

39 Jacques Camatte, "Against Domestication," trans. David Loneragan, in *This World We Must Leave*, ed. Alex Trotter (Brooklyn, NY: Autonomedia, 1995), 91–135.

40 See part 4 of Camatte, "Against Domestication," 113.

41 Jacques Camatte, "This World We Must Leave," in Trotter, *This World We Must Leave*, 158.

42 Georg Lukács, *The Young Hegel: Studies in the Relations between Dialectics and Economics*, trans. Rodney Livingstone (Cambridge, MA: MIT Press, 1977).

43 Lutz Niethammer, *Posthistoire: Has History Come to an End?*, trans. Patrick Camiller (New York: Verso, 1992).

44 Hegel, *The Philosophy of History*, 79.

45 Slavoj Žižek, "Catastrophes Real and Imagined," *In These Times*, March 31, 2003.

46 The joining of Camatte's conceptualization to Hardt and Negri is not arbitrary. Camatte's Marxism derives from the 1960s French upheavals as well as from his adherence to a post-1960s break from the Italian Marxism of Amadeo Bordiga, founder of the Italian Communist Party. By the 1950s, Bordiga was maintaining that the workers' movements of the nineteenth and twentieth centuries were, objectively, a movement of capital; Camatte follows Bordiga in his own formulation of the "community of capital" but breaks from Bordiga in the latter's party-centered "vanguardism." (For more on this, see David Black, "Has Capital Autonomized Itself from Humanity?," *Hobgoblin—Journal of Marxist-Humanism* 1 [spring/summer 1999]: n.p.) This traces a similar trajectory to that of the Italian *operaismo* and *autonomia* movements, to whose theories Negri has been central, and from which the theorization of *Empire* derives. For this, see John Kraniauskas, "Empire, or Multitude: Transnational Negri," *Radical Philosophy* 103 (September/October 2000); for a slightly different account of this trajectory, that links it to certain strands of breakaway American Trotskyism, see Jon Beasley-Murray, "Against Parochialism," *Radical Philosophy* 123 (January/ February 2004): 41–43. For an account of French Marxists/radicals after 1968, see Kristin Ross, *May '68 and Its Afterlives* (Chicago: University of Chicago Press, 2002).

47 Osborne, *Politics of Time*, 44.

48 Gilles Deleuze and Félix Guattari, *Anti-Oedipus: Capitalism and Schizophrenia*, trans. Robert Hurley, Mark Seem, and Helen R. Lane (Minneapolis: University of Minnesota Press, 1983), 191–92.

49 Deleuze and Guattari, *Anti-Oedipus*, 194.

50 Deleuze and Guattari, *Anti-Oedipus*, 194–95.

51 Read, *The Micro-Politics of Capital*.

52 Claude Meillasoux, *Maidens, Meal and Money: Capitalism and the Domestic Community* (Cambridge: Cambridge University Press, 1981), originally published in French in 1975; Samir Amin, *Unequal Development: An Essay on the Social Formations of Peripheral Capitalism*, trans. Brian Pearce (New York:

Monthly Review Press, 1976). I thank Ken Kawashima for bringing Meilla-soux's work to my attention.

53 There was a huge upsurge in comparative histories of India and China in the late 1980s and early 1990s that were ostensibly about the modern period but often were more about comparative empire than anything else. See, e.g., Peng Shuzhi, *Dongfang minzu zhuyi sichao* [Trends of the oriental nationalism] (Xi'an: Xibei daxue chubanshe, 1992); Tang Wenquan, *Dongfang de juexing: Jindai zhong yin minzu yundong dingwei guanzhao* [Oriental awakening: Exploration of the position of modern Chinese and Indian nationalist movements] (Changsha: Hunan chubanshe, 1991); He Xin, *Dongfang de fuxing* [Oriental renaissance], 2 vols. (Harbin: Heilongjiang renmin chubanshe/Heilongjiang jiaoyu chubanshe, 1989–92), esp. vol. 2. And so on. One is tempted to say that Prasenjit Duara's China/India juxtapositional comparative impulse in his *Rescuing History from the Nation* was an extension of this trend into U.S. academia. The comparative object of choice in economic history has oscillated between India and the Ottoman Empire. More recently, a series of conferences on the Qing and Ottoman Empires—one at New York University in 1999 and a follow-up in Istanbul in 2001 and several resultant publications (Peter Perdue, for one)—have given rise to a small cottage industry in comparative empire economics research.

54 Wu Dakun, "Guanyu yaxiya shengcan fangshi yanjiu de jige wenti" [Some questions concerning research on the Asiatic mode of production], *Xue-shu yanjiu* [Scholarly researches] 1 (1980): 11–18. See also Wu Dakun, "The Asiatic Mode of Production in History as Viewed by Political Economy in Its Broad Sense," in *Marxism in China*, ed. Su Shaozhi (Nottingham, UK: Spokesman, 1983), 53–77.

55 See Cui Zhiyuan, Wang Hui, and others on this issue.

56 Ke, "Ancient Chinese Society and the Asiatic Mode of Production," 16–25.

57 There are dozens of possible examples, but one citation will suffice here: Harrison E. Salisbury, *The New Emperors: China in the Era of Mao and Deng* (New York: Little, Brown, 1992).

58 The turn noted here can be seen from the move away from explicit discussions of the AMP to discussions of the semifeudal, semicolonial problem (which will be discussed further in the fourth essay of this volume). One can track these questions by reading from 1986 onward in the signature journal of academic history in China of that time, *Lishi yanjiu* [Researches on history] and then from the mid-1990s, in *Jindaishi yanjiu* [Researches in modern Chinese history], the journal mouthpiece of the Chinese Academy of Social Sciences, Modern History Institute. Despite much contention over the meaning and significance of the "semi" formulation, all participants to one degree or the next were concerned with normalizing China's history in the context of world history.

59 See, e.g., Su Kaihua, "The Asiatic Mode of Production and the Theory of the Five Modes of Production," in Brook, *The Asiatic Mode of Production in China*; Chen Qineng, "Guanyu chansheng zibenzhuyi de 'lishi biranxing' wenti" [On the question of the "inevitability" of capitalism], *Lishi yanjiu* [Researches on history] 1 (1982): 111–23; Qi Xin, "Guanliao zhengzhi de genyuan: Jianjie 'Guangyu yaxiya shengchan fangshi yanjiu de jige wenti'" [The roots of bureaucratism: Examining "Several questions about research on the Asiatic mode of production"], *Qishi niandai* [The '70s] 7 (1980): 24.

For a differently inflected discussion of the AMP's emergence in 1980s China, see Bill Brugger and David Kelly, *Chinese Marxism in the Post-Mao Era* (Stanford, CA: Stanford University Press, 1990), 19–30. For a selection of translated essays on the AMP in China from the 1930s onward, see those included in Brook, *The Asiatic Mode of Production*.

60 Wu Dakun, "The Asiatic Mode of Production," 76.

61 The endless rediscoveries of *tianxia* (all under heaven) and *datong* (one-worldism), excavated from various eras of China's imperial histories, are symptomatic of this nationalistic-culturalist postcolonial recuperative trend. I refrain from naming names.

62 One does not need to look far for these types of studies; I will cite only two of the more influential early ones: Timothy Brook, *Confusions of Pleasure: Commerce and Culture in Ming China* (Berkeley: University of California Press, 1999); Duara, *Rescuing History from the Nation*.

Chapter 3. The Economic as Transhistory

1 David Landes, "Why Europe and the West? Why Not China?," *Journal of Economic Perspectives* 20, no. 2 (spring 2006): 6.

2 Friedrich A. Hayek, *The Fatal Conceit: The Errors of Socialism*, ed. W. W. Bartley III (Chicago: University of Chicago Press, 1988).

3 See Lefebvre, *Critique of Everyday Life*, 1:94.

4 Javier Aranzadi, *Liberalism against Liberalism* (New York: Routledge, 2006), 105.

5 Karl Polanyi, *The Great Transformation* (New York: Beacon, 1957), 43, 68–76.

6 Yutaka Nagahara, "*Monsieur le Capital* and *Madame la Terre* Do Their Ghost-Dance: Globalization and the Nation-State," *South Atlantic Quarterly* 99, no. 4 (fall 2000): 944.

7 While the Chinese history iterations of market-centrism do not necessarily directly derive from Hayek, nevertheless, market-centrism has become a dominant form of inquiry into modern and early modern Chinese history in the past two decades. Thus, I do not claim that Song-Ming China scholars in the United States or Europe are necessarily Hayek admirers. And certainly not Pomeranz. I do wish to indicate for the China field the coincident re-

surgence of Hayekian emphasis on the historical role played by free markets and the rediscovery of Kyoto School scholars' work on Song early modernity in the turn to markets and consumption as a dominant mode of analysis for China's Song-Ming early-Qing period. The latter-day Kyoto School is the cornerstone of claims to China's historical "alternative modernity" (markets without capitalism, essentially) and to parity. This is the pure ideology of China studies as contemporary practice. See the first essay for more discussion. I should note here, so as to forestall misunderstanding: the appeal to alternative modernity of which I am speaking has nothing to do with socialism. I am fully aware that in the political and economic ideological battles in China, what is often called socialist modernity is sometimes also called alternative modernity by those who are ardent critics of the contemporary capitalist turn of the Chinese state and society. While I am not a fan of "socialist modernity" or "alternative modernity" as a way of naming, that is a separate issue from my critique of certain sinologists for their purported discovery of China's supposed alternative modernity dating from the Song dynasty.

8   Hayek's major works were translated into Chinese beginning in 1997 and have sold briskly from that time onward.

9   Liu Junning left China as a dissident in 1999 (for publishing *Res Publica*) and went to Harvard University's Fairbank Center for Chinese Studies. He returned to China to great acclaim in 2001 and became a senior researcher at the Chinese Academy of Social Sciences. He has since moved to the Institute of Chinese Culture under China's Ministry of Culture. The quotation here is from his blog of February 28, 2008, "Jingji ziyou: Ziyou zhi mu, xianzheng zhi lu—Du Ha-ye-ke" [Economic freedom: The mother of freedom, the road to constitutionalism—Reading Hayek], *Observechina*, originally accessed March 19, 2008, http://www.cicus.org/info/ArtShow.asp?ID=47965. NOTE: The URL has disappeared. I have been unable to find an alternative source for this blog.

10 For the ideological convergences and contemporary policy differences between the Chicago and Austrian Schools, see Mark Skousen, *Vienna and Chicago: Friends or Foes?* (New York: Capital Press, 2005); for a sustained discussion of methodological differences, see Aranzadi, *Liberalism against Liberalism*. The comeback of liberalism is a refrain for Liu. For a concentrated expression in English, see his "The Intellectual Turn: The Emergence of Liberalism in Contemporary China," in *China's Future: Constructive Partner or Emerging Threat?*, ed. Ted Galen Carpenter and James A. Dorn (Washington, DC: Cato Institute, 2000), 49–60.

11 Liu, "The Intellectual Turn," 52. Liu consistently juxtaposes the scourge of "redness" to the "greenness" of liberalism, as if to align free-market fundamentalism with environmentalism.

12 Carl Menger, *Principles of Economics* [1871] (Auburn, AL: Ludwig von Mises Institute, 2011).

13 "Carl Menger," accessed February 20, 2008, http://cepa.newschool.edu/het /profiles/menger.htm. See also Max Alter, *Carl Menger and the Origins of Austrian Economics* (Boulder, CO: Westview Press, 1990); and Karl Polanyi, "Carl Menger's Two Meanings of 'Economic,'" in *Studies in Economic Anthropology*, ed. George Dalton, Anthropological Studies 7 (Washington, DC: American Anthropological Association, 1971), 16–24.

14 Pioneered by Gustav von Schmoller from his position at Berlin University, this school's most famous adherent in the late Qing Chinese (and late Meiji Japanese) historical realm was Friedrich List, widely translated and treated as a guru of national economics. Schmoller's economics was based upon empiricism. Rejecting the universalism of "old historicism" (whether Hegelian or Marxist) as well as any positive (as opposed to normative) theory of economics, Schmoller and his group engaged in microresearch on political and economic history. By the 1870s, this consolidated into support for a corporatist state-industry-labor nexus favoring state intervention (on behalf of corporations).

15 For the derivation of this phrasing, see Moishe Postone, *Time, Labor, and Social Domination: A Reinterpretation of Marx's Critical Theory* (Cambridge: Cambridge University Press, 1996), 146.

16 This was essentially Böhm-Bawerk's question. See his *Karl Marx and the Close of His System: By Eugen von Böhm-Bawerk and Böhm-Bawerk's Criticism of Marx by Rudolf Hilferding*, ed. Paul M. Sweezy (New York: A. M. Kelley, 1949).

17 These extensions of Menger's insights are developed most by Böhm-Bawerk.

18 Postone, *Time, Labor, and Social Domination*, 132–35.

19 Deborah L. Walker, "Austrian Economics," in *The Concise Encyclopedia of Economics*, accessed February 23, 2008, http://www.econlib.org/library/Enc1 /AustrianEconomics.html.

20 Several books work to disentangle the apparently convergent theories of the Chicago and Austrian Schools. They aver that just because each espouses market fundamentalism does not mean that they arrive at their espousals in the same fashion, nor that they advocate the same methods of calculation, nor that they point in the same direction. Because my concern here—as with Wang's—is not economics per se but rather the ideology of the economic, these differences are less relevant to me. See Skousen, *Vienna and Chicago;* and Aranzadi, *Liberalism against Liberalism.*

21 Wang, "Zhengzhi jingjixue zai zhongguo," 124–29.

22 Wang, "Zhengzhi jingjixue zai zhongguo," 126–27. Wang translated some of Kniess's work (although he miswrites the name as Kneiss). Karl Kniess taught in Heidelberg in the mid-nineteenth century and was well known for his theories on the relationship of jurisprudence to political economy.

23 Wang, "Audili xuepai jingji xue," 151.

24 Luigi Cossa, a nineteenth-century Italian economist based in Padua, challenged Adam Smith–style liberalism in Italy by partially embracing the empiricism of German New Historicists, particularly as concerned their emphasis on the national economy. Several of his students soon migrated into Austrian School economics and became bulwarks of that form of liberalism in pre–World War I Italy. Robert Ingram was an early nineteenth-century English economist, known for disputing Malthus's population theories based on English specificities.

25 Wang, "Audili xuepai jingji xue," 150.

26 Osborne, *Politics of Time*, 193. This is Osborne's explication of Lefebvre's category of "everyday life"—*la vie quotidienne*.

27 On this, Wang was perhaps wrong. Mises, among others, defended his a priori theories based upon strict utilitarianism rather than ethics.

28 Wang, "Audili xuepai jingji xue," 153–54.

29 Wang, "Audili xuepai jingji xue," 155.

30 Aranzadi, *Liberalism against Liberalism*, 3, quoting Ludwig von Mises, *Human Action: A Treatise on Economics* (Irvington-on-Hudson, NY: Foundation for Economic Education, 1996).

31 My reference to Heideggerian *Being* is not casual; the second-generation Austrians, e.g., Mises, took much of their philosophical epistemology from Heidegger's *Being and Time*.

32 Wang, "Audili xuepai jingji xue," 158.

33 Wang, "Audili xuepai jingji xue," 162.

34 Wang, "Audili xuepai jingji xue," 161–63.

35 Postone, *Time, Labor, and Social Domination*, 137.

36 Harry Harootunian, "comment" on a panel at the Association for Asian Studies, Atlanta, GA, April 4, 2008. The comment was made with regard to 1930s Japanese philosopher Tosaka Jun.

37 However, by the 1920s even Ludwig von Mises complained that the specificity of Austrian School economics was being too rapidly assimilated into mainstream economics, thus causing the Austrians to lose their particular identity. See Karen I. Vaughn, *Austrian Economics in America: The Migration of a Tradition* (Cambridge: Cambridge University Press, 1998).

38 Wang, "Zhengzhi jingjixue zai zhongguo," 117, 122. Wang was writing during a time of maximal Nationalist Party (GMD) censorship; he thus references Marx as "a noted nineteenth-century economist and philosopher," and the Soviet Union goes unnamed as the "possibility" of an alternative.

39 Wang, "Audili xuepai jingji xue," 159.

40 Rosa Luxembourg, *The Accumulation of Capital* (London: Routledge, 1951).

41 Wang, "Zhengzhi jingjixue zai zhongguo," 121.

42 Wang, "Zhengzhi jingjixue zai zhongguo," 121.

43 Wang, "Zhengzhi jingjixue zai zhongguo," 122.

44 Wang, "Zhengzhi jingjixue zai zhongguo," 123–28.
45 At the time, Schumpeter still considered himself part of the Austrian School; he turned against them later in his career.
46 Wang, "Audili xuepai jingji xue," 160.
47 Wang, "Zhengzhi jingjixue zai zhongguo," 123.
48 Wang, "Audili xuepai jingji xue," 163.
49 Wang, "Audili xuepai jingji xue," 163.
50 Wang, "Jingji kexue lun," 3.
51 For Rousseau on crisis, see Koselleck, *Critique and Crisis*, 167–68.
52 Wang, "Audili xuepai jingji xue," 162–63.
53 Georg Lukács, "The Marxism of Rosa Luxembourg" [1923], in *History and Class Consciousness: Studies in Marxist Dialectics*, trans. Rodney Livingstone (Cambridge, MA: MIT Press, 1971), 34.
54 Lukács, "The Marxism of Rosa Luxembourg," 34.
55 Wang, "Audili xuepai jingji xue," 164.
56 Wang Yanan, "Lun Shehui kexue de yingyong" [On the utility of social science], in *Shehui kexue xinlun* [New essays on social science] (Fuzhou: Jingji kexue chubanshe, 1946), 38. The Southwest School was associated with Georg Simmel and Max Weber.
57 Wang, "Jingji kexue lun," 2.
58 To some theorists, Hayek is more British than Austrian, but Jeremy Shearmur makes a compelling, if brief, case for the Austrian roots of Hayek's thought, particularly with regard to his belief in "organic" institutions rather than designed ones, a theorization he derived from Carl Menger. Jeremy Shearmur, "The Austrian Connection: Hayek's Liberalism and the Thought of Carl Menger," in *Austrian Economics: Historical and Philosophical Background*, ed. Wolfgang Grassl and Barry Smith (New York: New York University Press, 1986), 210–14.
59 As Hayek put this in the mid-1940s, state intervention was the "road to serfdom."
60 Alter, *Carl Menger*, 23–77. Alter is much concerned to align Menger/the Austrians with German Romanticism, particularly with regard to their interest in introspective theorizing rather than empirical evidence.
61 Postone, *Time, Labor, and Social Domination*, 146. As he notes later, "Value . . . is not mediated by overtly social relations but, rather, *is itself a mediator*: it is the self-mediating dimension of commodities" (188).
62 Postone, *Time, Labor, and Social Domination*, 134.
63 Lefebvre, *Critique of Everyday Life*, 1:130.
64 Noting the importance of passion does not mean, however, that reducing economics to sentiment derived through a cataloging of practices of everyday life is any better as a theorizing or historicizing strategy. For the reductionist sentimental version, see Wen-hsin Yeh, *Shanghai Splendor: Economic Sentiments and the Making of Modern China, 1843–1949* (Berkeley: University of California Press, 2007).

65 Lefebvre, *Critique of Everyday Life*, 2:10–11.

66 Wang, "Audili xuepai jingji xue," 166.

67 Wang, "Audili xuepai jingji xue," 166.

68 Thus, unlike some postcolonial scholars, "decolonizing the mind" for Wang was not only a cultural or linguistic problem but an economic one as well.

69 Wang, "Audili xuepai jingji xue," 171.

70 Wang, "Audili xuepai jingji xue," 172. Wang's reference to slavishness here is not the Lu Xun variety (which pointed to a national character flaw). Rather, it points to the impulse to smooth out the sociopolitical violence produced by a historical necessity (conceptual appropriation) and historical experience (imperialist colonization).

71 Peter Osborne, "Marx and the Philosophy of Time," *Radical Philosophy* 147 (January/February 2008): 16.

72 Aranzadi, *Liberalism against Liberalism*, 21–22.

73 Vaughn, *Austrian Economics in America*, xi.

74 Osborne, *Politics of Time*, 46.

75 Vaughn, *Austrian Economics in America*, xi.

76 Aranzadi, *Liberalism against Liberalism*, 41.

77 Cited in Aranzadi, *Liberalism against Liberalism*, 105. For Bergson's original argument, see Henri Bergson, *Time and Free Will: An Essay on the Immediate Data of Consciousness,* trans. F. L. Pogson (London: George Allen and Unwin, 1919); *Duration and Simultaneity*, trans. Leon Jacobson (Manchester, UK: Clinamen Press, 1999); and *La pensée et le movement* [1934] (Paris: Flammarion, 2014). For analysis of Bergonism, see Osborne, *Politics of Time*, 214–15.

78 This distinguishes action/duration from a concept of the event.

79 See Lukács's extended discussion in *The Theory of the Novel*, trans. Anna Bostock (Cambridge, MA: MIT Press, 1999).

80 Georg Lukács, *History and Class Consciousness: Studies in Marxist Dialectics,* trans. Rodney Livingstone (Cambridge, MA: MIT Press, 1971), in particular "Reification and the Consciousness of the Proletariat."

81 Louis Althusser and Étienne Balibar, *Reading Capital*, trans. Ben Brewster (London: Verso, 1979), 96–97. See also Osborne, *Politics of Time*, 24–25.

82 In the Austrian School, Bergson is one philosophical source of temporality as duration; Heidegger's concept of contingence is another. Althusser reconfigured the notion of conjuncture as a politics of the temporal present, rather than merely, as in the Annales School, as an intersection of types of times (longue durée and eventfulness).

83 For indications on this as a disciplinary issue, see Yung-chen Chiang, *Social Engineering and the Social Sciences in China, 1919–1949* (Cambridge: Cambridge University Press, 2001); and, as an ideological issue, see Wang Hui, "On Scientism and Social Theory in Modern Chinese Thought," trans. Gloria Davies, in *Voicing Concerns: Contemporary Chinese Critical Inquiry*, ed. Gloria Davies (Lanham, MD: Rowman and Littlefield, 2001), 135–56.

84 This concept is borrowed from Roberto Schwarz, *Master on the Periphery of Capitalism*, trans. John Gledson (Durham, NC: Duke University Press, 2001), 46.

85 Wang Yanan, "Yanjiu shehui kexue yingyou de jige jiben renshi" [A few basic points of understanding in the study of social science], in *Shehui kexue xinlun* [New essays on social science] (Fuzhou: Jingji kexue chubanshe, 1946), 10.

86 Wang, "Yanjiu shehui kexue yingyou de jige jiben renshi," 15.

87 Wang, "Jingjixue yu zhexue," 59–62.

88 Wang, "Jingjixue yu zhexue," 67.

89 Wang, "Jingjixue yu zhexue," 71.

90 For Wang's specification of *fanchou*, see "Jingjixue yu zhexue," 71. For categories as structured forms of practice, see Postone, *Time, Labor, and Social Domination*, 37.

91 The one, clearly, is the bourgeois-Weberian mode; the other, the dominant Marxist mode. Indeed, as Walter Benjamin consistently, if unevenly, argued in theory and in his scholarly practice, the task of Marxist cultural critique was precisely *not* to efface the everyday in favor of a unified temporality but rather to rescue the everyday from social hegemony.

92 These issues are present—implicitly or explicitly—in much of the serious journalism of the day; one concentrated expression of the problem can be derived from a series of essays in *Wenhua pinglun* (Culture critique) published between January and April 1928. See, e.g., Zhu Jingwo, "Kexue de shehui guan" [A scientific perspective on the social], *Wenhua pinglun* 1 (January 1928): 34–52; 2 (April 1928): 48–71; and Peng Kang, "Zhexue de renwu shi shenma?" [What is the task of philosophy?], *Wenhua pinglun* 1 (January 1928): 14–24. *Wenhua pinglun* was published in Shanghai; a major contributor was Guo Moruo.

93 Zhu Jingwo, "Kexue de shehui guan," 1:36.

94 Marx and Engels were the first to connect technological and social change to a revolutionary experience located at the level of everyday life in the *Communist Manifesto*. Nevertheless, in subsequent Marxist theorizing and particularly in Communist practice, the problem of everyday/experience got assimilated to the problematic of class-consciousness in ways inimical to a further critique. Lefebvre, Benjamin, Ernst Bloch, Brecht, and so on wrote against this trend, yet it is only recently that the import of their works in this regard has gained attention.

95 Wang Yanan, "Lun wenhua yu jingji" [On culture and economics], in *Shehui kexue xinlun*, 68.

96 Wang, "Lun wenhua yu jingji," 68–69.

97 As we have seen, Wang Yanan was one of Weber's earliest critics in China (see second essay), even while more recently, in the wake of the rejection of Marxism, Maoism, and all radical theory, Weber's sociological system

and worldview have been aggressively translated and promoted, along with Hayek and others, in the China of the 1980s–1990s.

98 Wang, "Lun wenhua yu jingji," 72–73.

99 This vulgar relationship remains an article of faith among some historians in China. For example, see the last chapter of the first volume of Xu Dixin and Wu Chengming, eds., *Zhongguo zibenzhuyi de mengya* [The sprouts of capitalism in China], 3 vols. (Beijing: Renmin chubanshe, 2003).

100 I should clarify that Wang was not concerned in his essay with Liang Shuming's rural reconstruction work of the time; thus whether or not Wang's designation of Liang as exemplifying a form of national essence is adequate to an understanding of Liang as a totality is a moot point here.

101 Wang Yanan, "Lun Dongxi wenhua yu dongxi jingji: Ping Liang Shuming xiansheng de dongxi wenhua guan" [On Eastern-Western culture and Eastern-Western economy, part 1: Evaluation of Mr. Liang Shuming's view of Eastern-Western culture], in *Shehui kexue xinlun*, 76. Wang is referencing an essay by Liang originally published in Guilin's *Dagong bao*, "What Can China Contribute to the World?" This was initially paired with Lin Yutang's essay "Eastern-Western Culture and Psychological Construction." Wang discussed Liang's piece over Lin's because he considered Liang the more serious scholar.

102 Wang, "Ping Liang Shuming," 83, 82, 85.

103 Wang Yanan, "Zai lun dongxi wenhua yu dongxi jingji: Ping Qian Mu xiansheng de dongxi wenhua guan" [On Eastern-Western culture and Eastern-Western economy, part 2: Evaluation of Mr. Qian Mu's view of Eastern-Western culture], in *Shehui kexue xinlun*, 87–102. Wang is here addressing an essay by Qian Mu published in *Zhongguo qingnian* [Chinese youth] titled "Zhongguo wenhua chuantong zhi yanjin" [The evolution of Chinese cultural tradition].

104 Wang, "Ping Qian Mu," 91.

105 Wang, "Ping Qian Mu," 92.

106 Wang, "Ping Qian Mu," 100–101.

107 Wang Yanan, "San lun dongxi wenhua yu dongxi jingji: Ping Zhu Qianzhi xiansheng de dongxi wenhua guan" [On Eastern-Western culture and Eastern-Western economy, part 3: Evaluation of Mr. Zhu Qianzhi's view of Eastern-Western culture], in *Shehui kexue xinlun*, 1946), 103–11. Wang here addresses an essay by Zhu published in *Shidai zhongguo* [The era of China] titled "Jingji wenhua zhi san jixing" [Three basic forms of economy-culture].

108 Wang, "Ping Zhu Qianzhi," 107, 108.

109 Wang, "Ping Zhu Qianzhi," 110. Wang (wrongly) predicted that Liang Shuming's national essence advocacy was permanently on the wane and that Qian Mu's essence/use could only last a little longer. According to Wang, it

was Zhu's incoherent mixing and matching that was most dangerous. Little could he have predicted that all three versions of culturalism have returned with a vengeance, mixing and matching with one another as well as developing in their own philosophical and historical worlds.

110 Siegfried Kracauer, *History: The Last Things before the Last*, completed after the author's death by Paul Oskar Kristeller (Princeton, NJ: Markus Wiener, 1995), 163.

111 For a discussion of this aspect of Benjamin's concept of temporality, see Harry Harootunian, *History's Disquiet: Modernity, Cultural Practice, and the Question of Everyday Life* (New York: Columbia University Press, 2000), 99–105. I am also indebted to discussions with Manu Goswami on this issue.

112 By the mid-1940s and prior to the victory of the CCP in the civil war, Wang's target shifted to caution about "bourgeois economists" and Trotskyists' fascination with the commodity economy, and also about the attachment of "critical economists" (that is, CCP Marxists) to economic stage theories and the prospect of skipping stages altogether. See Wang Yanan, *Zhongguo banfengjian banzhimindi jingji xingtai yanjiu* [Researches on China's semifeudal, semicolonial economic formation] [1943] (Beijing: Renmin chubanshe, 1957), 43–53.

113 Peter Osborne, *Philosophy in Cultural Theory* (New York: Routledge, 2000), 10–13.

114 Wang, "Yanjiu shehui kexue yingyou de jige jiben renshi," 17.

115 Wang, "Yanjiu shehui kexue yingyou de jige jiben renshi," 19.

116 "Sociological calm" is a phrase borrowed from Schwarz, *Master on the Periphery*, 22.

117 Wang, "Yanjiu shehui kexue yingyou de jige jiben renshi," 13.

118 Wang, "Yanjiu shehui kexue yingyou de jige jiben renshi," 21.

119 Wang, "Yanjiu shehui kexue yingyou de jige jiben renshi," 21–22.

120 Wang Yanan, "Shehui kexue de yingyong" [The utility of social science], in *Shehui kexue xinlun*, 36.

121 As mentioned in the introduction to this volume, I am currently at work on a more fully researched monograph on Wang Yanan and his worlds of economic thinking. This will include a consideration of his very important work on bureaucracy, land relations, demography, and many other arenas. For a preliminary discussion of bureaucracy, see Karl, "Compradors."

Chapter 4. The Economic as Lived Experience

1 See introduction and the third essay in this book for more on Wang's biography.

2 Wang, "Zhongguo shehui jingjishi gang," 18–19. One could also consult here Wang's important *Zhongguo de dizhu fengjian jingji lungang* [Outline

of China's feudal landlord economy]. I am writing on the latter work in my monograph in progress.

3 As Tani Barlow has reminded me, her and Donald Lowe's promotion of "colonial modernity" for China studies in the early 1990s programmatic launch of the journal *positions* was a strategic move to try to force the China field in the United States to come to terms with the problem of the colonial in China's modern history. I acknowledge and am grateful for this necessary strategic intervention and yet wish to move beyond it.

4 V. I. Lenin, *Imperialism, the Highest Stage of Capitalism* (New York: International Publishers, 1985).

5 See the proceedings and documents of the Second Congress published under the title *Workers of the World and Oppressed Peoples, Unite!*, 2 vols., ed. John Riddell (New York: Pathfinder Press, 1991).

6 At a slightly earlier time, in Peru, Marxist activist José Mariátegui was theorizing in a similar vein. See his 1928 work *Seven Interpretive Essays on Peruvian Reality*, trans. Jorge Basadre (Austin: University of Texas Press, 1971).

7 Henri Lefebvre, *Introduction to Modernity* (London: Verso, 1995), 206.

8 One of the only English-language theorizations of semicolonialism as an economic form is Jürgen Osterhammel, "Semi-Colonialism and Informal Empire in Twentieth-Century China: Towards a Framework of Analysis," in *Imperialism and After: Continuities and Discontinuities*, ed. Wolfgang J. Mommsen and Jürgen Osterhammel (London: Allen and Unwin, 1986), 290–314. Osterhammel's theorization is hobbled by his assimilation of semicolonialism to the notion of "informal empire," thus containing it to a category of the political. More recently, semicolonialism has been reactivated in a postcolonial mode, as a form of hybrid cultural condition. For discussion in the latter idiom, see Shu-mei Shih, *The Lure of the Modern* (Berkeley: University of California Press, 2001).

9 Each of the semis had emerged in the 1920s; in February 1929 they were combined by the Chinese Communist Party Central Committee in its twenty-eighth directive ("Strategies for the Peasant Revolution"). The formulation was codified in Su Hua's (1933) and Zhang Wentian's usage (1932), and by Mao Zedong starting in December 1936. Su Hua, "Zhongguo ziben zhuyi jingji de fazhan" [Development in China's capitalist economy], *Zhongguo jingji* [Chinese economics] 1, no. 6 (September 1933): 1–19; Zhang Wentian, "Zhongguo jingji zhi xingzhi wenti de yanjiu—Ping Ren Shu jun de 'Zhongguo jingji yanjiu'" [Research on the question of the nature of China's economy—An evaluation of Mr. Ren Shu's *Research on China's Economy*], *Dushu zazhi* [Readings journal] 1, nos. 4/5 (1932): 4–8; Mao Zedong, "Zhongguo geming zhanzheng de zhanlüe wenti" [Strategy of the Chinese revolutionary war], in *Mao Zedong Xuanji* [Selected works of Mao Zedong] (Beijing: Renmin chubanshe, 1991), 1:154–225.

10 See Dirlik, *Revolution and History*, 96–97.
11 Chen, *Zhimindi yu banzhimindi* [Colonialism and semicolonialism] (Shanghai: Heibai congshu, 1937), 44–45.
12 Chen, *Zhimindi yu banzhimindi*, 45–64.
13 Chen, *Zhimindi yu banzhimindi*, 46–48.
14 Žižek, *The Sublime Object of Ideology*, chap. 1.
15 Wang Yanan, *Zhongguo jingji yuanlun* [Elements of the Chinese economy], 2nd ed. (Shanghai: Shenghuo shudian, 1947), chaps. 1–2. This book was later republished in 1955 and again in 1957, both under the new title: *Zhongguo banfengjian banzhimindi jingji xingtai yanjiu* [Researches on China's semifeudal, semicolonial economic formation] (Beijing: Renmin chubanshe, 1955). In the 1955 preface, Wang notes that, in response to critiques of and suggestions about the preliberation edition, in the revised edition he (1) provides an overall account of semifeudalism and semicolonialism; (2) clearly links the social history controversy to revolutionary and antirevolutionary thought, even as he features Mao more prominently in his accounts; (3) corrects the inadequate critique of the comprador economy and gives a better account of Sun Yatsen's subjective socialism; and (4) retains, despite the critique of his book by Marxists and Maoists, the analysis of the commodity and the commodity form as key. The book carries several more prefaces, for the Japanese and Russian translated editions, that address specific areas of concern to Marxists in those countries. Page citations hereafter in the text are to the 1947 edition, unless otherwise noted.
16 For more on Wang's theory of the comprador-bureaucratic class, see my forthcoming essay, "Compradors."
17 For a comment on Wang that downplays his politics, see Osterhammel, "Semi-Colonialism and Informal Empire," 296–97.
18 Wang, "Zhengzhi jingjixue zai zhongguo," 118.
19 David Harvey, *The Limits to Capital* (New York: Verso, 2007).
20 For the centrality of primitive accumulation to Marx, see Perelman, *Invention of Capitalism*, 30–31.
21 For a thorough discussion of formal and real subsumption, see Harry Harootunian, *Marx after Marx: History and Time in the Expansion of Capitalism* (New York: Columbia University Press, 2015), introduction and chap. 1.
22 Zhang, "Zhongguo jingji zhi xingzhi wenti de yanjiu," 4.
23 Zhang, "Zhongguo jingji zhi xingzhi wenti de yanjiu," 4.
24 Zhang Wentian, "Zhongguo jingji zhi xingzhi wenti de yanjiu," 4.
25 Zhang Wentian, "Zhongguo jingji zhi xingzhi wenti de yanjiu," 6.
26 Mao Zedong, "Lun fandui riben diguo zhuyi de cilüe" [On tactics against Japanese imperialism], in *Mao Zedong Xuanji* [Selected works of Mao Zedong], 133, 137, 138.

27 Mao Zedong, "The Chinese Revolution and the Chinese Communist Party," in *Selected Works of Mao Tse-tung* (Peking: People's Publishing House, 1967), 2:305–34.

28 For more on this version of Maoist politics, see Rebecca E. Karl, *Mao Zedong and China in the Twentieth-Century World: A Concise History* (Durham, NC: Duke University Press, 2010), chaps. 3–4.

29 Mao, "Chinese Revolution and the Chinese Communist Party," 310.

30 For this periodization of Lenin's thought, see Neil Harding, *Lenin's Political Thought: Theory and Practice in the Democratic Socialist Movement*, 2 vols. (London: Haymarket Press, 2009).

31 For more critical discussion of anachronism, see Dai Jinhua, "After the post-Cold War," trans. Li Jie, in *Works of Dai Jinhua*, ed. Lisa Rofel (Durham, NC: Duke University Press, forthcoming).

32 See François Furet and Denis Richet, *La Révolution française* (Paris: Hachette, 1986).

33 Yan Sun, *The Chinese Reassessment of Socialism, 1976–1992* (Princeton, NJ: Princeton University Press, 1999), chaps. 7 and 8.

34 Wang Jinglu "Zhongguo jindai shehui, jindai zichan jieji he zichan jieji geming" [China's modern society, modern bourgeoisie, and the bourgeois revolution]. *Lishi yanjiu* [Researches on history] 6 (1986): 51–61.

35 Li Shiyue, "Guanyu 'banzhimindi banfengjian' de jidian sixiang" [A few thoughts on 'semi-colonialism semi-feudalism']. *Lishi yanjiu* [Researches on history] 1 (1988): 52–60.

36 For the trend toward "rethinking radicalism" in Chinese academic discussion from the early 1990s onward, see Wang Hui, "The Year 1989 and the Historical Roots of Neoliberalism in China," trans. Rebecca E. Karl, *positions* 12, no. 1 (spring 2004): 37–40. I should mention here that my version of the academic debates through this period is quite idiosyncratic and not meant to be all-inclusive or comprehensive. For a more complete assessment of trends in recent PRC historiography, see Li Huaiyin, *Reinventing Modern China: Imagination and Authenticity in Chinese Historical Writing* (Honolulu: University of Hawai'i Press, 2012).

37 Chen Jinlong, "Ban zhimindi banfengjian gainian xingcheng guocheng kaoxi" [Considerations and analysis of the formation of the concept of semi-colonial semifeudal], *Jindaishi yanjiu* 4 (1996): 227–331.

38 Zhang Qinghai, "Lun dui banfengjian banzhimindi liangge gainian de lilun jieding" [On the theoretical specification of the two concepts *semifeudal* and *semicolonial*], *Jindaishi yanjiu* 6 (1998):226–34.

39 Zhang, "Lun dui banfengjian banzhimindi liangge gainian de lilun jieding," 233. At the time, the question of principle was still quite relevant as a question of political correctness and thus of party approval.

40 See Rancière, *Names of History*, where he argues that historical nominalism is inextricably related to political ideologies of class. See also Jim Chandler,

England in 1819: The Politics of Literary Culture and the Case of Romantic Historicism (Chicago: University of Chicago Press, 1998), 53–59.

41 Ma Min, "Guodu tezheng yu zhongguo jindai shehui xingtai" [Special characteristics of transition and early modern China's social formation], *Lishi yanjiu* [Researches on history] 1 (1989): 47, 51.

42 "Spontaneity" refers to the assumed smooth internalist transition in "normal" capitalism from merchant to industrial capital.

43 Ma Min, "Guodu tezheng," 48–49. Ma's essay was written prior to the USSR's dissolution.

44 Ma Min, "Guodu tezheng," 58.

45 The dispute over the progressive and regressive nature of imperialism/capitalism/feudalism in China echoes the 1930s debate, although in the latter case the debate shaped up between the CCP and Trotskyists. See Dirlik, *Revolution and History*, chapter 3.

46 Nie Xiwen, "Dui Zhongguo banzhimindi banfengjian shehui de xin renshi" [A new understanding of semicolonial, semifeudal society], *Xueshu yanjiu* [Scholarly researches] 1 (1992): 69, 66.

47 The point here is not that the contemporary Chinese state is monolithic; there are evidently many fractions and factions struggling for ascendance. This is clear in Xi Jinping's ongoing attempts to consolidate his power. My point is that in much academic theorizing about the relations of the state to social formations, the state is seen as standing above the social struggle itself.

48 Wang Xiaoming, *Zai xin yishi xingtai de longzhao xia: 90 niandai de wenhua yu wenxue fenxi* [Under the glare of the new ideology: Culture and literature in the 1990s] (Nanjing: Jiangsu renmin chubanshe, 2000), 15.

49 Tao Xisheng, "Zhongguo shehui daodi shi shenma shehui?" [What kind of society is China's anyway?], *Xin shengming* [New life] 1, no. 10 (October 1928): 2–14.

50 Dirlik, *Revolution and History*, 119.

51 For this analysis of Maoist developmental theory, see Karl, *Mao Zedong*, chapter 7.

52 Althusser and Balibar, *Reading Capital*, 273ff.

53 Barry Hindess and Paul Q. Hirst, *Pre-capitalist Modes of Production* (London: Routledge, 1975), 264–65.

54 Hypocolonialism asserts that China is the common colony of all imperialists and is thus in a more subordinated and more complex situation than full colonies.

55 Wu Qingyou, *Ziben zhuyi fazhan de bu pinghenglü* [Uneven rates of capitalist development] (Shanghai: Shenghuo shudian, 1937), 8. Wu is following Nikolai Bukharin relatively closely.

56 See Su, "Zhongguo ziben zhuyi jingji de fazhan."

57 As of July 2001, capitalists began to be formally accepted as members of the Communist Party.

58 See Wang's general discussion in the essay "Zhengzhi jingjishang de ren." Wang later reiterated and elaborated on this point in 1956 and 1957, during the dispute over population policy that led to Ma Yinchu's disgrace and political exile.

59 Wang, *Zhongguo jingji yuanlun*, chapter 2. For the comment about commerce in wartime, see Wang Yanan, "Zhongguo jingjishi yanjiu de xian jieduan" [The current phase of research on the economy in China], *Jingji kexue* [The science of economics] 5 (April 1943), reprinted in *Wang Yanan Wenji*, 4:40. The issue is linked, for Wang, to the inadequacies of the social history debate, for which he notes that arguing about historical stages before doing research commits the error of "putting theory before practice" (40). We can recall from Arif Dirlik's discussion that commercial capital was one of the more fraught questions dealt with at the time. See also my discussion in the third essay of this volume.

60 Wang, *Zhongguo jingji yuanlun*, 61–64.

61 Wang makes this distinction in a number of essays; for example, see "Guanyu zhongguo jingjixue jianli zhi keneng yu biyao de wenti" [On the possibility and necessity of establishing economics in China], *Dongnan ribao* [Southeast daily], November 14, 15, 18, 1944, reprinted in *Wang Yanan Wenji*, 1:126–37.

62 Wang Yanan, "You banfengjian banzhimindi jingji dao xin minzhu zhuyi jingji" [From semifeudal semicolonial economy to a new democratic economy], *Xin Zhonghua* [New China], 12, no. 15, reprinted in *Wang Yanan Wenji*, 3:484.

Chapter 5. The Economic as Culture and the Culture of the Economic

1 Yingjin Zhang, "Introduction," in *Cinema and Urban Culture in Shanghai, 1922–1943*, ed. Yingjin Zhang (Stanford, CA: Stanford University Press, 1999), 22.

2 Rancière, *Names of History*, 39.

3 Osborne, *Politics of Time*, 44.

4 Rancière, *Names of History*, 24–41, 58–59, 66.

5 Rancière, *Names of History*, 67.

6 For a recent (more sophisticated) example of a project like Zhang's, see Luo Gang and Lin Yun, "Zuowei 'shehui zhuyi chengshi' de 'shanghai' yu kongjian de zai shengcan: 'Chengshi wenben' yu 'Meijie wenben' de 'hudu' " [The socialist city of Shanghai and the reproduction of space: The conflations of urban text and media text], *Refeng xueshu* 4 (August 2010): 57–96.

7 The 1930s could be dated 1928–37, from the violent dissolution of the first United Front to the Japanese invasion; and the 1990s could begin with the 1987 "primary stage of socialism" theory, or the 1989 Tiananmen events, or Deng Xiaoping's 1992 "Southern Tour."

8 Marx, *Capital*, 1:711.

9 Harootunian, *History's Disquiet*; Harry Harootunian, *Overcome by Modernity: History, Culture, and Community in Interwar Japan* (Princeton, NJ: Princeton University Press, 2000).

10 For conditions surrounding the filming, editing, and release of *Crows and Sparrows*, see Leo Ou-fan Lee, "The Tradition of Modern Chinese Cinema: Some Preliminary Explorations and Hypotheses," in *Perspectives on Chinese Cinema*, ed. Chris Berry (London: British Film Institute, 1991), 10–11.

11 Most information on the making of *Once Upon a Time in Shanghai* was obtained in conversation with Peng Xiaolian, who also helpfully supplied me with a DVD of the film.

12 Zhu Yongde, "Nongmo zhongcai you yi zhang: Shang ying guoqing 50 zhou-nian huoli yingpian paiying huigu" [Another chapter of dark ink and bold colors: Reviewing the making of prize-winning Shanghai Studio films for the 50th anniversary], *Dianying xinzuo* [New films] 1 (2000): 9.

13 For the importance of nostalgia to post-Communist figurations of the past, see Svetlana Boym, *The Future of Nostalgia* (New York: Basic Books, 2002).

14 Carl Schmitt, *Political Romanticism*, trans. Guy Oakes (Cambridge, MA: MIT Press, 1986), 159. This is what he also encapsulates as "subjectivist occasionalism" (17–20).

15 Harootunian, *History's Disquiet*, 64.

16 Mao famously begins a 1925 essay: "Who are our enemies? Who are our friends? This is a question of the first importance for the revolution." See Mao Zedong, "Analysis of Classes in Chinese Society," accessed January 23, 2014, https://www.marxists.org/reference/archive/mao/selected-works /volume-1/mswv1_1.htm.

17 According to William Pietz, reification is one of four characteristics of the fetish, as it comes to be articulated in European thought through the pre- and post-Enlightenment periods. William Pietz, "The Origins of Fetishism: A Contribution to the History of Theory" (PhD diss., University of California, Santa Cruz, 1988), 34.

18 For a trenchant account of this process, see Qin Shao, *Shanghai Gone: Domicide and Defiance in a Chinese Megacity* (New York: Rowman and Littlefield, 2013).

19 Michel de Certeau, "Walking the City," in *The Practice of Everyday Life*, trans. Steven Rendall (Berkeley: University of California Press, 1984), 93.

20 Marx, *Capital*, 1:712.

21 For this formulation—which I have syntactically rearranged from the original—see Daniel Bensaïd, *An Impatient Life: A Memoir* (New York: Verso, 2015), 67.

Afterword

1 The Liu Junming and Wang Ruolin quotes come from a blog originally written by Liu that has now disappeared from the web.

2 This observation should be seen as distinct from, e.g., Andrew Sartori's usage of the term *culturalism* in the context of colonial Bengal. Sartori tracks the experience of dislocatedness to which an appeal to culturalism appears as an antidote through the years of British colonial transformation of Bengali society. Andrew Sartori, *Bengal in Global Concept History: Culturalism in the Age of Capital* (Chicago: University of Chicago Press, 2008). By contrast, my indictment of culturalism is about a version of a sure *locatedness* that announces itself in deracinated ahistorical terms.

3 Theodor W. Adorno, *Sound Figures*, trans. Rodney Livingston (Stanford, CA: Stanford University Press, 1999), 23.

4 Brian Magee, *The Tristan Chord: Wagner and Philosophy* (New York: Metropolitan Books, 2001), 208.

5 Magee, *Tristan Chord*, 209.

6 Jacques Attali, *Noise: The Political Economy of Music* (Minnesota: University of Minnesota Press, 2002).

7 Slavoj Žižek and Mladen Dolar, *Opera's Second Death* (New York: Routledge, 2002), 121, 123.

BIBLIOGRAPHY

Adorno, Theodor W. *Sound Figures*. Translated by Rodney Livingston. Stanford, CA: Stanford University Press, 1999.

Alliez, Éric. "What Is—or What Is Not—Contemporary French Philosophy, Today?" *Radical Philosophy* 161 (May–June 2010): 9–17.

Alter, Max. *Carl Menger and the Origins of Austrian Economics*. Boulder, CO: Westview Press, 1990.

Althusser, Louis, and Étienne Balibar. *Reading Capital*. Translated by Ben Brewster. London: New Left Books, 1979.

Amin, Samir. *Eurocentrism*. London: Zed Books, 1989.

———. *Unequal Development: An Essay on the Social Formations of Peripheral Capitalism*. Translated by Brian Pearce. New York: Monthly Review Press, 1976.

Anderson, Perry. *Lineages of the Absolutist State*. London: Verso, 1979.

Aranzadi, Javier. *Liberalism against Liberalism*. New York: Routledge, 2006.

Arrighi, Giovanni. *Adam Smith in Beijing: Lineages of the Twenty-First Century*. London: Verso, 2007.

Aston, T. H., and C. H. E. Philpin, eds. *The Brenner Debate: Agrarian Class Structure and Economic Development in Pre-industrial Europe*. Cambridge: Cambridge University Press, 1987.

Attali, Jacques. *Noise: The Political Economy of Music*. Minnesota: University of Minnesota Press, 2002.

Bailey, Anne M., and Josep R. Llobera, eds. *The Asiatic Mode of Production: Science and Politics*. London: Routledge and Kegan Paul, 1981.

Baudrillard, Jean. *For a Critique of the Political Economy of the Sign*. Translated by Charles Levin. St. Louis, MO: Telos Press, 1981.

Beasley-Murray, Jon. "Against Parochialism." *Radical Philosophy* 123 (January–February 2004): 41–43.

Benjamin, Walter. "Conversations with Brecht." In *Reflections*, edited by Peter Demetz, 203–19. New York: Random House, 1979.

Bensaïd, Daniel. *An Impatient Life: A Memoir*. New York: Verso, 2015.

———. *Marx for Our Times: Adventures and Misadventures of a Critique*. Translated by Gregory Elliott. London: Verso, 2002.

Bergson, Henri. *Duration and Simultaneity* [1923]. Translated by Leon Jacobson. Manchester, UK: Clinamen Press, 1999.

———. *La pensée et le mouvement*. 1934. Paris: Flammarion, 2014.

———. *Time and Free Will: An Essay on the Immediate Data of Consciousness*. Translated by F. L. Pogson. London: George Allen and Unwin, 1910.

Bewes, Timothy. *Reification; or, The Anxiety of Late Capitalism*. New York: Verso, 2002.

Black, David. "Has Capital Autonomized Itself from Humanity?" *Hobgoblin— Journal of Marxist-Humanism* 1 (spring/summer 1999): n.p.

Böhm-Bawerk, Eugen von. *Karl Marx and the Close of His System: By Eugen von Böhm-Bawerk and Böhm-Bawerk's Criticism of Marx by Rudolf Hilferding*, edited by Paul M. Sweezy. New York: A. M. Kelley, 1949.

Boym, Svetlana. *The Future of Nostalgia*. New York: Basic Books, 2002.

Brecht, Bertolt. "The Film, the Novel, and Epic Theatre." In *Brecht on Theatre: The Development of an Aesthetic*, edited and translated by John Willett, 47–50. New York: Hill and Wang, 1992.

Brook, Timothy, ed. *The Asiatic Mode of Production in China*. New York: M. E. Sharpe, 1989.

———. *Confusions of Pleasure: Commerce and Culture in Ming China*. Berkeley: University of California Press, 1999.

Brugger, Bill, and David Kelly. *Chinese Marxism in the Post-Mao Era*. Stanford, CA: Stanford University Press, 1990.

Burbank, Jane, and Fred Cooper. *Empires in World History: Power and the Politics of Difference*. Princeton, NJ: Princeton University Press, 2010.

Camatte, Jacques. "Against Domestication." Translated by David Loneragan. In *This World We Must Leave*, edited by Alex Trotter, 91–135. Brooklyn, NY: Automedia, 1995.

———. *This World We Must Leave: And Other Essays*. Edited by Alex Trotter. Brooklyn, NY: Autonomedia, 1995.

———. "This World We Must Leave." In *This World We Must Leave: And Other Essays*, edited by Alex Trotter. Brooklyn, NY: Autonomedia, 1995. 137–80.

Chandler, Jim. *England in 1819: The Politics of Literary Culture and the Case of Romantic Historicism*. Chicago: University of Chicago Press, 1998.

Chen Guangxing and Qian Yongxiang. "Quanqiuhua zhixia Taiwan de xueshu shuxie " [The production of scholarship in Taiwan under globalization]. *Dushu* [Readings] 2 (February 2005): 56–66.

Chen Hongjin. *Zhimindi yu banzhimindi* [Colonialism and semicolonialism]. Shanghai: Heibai congshu, 1937.

Chen Jinlong. "Banzhimindi banfengjian gainian xingcheng guocheng kaoxi" [Considerations and analysis of the formation of the concept of semicolonial semifeudal]. *Jindaishi yanjiu* [Researches on modern history] 4 (1996): 227–331.

Chen Qineng. "Guanyu chansheng zibenzhuyi de 'lishi biranxing' wenti" [On the question of the "inevitability" of capitalism]. *Lishi yanjiu* [Researches on history] 1 (1982): 111–23.

Chiang, Yung-chen. *Social Engineering and the Social Sciences in China, 1919–1949.* Cambridge: Cambridge University Press, 2001.

Chin, Tamara. *Savage Exchange: Han Imperialism, Chinese Literary Style, and Economic Imagination.* Cambridge, MA: Harvard University Press, 2015.

Clifford, James. *Routes: Travel and Translation in the Late Twentieth Century.* Cambridge, MA: Harvard University Press, 1997.

Cole, Robert. "To Save the Village." PhD diss., New York University, forthcoming.

Crawcour, Sydney. "The Tokugawa Period and Japan's Preparation for Modern Economic Growth." *Journal of Japanese Studies* 1, no. 1 (1974): 113–25.

Cumings, Bruce. "Boundary Displacement: The State, the Foundations, and Area Studies during and after the Cold War." In *Learning Places: The Afterlives of Area Studies,* edited by Masao Miyoshi and Harry Harootunian, 261–302. Durham, NC: Duke University Press, 2002.

Dai Jinhua. "After the post–Cold War." Translated by Li Jie. In *Works of Dai Jinhua,* edited by Lisa Rofel. Durham, NC: Duke University Press, forthcoming.

Day, Alexander. "Review: Philip Huang, *The Peasant Family and Rural Development in the Yangzi Delta, 1350–1988.*" Accessed May 15, 2015. http://www .academia.edu/9409110/Review_Philip_Huang_The_Peasant_Family_and _Rural_Development_in_the_Yangzi_Delta_1350-1988.

de Certeau, Michel. "Walking the City." In *The Practice of Everyday Life,* translated by Steven Rendall, 91–110. Berkeley: University of California Press, 1984.

Deleuze, Gilles, and Félix Guattari. *Anti-Oedipus: Capitalism and Schizophrenia.* Translated by Robert Hurley, Mark Seem, and Helen R. Lane. Minneapolis: University of Minnesota Press, 1983.

Dirlik, Arif. "Chinese Historians and the Marxist Concept of Capitalism: A Critical Examination." *Modern China* 8, no. 1 (January 1982): 105–32.

———. *Revolution and History: Origins of Marxist Historiography in China.* Berkeley: University of California Press, 1978.

Drayton, Richard. "Empire and Other Scales of Domination and Inequality: Towards an Intersectional *longue durée* Global History." Paper presented at CFP: The Future of Atlantic, Transnational, and World History, University of Pittsburgh, May 1–3, 2014.

Duara, Prasenjit. *Rescuing History from the Nation: Questioning Narratives of Modern China.* Chicago: University of Chicago Press, 1996.

Dushu bianji [*Dushu* editorial board], eds. *Yazhou de bing li* [Asia's pathology]. Beijing: Sanlian chubanshe, 2007.

Du Weizhi. "A Criticism of Research on Ancient China." *Dushu zazhi* [Readings journal] 1, nos. 2–3 (1932): n.p.

Elvin, Mark. *The Pattern of the Chinese Past: A Social and Economic Interpretation.* Stanford, CA: Stanford University Press, 1973.

Endo, Katsuhiko. "The Science of Capital: The Uses and Abuses of Human Sciences in Interwar Japan." PhD diss., New York University, 2004.

Furet, François, and Denis Richet. *La Révolution française* [1963]. Paris: Hachette, 1986.

Gates, Hill. *China's Motor: A Thousand Years of Petty Capitalism*. Ithaca, NY: Cornell University Press, 1996.

Godes, M. *Diskussia ob aziatskom sposobe proizvodstva* [A discussion of the Asiatic mode of production]. Moscow and Leningrad: Gosudarstvennoe sotsialno-ekonomicheskoe izdatelstvo, 1931.

Goswami, Manu. "Remembering the Future." *The American Historical Review* 113, no. 2 (2008): 417–24.

Gramsci, Antonio. *Selections from Cultural Writings*. Edited by David Forgacs and Geoffrey Nowell-Smith. Translated by William Boelhower. Cambridge, MA: Harvard University Press, 1985.

Gunder-Frank, Andre. *Re-Orient: Global Economy in the Asian Age*. Berkeley: University of California Press, 1998.

Guo Moruo. *Zhongguo gudai shehui yanjiu* [Research on ancient Chinese society]. Beijing: Renmin chubanshe, 1972.

Hanley, Susan B., and Kozo Yamamura. "A Quiet Transformation in Tokugawa Economic History." *Journal of Asian Studies* 30, no. 2 (1971): 373–84.

Harding, Neil. *Lenin's Political Thought: Theory and Practice in the Democratic Socialist Movement*. 2 vols. London: Haymarket Press, 2009.

Hardt, Michael, and Antonio Negri. *Empire*. Cambridge, MA: Harvard University Press, 2000.

Harootunian, Harry. *History's Disquiet: Modernity, Cultural Practice, and the Question of Everyday Life*. New York: Columbia University Press, 2000.

———. *Marx after Marx: History and Time in the Expansion of Capitalism*. New York: Columbia University Press, 2015.

———. *Overcome by Modernity: History, Culture, and Community in Interwar Japan*. Princeton, NJ: Princeton University Press, 2002.

Harvey, David. *The Limits to Capital*. New York: Verso, 2007.

Hayek, Friedrich A. *The Fatal Conceit: The Errors of Socialism*. Edited by W. W. Bartley III. Chicago: University of Chicago Press, 1988.

———. *The Road to Serfdom*. Chicago: University of Chicago Press, 1944.

He Ganzhi. *Zhongguo shehui xingzhi wenti lunzhan* [The debate on Chinese social history]. Shanghai: Sanlian chubanshe, 1939.

Hegel, G. W. F. *The Philosophy of History*. Translated by J. Sibree. New York: Dover, 1956.

Hevia, Jim. *Cherishing Men from Afar*. Durham, NC: Duke University Press, 1995.

He Xin. *Dongfang de fuxing* [Oriental renaissance]. 2 vols. Harbin: Heilongjiang renmin chubanshe/Heilongjiang jiaoyu chubanshe, 1989–92.

Hindess, Barry, and Paul Q. Hirst. *Pre-capitalist Modes of Production*. London: Routledge, 1975.

Huang, Philip [Zongzhi]. "Beilun shehui yu xiandai chuantong" [Social theory of paradoxes and modernity's tradition]. *Dushu* [Readings] 2 (2005): 3–14.

———. "Da fencha: Ouzhou, Zhongguo ji xiandai shijie jingji de fazhan" [The great divergence: Europe and China in the development of the modern global economy]. *Lishi yanjiu* [Researches on history] 4 (2002): 3–48.

———. "Development or Involution in Eighteenth-Century Britain and China?" Review of *The Great Divergence: China, Europe, and the Making of the Modern World Economy*, by Kenneth Pomeranz. *Journal of Asian Studies* 61, no. 2 (2002): 501–38.

———. *The Peasant Family and Rural Development in the Yangzi Delta, 1350–1988*. Stanford, CA: Stanford University Press, 1990.

Hu Peizhao. "Dang bian Yuanfu yu Guofu Lun" [Let's distinguish Yuanfu from Guofu Lun]. *Xueshu Yuekan* [Academic monthly] 9 (2012): n.p.

Ives, Peter. *Language and Hegemony in Gramsci*. Ann Arbor, MI: Pluto Press, 2004.

Ivy, Marilyn. *Discourses of the Vanishing*. Chicago: University of Chicago Press, 1995.

Jay, Martin. *Marxism and Totality: The Adventures of a Concept from Lukács to Habermas*. Berkeley: University of California Press, 1986.

Johnson, Walter. *River of Dark Dreams: Slavery and Empire in the Cotton Kingdom*. Cambridge, MA: Harvard University Press, 2013.

Karl, Rebecca E. "Compradors: The Mediating Middle of Global Capitalism in Twentieth-Century China and the World." In *Marxisms in Asia*, edited by Joyce Liu and Viren Murthy. New York: Routledge, forthcoming.

———. *Mao Zedong and China in the Twentieth-Century World: A Concise History*. Durham, NC: Duke University Press, 2010.

———. "On Comparability and Continuity: China, circa 1930s and 1990s." *boundary 2* 32, no. 2 (summer 2005): 169–200.

Ke Changji. "Ancient Chinese Society and the Asiatic Mode of Production." *Lanzhou daxue xuebao* [Journal of Lanzhou University] 3 (1983): 16–25.

Ko, Dorothy. *Teachers of the Inner Chambers: Women and Culture in Seventeenth-Century China*. Stanford, CA: Stanford University Press, 1994.

Koselleck, Reinhart. *Critique and Crisis: Enlightenment and the Pathogenesis of Modern Society*. Cambridge, MA: MIT Press, 1988.

———. *The Practice of Conceptual History: Timing History, Spacing Concepts*. Translated by Todd Samuel Presner et al. Stanford, CA: Stanford University Press, 2002.

Koyasu Nobukuni. *Dongya lun: Riben xiandai sixiang pipan* [The discourse of Asia: A critique of modern Japanese thought]. Translated by Zhao Jinghua. Jilin: Jilin renmin chubanshe, 2004.

———. "Riben jindai de dongya xushi" [Narrating Asia in modern Japan]. Translated by Zhao Jinghua. *Shijing* [Horizons], no. 14 (2004): 2–75.

Kracauer, Siegfried. *History: The Last Things before the Last*. Completed after the author's death by Paul Oskar Kristeller. Princeton, NJ: Markus Wiener, 1995.

Kraniauskas, John. "Empire, or Multitude: Transnational Negri." *Radical Philosophy* 103 (September–October 2000): 29–39.

———. "Transculturation and the Work of Translation." *Traces: A Multilingual Journal of Cultural Theory*, no. 1 (2000):95–108.

Landes, David. "Why Europe and the West? Why Not China?" *Journal of Economic Perspectives* 20, no. 2 (spring 2006): 3–22.

Lee, Leo Ou-fan. "The Tradition of Modern Chinese Cinema: Some Preliminary Explorations and Hypotheses." In *Perspectives on Chinese Cinema*, edited by Chris Berry, 6–21. London: British Film Institute, 1991.

Lefebvre, Henri. *Critique of Everyday Life*. Vol. 1, *Introduction*. Translated by John Moore. New York: Verso, 2000.

———. *Critique of Everyday Life*. Vol. 2, *Foundations for a Sociology of the Everyday*. Translated by John Moore. London: Verso, 2002.

———. *Introduction to Modernity*. London: Verso, 1995.

Lenin, V. I. *Imperialism, the Highest Stage of Capitalism*. New York: International Publishers, 1985.

Li Huaiyin. *Reinventing Modern China: Imagination and Authenticity in Chinese Historical Writing*. Honolulu: University of Hawai'i Press, 2012.

Lin Chun. *China and Global Capitalism: Reflections on Marxism, History, and Contemporary Politics*. New York: Palgrave Macmillan, 2013.

———. "Marxism and the Politics of Positioning China in World History." *Inter-Asia Cultural Studies* 13, no. 3 (2012): 438–66.

———. *Transformations in Chinese Socialism*. Durham, NC: Duke University Press, 2006.

Lin Guangquan. "The Asiatic Mode of Production and Ancient Chinese Society: A Criticism of Umberto Melotti's Distortion of Chinese History in His Book 'Marx and the Third World.'" Translated by V. Young. *Chinese Law and Government* 22, no. 2 (1989): 47–70.

Li Shiyue. "Guanyu 'banzhimindi banfengjian' de jidian sixiang" [A few thoughts on 'semi-colonialism semi-feudalism']. *Lishi yanjiu* [Researches on history] 1 (1988): 52–60.

Little, Daniel. "The Involution Debate: New Perspectives on China's Rural Economic History." Accessed May 15, 2015. http://www-personal.umd .umich.edu/~delittle/new%20perspectives%20short%20journal%2 oversion.htm.

Liu Junning. "The Intellectual Turn: The Emergence of Liberalism in Contemporary China." In *China's Future: Constructive Partner or Emerging Threat?*, edited by Ted Galen Carpenter and James A. Dorn, 49–60. Washington, DC: Cato Institute, 2000.

———. "Jingji ziyou: Ziyou zhi mu, xianzheng zhi lu—Du Ha-ye-ke" [Economic freedom: The mother of freedom, the road to constitutionalism—Reading Hayek]. Observechina. Accessed March 19, 2008. http://www.cicus.org/info /ArtShow.asp?ID=47965.

———. "The New Trinity: The Political Consequences of WTO, PNTR, and the Internet in China." *Cato Journal* 21, no. 1 (spring/summer 2001): 151–60.

Liu Xiaofeng, and Lin Liwei, eds. *Jingji lunli yu jinxiandai zhongguo shehui* [Economic ethics and modern Chinese society]. Hong Kong: Hong Kong University Press, 1998.

———, eds. *Zhongguo jinxiandai jingji lunli de bianqian* [The changes in China's modern economic ethics]. Hong Kong: Hong Kong University Press, 1998.

Li Yining. *Economic Reform and Development in China*. Cambridge: Cambridge University Press, 2012.

Li Zehou, and Liu Zaifu. *Gaobie geming* [Good-bye to revolution]. Hong Kong: Cosmos Books, 1995.

Lukács, Georg. *History and Class Consciousness: Studies in Marxist Dialectics*. Translated by Rodney Livingstone. Cambridge, MA: MIT Press, 1971.

———. "The Marxism of Rosa Luxembourg." [1923]. In *History and Class Consciousness: Studies in Marxist Dialectics*, translated by Rodney Livingstone, 27–45. Cambridge, MA: MIT Press, 1971.

———. "Reification and the Consciousness of the Proletariat" [1923]. In *History and Class Consciousness: Studies in Marxist Dialectics*, translated by Rodney Livingstone, 83–222. Cambridge, MA: MIT Press, 1971.

———. *The Theory of the Novel*. Translated by Anna Bostock. Cambridge, MA: MIT Press, 1999.

———. *The Young Hegel: Studies in the Relations between Dialectics and Economics*. Translated by Rodney Livingstone. Cambridge, MA: MIT Press, 1977.

Luo Gang, and Lin Yun. "Zuowei 'shehui zhuyi chengshi' de 'shanghai' yu kongjian de zai shengcan: 'Chengshi wenben' yu 'Meijie wenben' de 'hudu'" [The socialist city of Shanghai and the reproduction of space: The conflations of urban text and media text]. *Refeng xueshu* 4 (August 2010): 57–96.

Luxembourg, Rosa. *The Accumulation of Capital*. London: Routledge, 1951.

Lü Xingyu. *Xiangcun yu geming: Zhongguo xin ziyou zhuyi pipan sanshu* [The villages and revolution: Three essays on the critique of Chinese neoliberalism]. Shanghai: Huadong shida chubanshe, 2012.

Magee, Brian. *The Tristan Chord: Wagner and Philosophy*. New York: Metropolitan Books, 2001.

Ma Min. "Guodu tezheng yu zhongguo jindai shehui xingtai" [Special characteristics of transition and early modern China's social formation]. *Lishi yanjiu* [Researches on history] 1 (1989): 47–59.

Mann, Susan. *Precious Records: Women in China's Long Eighteenth Century*. Stanford, CA: Stanford University Press, 1997.

Manning, Patrick. "Asia and Europe in the World Economy: Introduction." *American Historical Review* 107, no. 2 (2002): 419–24.

Mao Zedong [Tse-tung]. "Analysis of the Classes in Chinese Society." 1925. Accessed January 23, 2014. https://www.marxists.org/reference/archive/mao/selected-works/volume-1/mswv1_1.htm.

———. "The Chinese Revolution and the Chinese Communist Party." In *Selected Works of Mao Tse-tung*, 2:305–34. Peking: People's Publishing House, 1967.

———. "Lun fandui riben diguo zhuyi de cilüe" [On tactics against Japanese imperialism]. In *Mao Zedong Xuanji* [Selected works of Mao Zedong], 1:128–53. Beijing: Renmin chubanshe, 1991.

———. "Zhongguo geming zhanzheng de zhanlüe wenti" [Strategy of the Chinese revolutionary war]. In *Mao Zedong Xuanji* [Selected works of Mao Zedong], 1:154–225. Beijing: Renmin chubanshe, 1991.

Mariátegui, José. *Seven Interpretive Essays on Peruvian Reality*. Translated by Jorge Basadre. Austin: University of Texas Press, 1971.

Marx, Karl. *Capital*. Vol. 1. Translated by Ben Fowkes. New York: Penguin, 1990.

———. *Capital*. Vol. 3. Translated by David Fernbach. New York: Penguin, 1991.

———. *A Contribution to the Critique of Political Economy*. New York: International Publishers, 1979.

———. *The Eighteenth Brumaire of Louis Bonaparte*. New York: International Publishers, 1994.

———. *Grundrisse: Foundations of the Critique of Political Economy*. Translated with a foreword by Martin Nicolaus. New York: Penguin, 1993.

Masao Miyoshi. "Ivory Tower in Escrow." In *Learning Places: The Afterlives of Area Studies*, edited by Masao Miyoshi and Harry Harootunian, 19–60. Durham, NC: Duke University Press, 2002.

Mauss, Marcel. *A General Theory of Magic*. London: Routledge and Kegan Paul, 1972.

Ma Yinchu, *Zhongguo jingji gaizao* [Transformation of the Chinese economy]. Shanghai: Shangwu yinshuguan, 1935.

Meek, Ronald. *Social Science and the Ignoble Savage*. Cambridge: Cambridge University Press, 1976.

Meillasoux, Claude. *Maidens, Meal and Money: Capitalism and the Domestic Community*. Cambridge: Cambridge University Press, 1981.

Melotti, Umberto. *Marx and the Third World*. Translated by Pat Ransford. Atlantic Highlands, NJ: Humanities Press, 1977.

Menger, Carl. *Principles of Economics* [1871]. Auburn, AL: Ludwig von Mises Institute, 2011.

Mises, Ludwig von. *Human Action: A Treatise on Economics*. Irvington-on-Hudson, NY: Foundation for Economic Education, 1996.

Nagahara, Yutaka. "*Monsieur le Capital* and *Madame la Terre* Do Their Ghost-Dance: Globalization and the Nation-State." *South Atlantic Quarterly* 99, no. 4 (fall 2000): 929–61.

Negri, Antonio, and Danilo Zolo. "Empire and the Multitude: A Dialogue on the New Order of Globalization." *Radical Philosophy* 120 (July–August 2003): 23–37.

Niethammer, Lutz. *Posthistoire: Has History Come to an End?* Translated by Patrick Camiller. New York: Verso, 1992.

Nie Xiwen. "Dui Zhongguo banzhimindi banfengjian shehui de xin renshi" [A new understanding of semicolonial, semifeudal society]. *Xueshu yanjiu* [Scholarly researches] 1 (1992): 64–69.

Osborne, Peter. "Marx and the Philosophy of Time." *Radical Philosophy* 147 (January–February 2008): 15–22.

———. *Philosophy in Cultural Theory.* New York: Routledge, 2000.

———. *The Politics of Time: Modernity and Avant-Garde.* London: Verso, 1995.

Osterhammel, Jürgen. "Semi-Colonialism and Informal Empire in Twentieth-Century China: Towards a Framework of Analysis." In *Imperialism and After: Continuities and Discontinuities,* edited by Wolfgang J. Mommsen and Jürgen Osterhammel, 290–314. London: Allen and Unwin, 1986.

Oya, Carlos, Jingzhong Ye, and Qian Forrest Zhang, eds. "Agrarian Change in Contemporary China." Special issue, *Journal of Agrarian Change* 15, no. 3 (July 2015).

Pan Guangzhe. "Xiangxiang 'xiandai hua': 1930 niandai Zhongguo sixiangjie de jiepou" [The imaginary of "modernization": An anatomy of the 1930s Chinese intellectual world]. *Xin Shixue* [New history journal] 1, no. 5 (2005): 85–124.

Pels, Peter. "Magic and Modernity." In *Magic and Modernity: Interfaces of Revelation and Concealment,* edited by Birgit Meyer and Peter Pels, 1–38. Stanford, CA: Stanford University Press, 2003.

Peng Kang. "Zhexue de renwu shi shenma?" [What is the task of philosophy?]. *Wenhua pinglun* [Culture critique] 1 (January 1928): 14–24.

Peng Shuzhi. *Dongfang minzu zhuyi sichao* [Trends of the oriental nationalism]. Xi'an: Xibei daxue chubanshe, 1992.

Perelman, Michael. *The Invention of Capitalism: Classical Political Economy and the Secret History of Primitive Accumulation.* Durham, NC: Duke University Press, 2000.

Pietz, William. "The Origins of Fetishism: A Contribution to the History of Theory." PhD diss., University of California, Santa Cruz, 1988.

Polanyi, Karl. "Carl Menger's Two Meanings of 'Economic.'" In *Studies in Economic Anthropology,* edited by George Dalton, 16–24. Anthropological Studies 7. Washington, DC: American Anthropological Association, 1971.

———. *The Great Transformation.* New York: Beacon, 1957.

Pomeranz, Kenneth. "Beyond the East-West Binary." *Journal of Asian Studies* 61, no. 2 (2002): 539–90.

Postone, Moishe. "Lukács and the Dialectical Critique of Capitalism." Paper delivered at the NYU Social Theory Workshop, April 5, 2002.

———. *Time, Labor, and Social Domination: A Reinterpretation of Marx's Critical Theory.* Cambridge: Cambridge University Press, 1996.

Qin Hui. *Zouchu dizhi* [Out of imperial autocracy]. No publisher. 2015.

Qi Xin. "Guanliao zhengzhi de genyuan: Jianjie 'Guangyu yaxiya shengchan fangshi yanjiu de jige wenti'" [The roots of bureaucratism: Examining "Several questions about research on the Asiatic mode of production"]. *Qishi niandai* [The '70s] 7 (1980): 24–27.

Rancière, Jacques. *The Names of History: On the Poetics of Knowledge.* Translated by Hassan Melehy. Minneapolis: University of Minnesota Press, 1994.

Read, Jason. *The Micro-Politics of Capital: Marx and the Prehistory of the Present.* Albany: State University of New York Press, 2003.

Riddell, John, ed. *Workers of the World and Oppressed Peoples, Unite!* 2 vols. New York: Pathfinder, 1991.

Rosenberg, Justin. *The Follies of Globalisation Theory.* London: Verso, 2002.

Ross, Kristin. *May '68 and Its Afterlives.* Chicago: University of Chicago Press, 2002.

Salisbury, Harrison E. *The New Emperors: China in the Era of Mao and Deng.* New York: Little, Brown, 1992.

Sartori, Andrew. *Bengal in Global Concept History: Culturalism in the Age of Capital.* Chicago: University of Chicago Press, 2008.

Sautman, Barry, and Yan Hairong. "The 'Right Dissident': Liu Xiaobo and the 2010 Nobel Peace Prize." *positions: east asia cultures critique* 19, no. 2 (2011): 581–613.

Schmitt, Carl. *Political Romanticism.* Translated by Guy Oakes. Cambridge, MA: MIT Press, 1986.

Schwarz, Roberto. *Master on the Periphery of Capitalism.* Translated by John Gledson. Durham, NC: Duke University Press, 2001.

———. *Misplaced Ideas: Essays on Brazilian Culture.* London: Verso, 1992.

Scott, Joan. "Gender: A Useful Category of Historical Analysis." *American Historical Review* 91, no. 5 (1986): 1053–75.

Shao, Qin. *Shanghai Gone: Domicide and Defiance in a Chinese Megacity.* New York: Rowman and Littlefield, 2013.

Shearmur, Jeremy. "The Austrian Connection: Hayek's Liberalism and the Thought of Carl Menger." In *Austrian Economics: Historical and Philosophical Background*, edited by Wolfgang Grassl and Barry Smith, 158–68. New York: New York University Press, 1986.

Shih, Shu-mei. *The Lure of the Modern.* Berkeley: University of California Press, 2001.

Skousen, Mark. *Vienna and Chicago: Friends or Foes?* New York: Capital Press, 2005.

Smith, Adam. *The Wealth of Nations* [1776]. New York: Bantam Classics, 2003.

Smith, Thomas. *The Agrarian Origins of Modern Japan.* Stanford, CA: Stanford University Press, 1959.

Su Hua. "Zhongguo ziben zhuyi jingji de fazhan" [Development in China's capitalist economy]. *Zhongguo jingji* [Chinese economics] 1, no. 6 (September 1933): 1–19.

Su Kaihua, "The Asiatic Mode of Production and the Theory of Five Modes of Production." In *The Asiatic Mode of Production in China*, ed. Timothy Brook. New York: M. E. Sharpe, 1989.

Tang Wenquan. *Dongfang de juexing: Jindai zhong yin minzu yundong dingwei guanzhao* [Oriental awakening: Exploration of the position of modern Chinese and Indian nationalist movements]. Changsha: Hunan chubanshe, 1991.

Tao Xisheng. "Zhongguo shehui daodi shi shenma shehui?" [What kind of society is China's anyway?]. *Xin shengming* [New life] 1, no. 10 (October 1928): 2–14.

Tomba, Massimiliano. *Marx's Temporalities*. Translated by Peter D. Thomas and Sara R. Farris. Chicago: Haymarket Books, 2013.

Tu Chenglin. "The Asiatic Mode of Production in World History Perspective: From a Universal to a Particularistic View of History." *Social Sciences in China* 35, no. 2 (2014): 5–25.

Vaughn, Karen I. *Austrian Economics in America: The Migration of a Tradition*. Cambridge: Cambridge University Press, 1998.

Vilar, Pierre. "Marxist History, a History in the Making: Towards a Dialogue with Althusser." In *Althusser: A Critical Reader*, edited by Gregory Elliott, 10–43. Oxford: Blackwell, 1994.

Walker, Deborah L. "Austrian Economics." In *The Concise Encyclopedia of Economics*. Accessed February 23, 2008. http://www.econlib.org/library/Enc1 /AustrianEconomics.html.

Wang Hui. "On Scientism and Social Theory in Modern Chinese Thought." Translated by Gloria Davies. In *Voicing Concerns: Contemporary Chinese Critical Inquiry*, edited by Gloria Davies, 135–56. Lanham, MD: Rowman and Littlefield, 2001.

——. "The Year 1989 and the Historical Roots of Neoliberalism in China." Translated by Rebecca E. Karl. *positions* 12, no. 1 (spring 2004): 7–69.

Wang Jinglu. "Zhongguo jindai shehui, jindai zichan jieji he zichan jieji geming" [China's modern society, modern bourgeoisie, and the bourgeois revolution]. *Lishi yanjiu* [Researches on history] 6 (1986): 51–61.

Wang Xiaoming. *Zai xin yishi xingtai de longzhao xia: 90 niandai de wenhua yu wenxue fenxi* [Under the glare of the new ideology: Culture and literature in the 1990s]. Nanjing: Jiangsu renmin chubanshe, 2000.

Wang Yanan. "Guanyu zhongguo jingjixue jianli zhi keneng yu biyao de wenti" [On the possibility and necessity of establishing economics in China]. *Dongnan ribao* [Southeastern daily news] November 14, 15, 18, 1944. Reprinted in *Wang Yanan Wenji* 1:126–37.

——. "Jingji kexue lun" [On economics]. In WYNJJ, 1–7.

——. "Jingjixue yu zhexue" [Economics and philosophy]. In WYNJJ, 59–71.

——. "Lun Dongxi wenhua yu dongxi jingji: Ping Liang Shuming xiansheng de dongxi wenhua guan" [On Eastern-Western culture and Eastern-Western economy part 1: Evaluation of Mr. Liang Shuming's view of Eastern-Western culture]. In *Shehui kexue xinlun*, 75–85.

——. "Lun Shehui kexue de yingyong" [On the utility of social science]. In *Shehui kexue xinlun*, 35–62.

——. "Lun wenhua yu jingji" [On culture and economics]. In *Shehui kexue xinlun*, 63–74.

——. *Makesi zhuyi de renkou lilun yu Zhongguo renkou wenti* [Marxist population theory and China's demographic problems]. Beijing: Kexue chubanshe, 1956.

———. "San lun dongxi wenhua yu dongxi jingji: Ping Zhu Qianzhi Xiansheng de dongxi wenhua guan" [On Eastern-Western culture and Eastern-Western economy, part 3: Evaluation of Mr. Zhu Qianzhi's view of Eastern-Western culture]. In *Shehui kexue xinlun*, 103–11.

———. *Shehui kexue xinlun* [New essays on social science]. Fuzhou: Jingji kexue chubanshe, 1946.

———. *Wang Yanan Jingji Sixiangshi lunwen ji* (WYNJJ) [Collected essays on economic thought of Wang Yanan], edited by Xiamen Daxue jingji yanjiusuo. Shanghai: Renmin chubanshe, 1981.

———. *Wang Yanan wenji* [Selected works of Wang Yanan], edited by Wang Yanan wenji collective. 5 vols. Fuzhou: Fujian jiaoyu chubanshe, 1987–89.

———. "Yanjiu shehui kexue yingyou de jige jiben renshi" [A few basic points of understanding in the study of social science]. In *Shehui kexue xinlun*, 1–22.

———. "You banfengjian banzhimindi jingji dao xin minzhu zhuyi jingji" [From semifeudal semicolonial economy to a new democratic economy]. *Xin Zhonghua* 12, no. 15 (1947). Reprinted in *Wang Yanan wenji*, 3:483–95.

———. "Zai lun dongxi wenhua yu dongxi jingji: Ping Qian Mu xiansheng de dongxi wenhua guan" [On Eastern-Western culture and Eastern-Western economy, part 2: Evaluation of Mr. Qian Mu's view of Eastern-Western culture]. In *Shehui kexue xinlun*, 87–102.

———. "Zhengzhi jingjixue shang de ren" [Man in political economics]. In WYNJJ, 8–22.

———. "Zhengzhi jingjixue zai Zhongguo" [Political economy in China]. In WYNJJ, 117–47.

———. *Zhongguo banfengjian banzhimindi jingji xingtai yanjiu* [Researches on China's semifeudal, semicolonial economic formation] [1947]. First revision. Beijing: Renmin chubanshe, 1955.

———. *Zhongguo banfengjian banzhimindi jingji xingtai yanjiu* [Researches on China's semifeudal, semicolonial economic formation] [1947]. Second revision. Beijing: Renmin chubanshe, 1957.

———. *Zhongguo de dizhu fengjian jingji lungang* [Outline of China's feudal landlord economy]. In *Wang Yanan wenji* [Selected works of Wang Yanan], 4:63–126.

———. *Zhongguo guanliao zhengzhi yanjiu* [Research into China's bureaucratic polity] [1948]. Beijing: Shangwu yinshuguan, 2010.

———. "Zhongguo jingjishi yanjiu de xian jieduan" [The current phase of research on the economy in China]. *Jingji kexue* [Economic sciences] 5 (April 1943). Reprinted in *Wang Yanan Wenji* 4:38–41.

———. "Zhongguo jingjixuejie de Audili xuepai jingjixue" [Austrian School economics in Chinese economics circles]. In WYNJJ, 148–71.

———. *Zhongguo jingji yuanlun* [Elements of the Chinese economy] [1943]. 2nd ed. Shanghai: Shenghuo shudian, 1947.

———. "Zhongguo shehui jingjishi gang: Xulun" [An outline of China's socio-economic history: preface] [1937]. In *Wang Yanan Wenji* 4:3–19.

Weber, Max. *The Religion of China.* Translated and edited by Hans H. Gerth. New York: The Free Press, 1968.

Wong, R. Bin. *China Transformed: Historical Change and the Limits of European Experience.* Ithaca, NY: Cornell University Press, 1997.

Wood, Ellen Meiskins. *Empire of Capital.* London: Verso, 2003.

Wu Dakun. "The Asiatic Mode of Production in History as Viewed by Political Economy in Its Broad Sense." In *Marxism in China*, edited by Su Shaozhi, 53–77. Nottingham, UK: Spokesman, 1983.

———. "Bo Ka'er Weitefu de 'Dongfang zhuanzhi zhuyi'" [Refuting Karl Wittfogel's *Oriental Despotism*]. *Lishi yanjiu* [Researches on history] 4 (1982): 27–36.

———. "Guanyu yaxiya shengchan fangshi yanjiu de jige wenti" [Some questions concerning research on the Asiatic mode of production]. *Xueshu yanjiu* [Scholarly researches] 1 (1980): 11–18.

Wu Qingyou. *Ziben zhuyi fazhan de bu pinghenglü* [Uneven rates of capitalist development]. Shanghai: Shenghuo shudian, 1937.

Xu Dixin and Wu Chengming, eds. *Zhongguo zibenzhuyi de mengya* [The sprouts of capitalism in China]. 3 vols. Beijing: Renmin chubanshe, 2003.

Yan Fu. *Yuanfu* [The origin of wealth]. Shanghai: Nanyang gongxue yishuyuan, 1902.

Yan Hairong and Chen Yiyuan. "Agrarian Capitalization without Capitalism? Capitalist Dynamics from Above and Below in China." *Journal of Agrarian Change* 15, no. 3 (July 2015): 366–92.

Yan Sun. *The Chinese Reassessment of Socialism, 1976–1992.* Princeton, NJ: Princeton University Press, 1999.

Yeh, Wen-hsin. *Shanghai Splendor: Economic Sentiments and the Making of Modern China, 1843–1949.* Berkeley: University of California Press, 2007.

Zhang Qinghai, "Lun dui banfengjian banzhimindi liangge gainian de lilun jieding" [On the theoretical specification of the two concepts semifeudal and semicolonial]. *Jindaishi yanjiu* [Researches on modern history] 6 (1998): 226–34.

Zhang Wentian. *Zhang Wentian xuanji* [Selected works of Zhang Wentian]. Beijing: Renmin chubanshe, 1985.

———. "Zhongguo jingji zhi xingzhi wenti de yanjiu—Ping Ren Shu jun de 'Zhongguo jingji yanjiu'" [Research on the question of the nature of China's economy—An evaluation of Mr. Ren Shu's *Research on China's Economy*]. *Dushu zazhi* [Readings journal] 1, nos. 4–5 (1932): 4–8.

Zhang, Yingjin, ed. *Cinema and Urban Culture in Shanghai, 1922–1943.* Stanford, CA: Stanford University Press, 1999.

Zhao Lisheng, "The Well-Field System in Relation to the Asiatic Mode of Production." In *The Asiatic Mode of Production in China*, ed. Timothy Brook, 65–84. New York: M. E. Sharpe, 1989.

Zhu Jingwo. "Kexue de shehui guan" [A scientific perspective on the social]. *Wen-hua pinglun* [Culture critique] 1 (January 1928): 34–52; 2 (April 1928): 48–71.

Zhu Yongde. "Nongmo zhongcai you yi zhang: Shang ying guoqing 50 zhounian huoli yingpian paiying huigu" [Another chapter of dark ink and bold colors: Reviewing the making of prize-winning Shanghai Studio films for the 50th anniversary]. *Dianying xinzuo* [New films] 1 (2000): 8–10.

Žižek, Slavoj. "Catastrophes Real and Imagined." *In These Times*, March 31, 2003.

———. *The Sublime Object of Ideology*. London: Verso, 1989.

Žižek, Slavoj, and Mladen Dolar. *Opera's Second Death*. New York: Routledge, 2002.

INDEX

Adorno, Theodor W., 164, 197n3
Alliez, Éric, 113, 133
Althusser, Louis, 95, 172n15
Amin, Samir, 65, 175n32, 180n52
Aranzadi, Javier, 182n4, 183n10, 184n20,
    185n30, 187n72, 187nn76–77
Asiatic Mode of Production, the, 17,
    31, 40, 49, 70, 73, 132, 175n3, 176n4,
    176n7, 177n13, 178n28, 179n33,
    179n35, 181n54, 181n56, 182nn59–60;
    as the AMP, 31, 40, 42–60, 63–72,
    74, 175n3, 176nn7–8, 177n19, 177n21,
    178n28, 179n33, 181n58, 182n59

Baudrillard, Jean, 8, 169n19
Benjamin, Walter, 7, 108, 188n91,
    188n94, 190n111
Bensaïd, Daniel, 9, 160, 169n21, 197n21
Bergson, Henri, 95, 187n77, 187n82; and
    Bergsonianism, 95
Bewes, Timothy, 57, 178n29, 179n36
Böhm-Bawerk, Eugen von, 79–80, 82,
    92, 184nn16–17
Brecht, Bertolt, 19, 141, 188n94
Brook, Timothy, 176n7, 177n17, 182n59,
    182n62

Camatte, Jacques, 61–63, 65, 179n39,
    180nn40–41, 180n46
capitalism, 2, 14–15, 17, 27–30, 33–39,
    41–48, 51–52, 54–55, 57, 60–62,
    64–66, 68, 71–72, 76, 80–82, 84,
    85–90, 93–94, 97, 103, 107, 111, 113–17,

118–22, 125–27, 131–38, 140, 143,
154, 158, 163, 171n4, 173n18, 174n3,
175nn26,27, 175n32, 176n6, 177n21,
178n24, 178n26, 178n29, 180–81n52,
182n7, 183n59, 188n84, 189n99, 191n4,
192nn20–21, 194n42, 194n45; and
modern capitalism, 28, 89, 129; and
global capitalism, 14–15, 30, 33, 39,
55, 69, 117–19, 122, 138, 161, 176n8,
190n121; and post–Mao capitalism,
70; and Eurocentric capitalism,
71; and liberal capitalism, 76; and
comprador-bureaucratic capitalism,
118; and Confucian-style capitalism,
170n30; and imperialist capitalism,
2, 17, 36, 65, 117–18, 123, 126; and
party-led capitalism, 157; as anticapitalism, 76
capitalist mode of production (CMP),
62–63, 65
Chen Hongjin, 117–18, 192nn11–13
Chen Jinlong, 128, 193n37
Crawcour, Sydney, 35, 175n28
culture, 4, 13, 17, 23–24, 47, 56, 67, 72,
99–106, 115, 143, 158, 163–64, 170n34,
178n25, 182n62, 188n95, 194n48,
196n9; and "Eastern-Western Culture," 100, 189n101, 189n103, 189n107;
and "Eastern Culture," 100, 103; and
Chinese culture, 103–4, 183n9; and
Western culture, 104, 110; and native
culture, 110; and world culture, 163
Cumings, Bruce, xi, 172n10

Mao Zedong, 17, 42, 45, 57, 67, 78, 113, 124–27, 130–32, 135, 137, 140, 158, 160, 167n1, 168n6, 181n57, 191n9, 192n15, 193nn26–29, 194n51, 196n16; and Maoism, 4, 12, 22, 43–44, 47, 54, 58, 66, 68–69, 78, 102, 126–27, 131, 134, 148, 157, 171n4, 171n31, 188n97, 192n15, 193n28, 194n51

market, the, 17, 48, 73–75, 77–80, 85–86, 91–92, 94–96

Marx, Karl, 1, 3–7, 28, 46–53, 59, 61–62, 64, 67, 70, 80, 83, 91–92, 122, 144, 153, 167n1, 169n12, 169n14, 169nn16–17, 169n21, 174n25, 177nn14–15, 177n18, 178n28, 179n37, 180n50, 184nn15–16, 185n38, 187n71, 188n94, 192nn20–21, 196n8, 197n20; and Marxism, 7, 12, 17, 21, 31, 34, 41–43, 50–51, 53, 55, 57–61, 68, 77, 84, 88–89, 92, 102, 106, 108, 111, 113, 128, 135–36, 154, 167n1, 168n10, 170n28, 172n15, 175nn2–3, 176nn6–7, 177nn20–21, 178nn27–28, 179n31, 180n46, 181n54, 182n59, 184n14, 186nn53–54, 187n80, 188n91, 188n94, 188n97, 190n112, 190n121, 191n6, 192n15; and Marxian, 34, 60, 61, 76, 79

Ma Yinchu, 3, 106, 168n6, 168n8, 195n58

Meek, Ronald, 47, 177n17

Meillasoux, Claude, 69, 180n52

Melotti, Umberto, 57, 67, 178n28

Menger, Carl, 79, 94–95, 183n12, 184n13, 184n17, 186n58, 186n60

Mises, Ludwig von, 80, 83, 94–95, 183n12, 185n27, 185nn30–31, 185n37

modernization, 5, 24–25, 28–30, 32–36, 42, 58, 60–61, 67–68, 71, 104, 110, 143–44, 157–59, 171n1, 171n4; and modernity, 7–11, 24, 32, 42, 76, 94, 96, 98–99, 107, 114, 123, 144, 169n18, 169n24, 173n19, 190n111, 191n7, 196n9; as alternative modernity, 56, 71, 158, 182–83n7; as colonial

modernity, 114, 191n3; as bourgeois modernity, 158; as Eurocentric capitalist modernity, 159; as hybrid modernity, 158; and modernization theory, 19–20, 55, 61, 63, 108, 123, 131, 133, 136, 140; and modernizationism, 25, 42–43, 61, 68, 78, 100

neo-Kantian, 101, 103, 105; and neo-Kantianism, 105

neoliberalism, ix, 17, 22–24, 39, 45, 135, 157, 176n8, 193n36

Nie Xiwen, 130, 194n46

orient, the, 51, 54, 55, 67, 181n53

Osborne, Peter, 54, 63, 82, 94, 142, 169n24, 172n8, 178n23, 180n47, 185n26, 187n71, 187n74, 187n77, 187n81, 190n113, 195n3

Pomeranz, Kenneth, 24–26, 28–31, 33, 37–38, 73–76, 172n16, 173n17, 174n25, 175n31, 182n7

precapitalism, 7, 29, 46–48, 51–53, 59, 68, 76, 86, 116–17, 173n18, 173n22

primitive accumulation, 53, 66, 68, 132, 136, 138, 140, 152, 168n10, 171n4, 175n32

Qian Mu, 100, 103–4, 189nn103–6

Qin Hui, 127, 174n27, 176n8

Rancière, Jacques, 142, 171n3, 194n40, 195n2, 195nn4–5

Rosenberg, Justin, 61, 179n38

Schmitt, Carl, 147, 196n16

Schwarz, Roberto, 11, 13, 170n34, 171n38, 188n84, 190n116

semicolonialism, 17, 113–18, 122–27, 129, 133, 136–37, 140, 143–44, 150, 158, 191n8, 192n1, 192n15; and colonialism, 23, 45, 81, 192n11; and postcolonialism, 55